⑤ 154742 2

A FULL STUDY OF OUR FAMILIES OF WORDS

BOOK OF ROOTS

Duane Beeler

© 1988 Duane Beeler

BOOK OF ROOTS/FAMILIES OF WORDS

Union Representative
2202 Cedar Road
Homewood, IL 60430

book design ● the bernstein design group, inc./chicago

ISBN 0-918515-00-9

I wish to thank three top classicists and etymologists of the midwest: Farrand Baker, Raymond Den Adel, and George Vander Weyden.

Also, the scholars Robert Bunge, Jay Faermark, Lois Hull, Carol Ising, Dominic Martia, Harry Price, Sylvia Thompson, and Fred Wranovics.

I have held the threads of this fabric in my hands and sought the final pattern, and although now it may be a fabric with a coarse, rough work, the threads were nonetheless chosen with care and according to certain rules.

VINCENT VAN GOGH

TABLE OF CONTENTS

SAY WHAT YOU MEAN

Easy Words, Hard Words, And Right Words 1
The Importance Of Vocabulary Building 6
The Poetry Of The Root Concept 8
The Root Concept In Teaching Vocabulary 10
Learning Latin 12
English History And The English Language 12

THE MEANING BEHIND THE MEANING 19

THE MEANING OF AFFIXES

Prefixes 33
Suffixes 37
Suffixes By Parts Of Speech 42

THE MEANING OF ROOTS

Simplified Major Roots 49
Roots With Selected Derivatives 55
Major Roots 67
Minor Roots 243

CHARTS

Some Words Starting With CON 3
Introduction To The Root System 5
Some Of The 150 Words From The Root DUC 7
Greek Roots Used In The Sciences 11

SAY WHAT YOU MEAN

SAY WHAT YOU MEAN

English may well be the most precise language in the world. It contains words that, singly or in combination, enable us to express virtually any shade of meaning without ambiguity.

However, this characteristic of English is a two-edged sword.

When we use the right words, English gives us an unequaled facility for putting our thoughts into words and communicating exactly what we want to say.

EASY WORDS, HARD WORDS, AND RIGHT WORDS

But English can be very unforgiving when we use the wrong words, as Mark Twain's oft-quoted comment points out: "The difference between the right word and the almost right word is the difference between lightning and a lightning bug."

Using the right word can be both easy and difficult.

It's easy to use high-frequency, simple words that we depend on for everyday conversation. These are the words we use even if we could not read or write.

Children learn the structure of the language and pick up the simple words by age six. They do it by listening to the talk of their parents, and by verbal mimicry.

In learning English, children are learning a language composed of two main sources of words, Anglo-Saxon and Latin.

Anglo-Saxon was the language of the Germanic tribes that settled England in the fifth century A.D. Thus, English and German are linguistic cousins.

Anglo-Saxon words form the foundation and structure of the English language. They are indispensable. We cannot speak, read or write English without using them.

Anglo-Saxon words include the prepositions (in, on, at, near, over, under), conjunctions (and, but, or, nor, of, for), pronouns (he, she, it), and many other simple words such as good, bad, great, small, man, woman, night, day, sea, land, winter, summer.

The easy words are almost all of Anglo-Saxon origin. Words derived from Anglo-Saxon constitute 62% of the thousand words most commonly used. Yet these words might total no more than 10% of all the words of an unabridged dictionary. A dictionary of 140,000 words has this breakdown: Latin 36%, French 21%, Anglo-Saxon 14%, Greek 4½%, Scandinavian 2%, and Spanish 2%.

So while the very heart of the language can be traced back to native Anglo-Saxon origins, borrowed words compose the greatest part of our vocabulary. These are mainly Latin words, taken directly from Latin or coming through the French.

Some of these Latin words are so complicated that we need the dictionary to get an accurate understanding of their meaning, even though other Latin words are so elemental that we are unaware they are Latin, as the chart on the facing page shows.

Although we learned the simple Anglo-Saxon words in our youth, learning the difficult words of other origin presents a perpetual problem. That is why our language is both easy and hard.

It might appear that the dictionary is what we need to teach us these hard words. Certainly, the unabridged dictionary is the most valuable book for the home or office, and perfect for its purpose: to find all words by their spellings, and to learn their meanings, pronunciations, and origins.

But for the purpose of learning the more difficult words—the words of Latin origin—the dictionary has limits because of its alphabetical order. We are unable to find words related to the word we are studying, because many of them have different prefixes and begin with different letters. If we wanted to learn a hundred related words, we would have to spend hours searching word by word through the dictionary.

How can we learn these difficult words of Latin origin that total as much as 60% of all of our words? Well, we can begin by examining the way the language was formed.

SOME WORDS STARTING WITH CON (THE PREFIX CON MEANS *TOGETHER, WITH*)

WORD	ROOT	ROOT MEANING	WORD MEANING
concentrate	CENT	*center*	come to a common center
concept	CEPT	*take in*	a generalized idea of a class
concern	CERN	*sift*	to be of importance to us
concert	CERT	*strive*	to settle by mutual opinions
conciliate	CIL	*a meeting*	to win over; make friendly
concise	CIS	*cut off*	brief and to the point
concommitant	COM	*accompany*	accompaniment, exist together
concrete	CRE	*grow*	formed into a solid mass
concur	CUR	*run*	to be in accord
concussion	CUSS	*shake*	the act of violently shaking
condemn	DEMN	*harm*	to pass an adverse judgment
condense	DENS	*dense*	make compact or compress
condition	DIT	*speak*	a requirement before an act
condone	DON	*give*	forgive or overlook
conducive	DUC	*lead*	contribute to a result
confer	FER	*bring*	to consult together
confide	FID	*trust*	share secrets with another
confine	FIN	*boundary*	to restrain within limits
confirm	FIRM	*strengthen*	to make firm or certain
conflict	FLIG	*strike*	to clash; be antagonistic
conform	FORM	*fashion*	to be in accordance with
confound	FUND	*pour*	to throw into discord
confuse	FUS	*pour*	to mix up
congeal	GEL	*freeze*	change a liquid to a solid
congenial	GEN	*same nature*	compatible
congest	GEST	*overcrowd*	to collect into a mass
conglomerate	GLOM	*in a ball*	gather parts into a ball
congratulate	GRAT	*joy*	compliment and wish joy
congruence	GRU	*agree*	agreement, harmony
conjure	JUR	*conspire*	to appeal, to entreat solemnly
connect	NECT	*bind*	join, fasten, link, couple
connive	NIV	*wink*	co-operate in wrong doing
conquest	QUE	*seek*	act of overcoming opposition
conscience	SCI	*know*	feeling of right and wrong
conserve	SERV	*save*	to keep safe
consist	SIST	*stand*	be composed of
consolidate	SOLI	*solid*	make solid; unite
conspicuous	SPIC	*observe*	easy to see
conspiracy	SPIR	*breathe*	planning together secretly
constant	STAN	*stand*	remaining the same

Whatever people do, they tend to do in the easiest way possible. It is logical, in the development of a language, that people would find it easier to add prefixes or suffixes before or after key words to explain a new idea, than to create and learn entirely new words.

These key words, sometimes stripped down, began to function as "roots," which, with slight modifications, could generate whole families of words.

Each word had an original and basic meaning, but, by adding a prefix or suffix or combining the root with another root, the root meaning could branch into many new words and ideas, with meanings close to the original root or even entirely different.

Just to list a few roots and their meanings will start our imagination to flow: FAL *deceive*, FID *faith*, FRIG *cold*, FUG *flee*, FUM *smoke*. Each root generates a family of words with as few as ten words or as many as two hundred. The chart on the facing page will suggest the scope of the roots.

We need only to look at American Indians, a people of many tribes and languages, who combined roots to form words with which we are very familiar:

MISSISSIPPI   "big river"   [*Obj*]   (misi *big* + sipi *river*)
MISSOURI   "muddy water"   [*Sioux*] (mni *water* + shoshay *muddy*)
MINNESOTA   "clear water"   [*Sioux*] (mni *water* + sota *clear*)

All languages have families of words that branch off from roots. Because of the way the English language was expanded—with a huge influx of Latin words about five hundred years ago—a broad system of word families developed. A limited number of effective prefixes spawned a wide spectrum of words enabling us to explain our most complex and sophisticated concepts.

The genius of the root concept is that, instead of learning thousands of words entirely different from each other, now it is possible to know many words by just learning the essential roots. Most of our difficult words belong to families that can be traced to these roots. In learning the root we will become familiar with the whole family.

We need to know thousands of difficult words. To learn them, we need a system like the PERIODIC TABLE OF THE ELEMENTS—in which all the elements fall into predictable places because of their physical and chemical properties.

INTRODUCTION TO THE ROOT SYSTEM

CED	*yield*	cede, concede, intercede, precede, proceed.
CLAM	*shout*	clamor, acclaim, acclamation, declamation.
CLUD	*shut*	include, conclude, exclude, preclude, occlude.
CREA	*create*	creativity, creature, procreate, recreate.
DUC	*lead*	conductor, deduce, educate, induce, produce.
EQU	*equal*	equality, equate, equator, adequate.
FEND	*keep off*	fend, fender, defend, offend, indefensible.
FIRM	*strong*	firm, affirm, confirm, infirm, infirmary.
FIX	*fix*	fixation, fixture, crucifix, prefix, suffix.
FORM	*shape*	conform, deform, inform, reform, transform.
FORT	*strong*	fortitude, comfort, effort, enforce, reinforce.
FRONT	*front*	affront, confront, affrontery, front, frontier.
JECT	*throw*	deject, inject, interject, object, project.
MEM	*memory*	commemorate, memento, memoir, remember.
MENT	*mind*	mental, mentality, comment, vehement.
MOR	*manner*	moral, immoral, demoralize, morose, mores.
PEND	*hang*	pendulum, depend, expend, impend, spend.
PORT	*carry*	portable, deport, export, import, report.
PRESS	*press*	compress, depress, express, impress.
PROV	*prove*	approve, disprove, improve, provable.
SCEND	*climb*	ascend, reascend, descend, condescend.
SCRIB	*write*	scribble, scripture, describe, prescribe.
SEN	*feel*	sense, sensation, sensitive, sensual.
SERV	*serve*	deserve, disservice, servile, service.
SPEC	*see*	expect, inspect, prospect, respect, suspect.
SPIR	*breathe*	aspire, conspire, expire, inspire, perspire.
SIGN	*sign*	assign, consign, design, resign, signature.
SIST	*stand*	assist, consist, desist, exist, insist, persist.
TEND	*stretch*	attend, contend, extend, intend, portend.
TEST	*witness*	attest, contest, detest, incontestable, testify.
TON	*tone*	astonish, baritone, intonation, monotonous.
TORT	*twist*	contort, distort, extort, retort, torture.
TRACT	*draw*	attract, contract, distract, extract, protract.
UNI	*one*	uniform, unify, unity, unique, union.
VAL	*value*	convalescent, equivalent, prevalent, valid.
VERS	*turn*	adverse, converse, inverse, obverse.
VIA	*way*	via, viaduct, deviate, obviate, trivial.
VIS	*see*	advise, revise, supervise, visage, visible.
VIV	*life*	vivacity, vivid, convivial, revive, survive.
VOC	*call*	vocal, advocate, invocation, provocation.
VOL	*roll*	convolve, devolve, evolve, involve, revolt.

But words are elements of speech, not elements of science. *So we must discern some properties of words that will lead logically to an understanding of their meaning.* If we know how words are constructed and how their parts relate to each other, we have the foundation of word learning and thus of language learning.

Most of the words in this book consist of the building blocks that determine their meanings. These building blocks are the root, the prefix, and the suffix.

Since these elements are limited in number, and thus manageable, a knowledge of them can help us to learn and understand the meaning of countless words.

THE IMPORTANCE OF VOCABULARY BUILDING

Our vocabulary needs are enormous. Every year knowledge explodes, and communication demands more awareness and skill. A definitive study of a Swedish peasant some years ago showed that he knew 26,000 words. Today anyone active in social and business life must know many more than that.

By learning concepts, we can deal more effectively with our complex physical and social world. Concepts let us simplify a mass of material by dividing it into meaningful categories. We use concepts as we go about making meaningful associations. We notice which things are similar and which things are different. We make lists and categorize. We discriminate. Students are high school graduates, or college graduates, or Ph.Ds. Or jocks or nerds. We constantly categorize.

The simplest concept will cover a group of objects that have something in common. The root concept is one such concept: all words containing the same root belong to the same family of words.

Through the root concept we can learn the meaning of words through their component parts. The value of the root concept is that it alerts us to the way the word is put together, and thus to its meaning. On the facing page we see that the root DUC "to lead" ties together many words we know but whose relationship we may never have realized.

Knowing the meaning of the root and the prefixes enables us to know the general meanings of all the derivative words. Such knowledge gives us the power to express our ideas and feelings, the power to understand and, most important, the power to learn for a lifetime.

SOME OF THE 150 WORDS FROM THE ROOT DUC *TO LEAD*

ABDUCE (ab *from* + ducere *to lead*) *"to lead away"; to kidnap,* abduct, abduction, abductor.
ADDUCE (ad *to* + ducere *to lead*) *"to lead to"; to offer as reason or proof; an example,* adducent, adducer, adducible, adduct, adduction.
CIRCUMDUCT *to revolve around an axis,* circumduction.
CONDUCE (con *together* + ducere *to lead*) *"to bring together"; to contribute to as a result,* conducent, conductibility, conducible.
CON′DUCT *(n) personal behavior.*
CONDUCT′ *(v) to guide, to escort,* conductance, conductibility, conductible, conduction, conductive, conductivity, conductor.
DEDUCE (de *from* + ducere *to lead*) *"to draw from"; to conclude from what precedes,* deducement, deductibility, deductible.
DEDUCTION *from the general theory to arrive at specific facts,* deduct, deductible, deductive, deductively.
DUCTILE *can be stretched without breaking,* ductilely, ductileness.
EDUCE (e *out* + ducere *to lead*) *"to draw out"; to evolve; to infer from the data,* educible, educt, eduction, eductor.
EDUCATE *to give knowledge and training to,* educability, educable, education, educational, educationally, educative, educator, educatress.
INDUCE *to lead by persuasion; to prevail on,* induced, inducement.
INTRODUCE (intro *within* + ducere *to lead*) *to bring or conduct a person in; to add a new feature,* introducement, introducer, introduction, introductive, introductively, introductor, introductorily.
INDUCT *to lead in; to initiate,* inductance, inductee, inductor.
INDUCTIVE *from individual facts to arrive at general principles; electrical and magnetic induction,* inductively, inductivity.
PRODUCE (pro *forward* + ducere *to lead*) *"to lead forward", to bring to view; to generate,* produced, producer, productibility, producible, producibleness, product, productibility, productile, production.
REPRODUCE *to bring into existence again,* reproducer, reproducible, reproduction, reproductive, reproductiveness, reproductory.
REDUCE *to diminish; to classify; to degrade,* reduceable, reduced, reducent, reducer, reducibility, reducible, reducibleness, reducibly.
SEDUCE (se *apart* + ducere *to lead*) *"to lead astray"; to persuade to do wrong,* seduceable, seducement, seducer, seducible, seducingly.
SUBDUCE (sub *under* + ducere *to lead*) *to bring into subjection,* subduable, subdual, subduct, subduction, subdue, subduer.
TRADUCE *to slander, to vilify,* traducement, traducent, traducer.
ALSO: duke, duchess, dukedom, duchy, ducal, ducat; aqueduct, viaduct, conduit.

About English, it has been said: "We speak German and write Latin." There is a measure of truth in the saying, because we use so many simple Anglo-Saxon words in our everyday speech, and so many Latin words in our formal speech and writing.

English is a fortunate combination of Anglo-Saxon and Latin. Both have dwelt together successfully for centuries. Sometimes it takes a close search to find which are Latin and which Anglo-Saxon. Each contributes to the total meaning. Many of the simple necessary words are Anglo-Saxon. Latin often furnishes the words when it is necessary to express subtlety, precision, and grandiloquence.

To see how native English (Anglo-Saxon) words and borrowed Latin words work together, look at the opening lines of our Declaration of Independence of July 4, 1776. (The Latin words are bold-face.):

When in the **course** of **human events** it becomes **necessary** for one **people** to **dissolve** the **political** bonds which have **connected** them with another, and to **assume** among the **powers** of the earth, the **separate** and **equal station** for which the Laws of **Nature** and of **Nature's** God entitles them, a **decent respect** to the **opinions** of mankind **requires** that they should **declare** the **causes** which **impel** them to the **separation**——We hold these truths to be self-**evident,** that all men are **created equal,** that they are **endowed** by their **Creator** with **certain unalienable** Rights, that among these are Life, **Liberty** and the **pursuit** of Happiness——

THE POETRY OF THE ROOT CONCEPT

As language develops, it takes the easiest course, going from the known to the unknown. It is easier to describe a new thought by using well-known words, or variants of them, rather than to create new words which very few would know. This impulse has also been a stimulus for the development of words into families.

Early words were concerned with the physical world of the people: animals, crops, equipment, occupations, the body, time, distance. But as societies develop, they become concerned with the abstract world of ideas and planning. We have used some of our old words to fill our new needs.

"Fluid," meaning liquid, now covers fluency of words and ideas. "Inflame," to set on fire, now means to excite intensely. "Flowery," abounding in blossoms, is also highly embellished language. "Manipulate," effective use of hands, now includes artful control and shrewd use of influence.

So a number of words that describe the physical world now also describe our abstract world. With the passage of time, words have taken on meanings never thought of in early days.

To show the evolution in the meaning of words, let us first define the words explaining this change.

The *literal* meaning of a word is based on its general or ordinary meaning. When a word becomes *figurative* it represents one concept in terms of another which may be compared to it. This change of meaning—generally from a physical function to a mental function—is often achieved by a metaphor. The *metaphor* (meta *over* + phero *bear*) is a figure of speech in which one thing is identified with another, by being spoken of as if it were that other.

We use metaphors all the time. We say money is "hot" or "dirty"; that assets are "frozen." We say: "Plan after plan galloped across his brain," using the rapid gait of the horse to demonstrate the onrush of ideas; or we may say: "He cruised from idea to idea," to indicate a slow sampling.

To show how meanings of words change, we choose a small family of words with the root TEXT, meaning weave or woven. There are five core words from this root. The five core words are:

TEXTILE *woven fabrics.*
TEXTURE *the arrangement or character of a woven fabric; the surface quality of a work of art.*
TEXT *printed matter on a page or book.*
CONTEXT *parts of a sentence just before or after a specified word or passage that may determine or alter its meaning.*
PRETEXT *a fictitious reason rather than the real reason.*

Because this family of words is small, we can document exactly the tendency of a root to be stretched to explain behavior beyond its original meaning.

This shows all the ways that words can change their meanings: some words retain their meanings; other words retain their meanings and take on new meanings; and other words take on new meanings and lose their old meanings.

The use of metaphor as a means of creating new words makes the process of word development identical to a basic process of poetry. Metaphor is the medium of poetry. It gives poetry its power to startle and inspire. By the use of metaphor, language itself develops in the same way a poet creates.

For us, it is important to understand, through awareness of the metaphor concept, how some words acquire new meanings in addition to their original meanings. This shows how language can grow and change to meet the needs of a people, even though the change may take centuries.

THE ROOT CONCEPT IN TEACHING VOCABULARY

To develop a love of a language and to muster the great resources of the Anglo-Saxon and the Latin foundations of English, students should be indoctrinated early into the meanings of individual words and the realization that many words are members of families that have distinguishing features. If this were done, word learning would become a game in which students, by astounding their parents with new-found knowledge, would be constantly motivated to learn more.

A first step could be the Greek roots on the facing page. These roots are so intertwined in our conversation that we use them every day of our lives. They will be a valuable supplement to the knowledge of Latin roots available in this book.

Word learning has suffered because teachers are themselves unaware of the value of the root concept. No book thoroughly covers this subject. True, the basic information for each word **is** contained in the unabridged dictionaries. But the prefix system—the progenitor of the many siblings of the family system—makes the tracing of each family an onerous task.

That's why this book is valuable for anyone who is interested in studying the English language. It is especially helpful for high school and college students, for people who are learning English as a second language, and for anyone who is studying a Romance language.

If teachers are not aware of the dominance of the root system, how can they be expected to teach and inspire their students about these roots? If a teacher does not know of the pervasiveness of the root concept, how can the teacher impart the wonder, the magnitude, and the usefulness of the concept?

Unfortunately, there are no books covering our families of words. Our language itself is a national treasure like our national park system or the Constitution. It should be known and treasured and passed on to our heirs. And yet many of us view our language with blurred vision.

In the unabridged dictionary, the alphabetical arrangement aims at helping us find the definitions and history of the word, after we've

GREEK ROOTS USED IN THE SCIENCES

ACRO	height	LOGOS	reason, speech
ANTHRO	man	MACRO	large
ANTI	against	MECH	machine
ARCH	chief, ruler	MEGA	big
ATMOS	vapor	META	beyond
ASTRO	star	METER	measure
AUTO	self	MICRO	small
AXIOM	evident truth	MISO	hate
BAROS	weight	MONO	one
BIBLO	book	MORPH	form
BIO	life	MYTH	story, legend
CARDI	heart	NARC	numbness, stupor
CHROME	color	NEUR	nerve
CHRONO	time	NOM	law
COSMOS	order	NYM	name
CRACY	rule	OLOGY	branch of learning
DERM	skin	ORTHO	straight, regular
DIA	across	OSTEO	bone
DOX	opinion	OSMOS	an impulse
DYNA	power	OSIS	condition, disease
EPI	upon	PAN	all
ERG	energy unit	PARA	like
ETHI	custom	PATH	feeling
EU	good, well	PNEUMA	breath
GAMOS	marriage	PHILO	love
GE	earth	PHOB	fear
GEN	birth	PHON	sound
GNO	know	POLIS	a city
GON	angle	POLY	many
GRAM	writing	PROTO	first
GRAPH	writing, drawing	PSEUDO	false
GYN	woman	PSYCH	mind, soul
HEMA	blood	SCOP	see
HETERO	other, different	SOMA	body
HOLO	whole, entire	SOPH	wise
HOMO (L)	man	SYN	with, together
HOMO	same, equal	TECH	art
HYDRA	water	TELE	far
HYPER	over, too much	THEO	god
HYPO	under	THERA	cure
ISO	equal	THERM	heat
ITIS	inflammation	ZO	animal

already heard the word and our interest in it has been piqued. The study of roots in this book enables us to learn words we never knew before by linking them to words in their family.

LEARNING LATIN

Latin is the fountainhead of that part of the language we need to learn—the simple Anglo-Saxon words having been learned the early years of school. The study of word roots derived from Latin is an essential, easy and logical way to learn more about our language.

Families of words from Latin should be studied as *families*. The main reason why students cannot get a comprehensive grasp on words is that this credo is not known and applied.

The majority of our words of Latin origin belong to families. Each family is identified and defined by a root that appears in all the related words. The root is the gene running through the family that ties all the derivative words to the family.

Students graduating from high school and college are unaware of the widespread family system of words in our language. Since they do not learn a system to follow, students become frustrated and then bored. They have been unable to acquire a philosophical acquaintance with their own language!

Those who have studied Latin recognize its great value in learning English.

But Latin has steadily disappeared in high schools, colleges, and even Catholic universities, whose churches now conduct Mass in English or the language of the congregation.

Even if we haven't learned Latin, we can easily study Latin roots in the English language, thereby extracting an essential value of the ancient language.

ENGLISH HISTORY AND THE ENGLISH LANGUAGE

In the *Book of Roots* we become acquainted with hundreds of word families that can be traced back to Latin. To thoroughly appreciate the full richness of English, it helps to also know a little about some other important influences on the language we speak and write today.

Over the years, there have been many influences on the English language.

The Celts were the first known settlers on the island, and brought with them their Celtic language. The Romans invaded in 54 B.C., but soon withdrew. In A.D. 43, the Romans conquered the Celts and ruled England until A.D. 410.

In A.D. 449, the Germanic tribes (Angles, Saxons and Jutes) invaded England. Their Anglo-Saxon language became the language of the land. A few Celtic words linger in our language: cradle, cart, down, pillow, pill; some Celtic place-names; and 14 rivers named Avon (Celtic for water).

Christianity came to England in 597. It brought the Latin alphabet, replacing the earlier Runic. From 700 to the close of the Old English period in 1150, some 450 Latin words appeared in English writing (although most would later disappear from non-use).

The Normans defeated the English in the Battle of Hastings in 1066. The Normans were from Gaul, but had settled there from Norway, and had adopted an early form of French. Consequently, England had three languages simultaneously for the next two centuries: English was the language of the people, French became the literary language, and Latin continued to be the language of the church and the law.

English returned to the courtroom in 1361 (although written records were still in Latin). English replaced French in the schools in 1395.

The term Renaissance has been given to the fourteenth, fifteenth and sixteenth centuries in Europe when a revival of art and classical languages in Italy stimulated learning and literature throughout Europe, bringing the continent from the medieval period into the modern one.

This was the period of the great borrowing by the English from the Latin and French in the final formation of the language.

The great changes in the language can be noted by comparison of translations of the Bible in each century. The quotation is Matthew vi. 9-13 (The Lord's Prayer):

THE WYCLIFFE BIBLE (1397)
Oure fadir that art in heuenes, halewid be thi name; thi kyngdoom come to; be thi wille don in erthe as in heuene; 3yue to vs this dai oure breed ouer othir substaunce; and for3yne to vs oure dettis, as we for3yuen to oure detourid; and lede us nott into temptacion, but delyvre vs from yvell. Amen.

THE TYNDALE BIBLE (1525)

O oure father which art in heven, halewed be thy name. Let thy kingdom come. Geve vs this daye oure dayly breade. And forgeve vs oure treaspases, even as we forgeve them which treaspas vs. Lede vs nott into temptacion, but delyvre vs from yvell. Amen.

KING JAMES AUTHORIZED BIBLE (1611)

(After this manner therefore pray ye:) Our father which art in heaven. Hallowed be thy name. Thy Kingdom Come. Thy will be done in earth, as it is in heaven. Give us this day our daily bread, And forgive our debts, as we forgive our debtors, And lead us not into temptation, but deliver us from evil. (For thine is the kingdom, and the power, and the glory, for ever.) Amen.

The Authorized Bible, the best known English book, used less than 6,000 words, 94% of them being native Anglo-Saxon words. This vocabulary has been a stimulant to writers such as Hemingway, who used a style of telling a story with simple short words.

In the fifteenth century, there were four separate English dialects in the four areas of England; often, a resident of one district could not be understood in another. The printing press was introduced into England in 1475 and became the instrument for stabilizing the language and standardizing the spelling, enabling the London-Oxford dialect to prevail.

The first English dictionary, with 2,500 words, was published in 1603, around the time Shakespeare was reaching his peak. Shakespeare's influence on the language was monumental; his works contain the first recorded use of more than 1,700 different words.

In 1755 Samuel Johnson published his landmark two-volume dictionary; this fixed the spelling and usage of words. The language had come of age.

With the expansion of English colonies around the world, the English language took root in many climes. North America contains the largest English speaking population, in the U.S. and Canada. American English (or just American to some scholars) has benefitted from contributions from many languages, including Yiddish, the Slavic languages, American Indian languages, Chinese and numerous exotic dialects and tongues. These contributions add richness and variety to the basic storehouses of words from Anglo-Saxon and Latin origins.

This brief sketch can only suggest the rich, complex history of the

English language. Throughout its development into its present form, English has continued to rely on its two main linguistic influences, Anglo-Saxon and Latin.

The original Anglo-Saxon structure of the English language has persisted, while the vocabulary is now dominated quantitatively by derivatives from Latin directly and through the French. This book will guide us through these derivatives, as we meet each family grouped around its root.

THE MEANING BEHIND THE MEANING

THE MEANING BEHIND THE MEANING

All words are of Latin origin unless otherwise noted.
ABERRATION (ab *from* + errare *to wander*) a deviation from the right or true way.
ABOMINATE (ab *away* + omen *a foreboding*) to loathe or despise.
ABSTEMIOUS (abs *from* + temetum *strong drink*) eating and drinking sparingly; avoiding excess.
ACCUMULATE (ad *to* + cumulare *to heap*) to heap up: money, misery, friends.
ACCURATE (ad *to* + cura *take care*) if one takes care, hopefully it will be done right.
ACUMEN (acumen *a point, a sting*) quickness of insight; keenness of intellect.
ADMONITION (ad *to* + monere *to warn*) a caution or warning.
AFFABILITY (ad *to* + fari *to speak*) ease and courteousness of manner.
AFFLUENT (ad *to* + fluere *to flow*) flowing freely; abounding in wealth.
AGGRAVATE (ad *to* + gravis *heavy*) to make worse; to exasperate or irritate.
AGGREGATE (ad *to* + gregare *to herd*) to collect into a body; the entire sum.
AGONY (*Gr.* agonia *a contest*) intense suffering of body or mind.
AMBIENCE (*Fr.* ambiance) the mood, character, atmosphere of an environment or milieu.

AMBIGUOUS (ambi *around* + agere *to drive*) capable of more than one meaning.
AMBITION (ambire *to go about*) Romans had to go about and solicit votes for election; now this means desire for any achievement.
AMBULANCE (ambulare *to walk*) the early ambulance was a movable hospital for the walking wounded.
ANACHRONISM (*Gr.* ana *against* + chronos *time*) anything incongruous because it is not fitting for that point in time.
ANATOMY (*Gr.* ana *up* + temnein *to cut*) "to cut up;" dissecting the body is now a science.
ANESTHETIC (an *without* + aisthesis *feeling*) "without feeling" and insensible to pain.
ANGUISH (angere *to choke*) excruciating pain of mind or body.
ANTIPATHY (anti *against* + pathein *to feel*) an instinctive aversion or dislike.
APROPOS (*pro before* + ponere to *place*) opportune; at the right time; "by the way."
ARCANE (arcere *to shut up*) hidden, secret; known only to a few.
ARRIVE (ad *to* + ripa *shore*) "to come to shore" now means to come by any means.
ASPERSION (ad *to* + spargere *to strew*) to spread false or harsh rumors; to slander; a calumny.
ASTONISH (ad *to* + tonare *to thunder*) to strike with sudden surprise; to be "thunderstruck."
AUCTION (auctio *an increasing*) the technique of the auction is to increase the price.
AUSPICIOUS (avis *bird* + specere *to see*) in Rome, bird flights foretold the future; now an auspicious sign is an indication of success.
AUTOMOBILE (auto *self* + mobilis *movable*) a self-propelling machine.
AVUNCULAR (avunculus *uncle*) pertaining to, or like an uncle.
CALCULATE (calculus *a pebble*) formerly, to add or subtract was done with small stones.
CANDIDATE (candidus *white*) in ancient Rome, candidates for office always wore white. Our "candid" was first a "white" response, but now means open and frank.
CAPRICIOUS (capra *goat*) unreasonable change of behavior, like a leaping goat.

CARDINAL (cardo *a hinge*) cardinal rules or principles or facts are those upon which everything depends (or hinges).

CARNATION (carnis *flesh*) originally a flesh-colored flower; now it is dark red.

CARNIVAL (carn *meat* + levare *to take away*) celebration just before Lent when meat was taken away; now, any festival.

CELIBACY (caelibatus *a single life*) being unmarried; a person bound by vows to remain single.

CHIMERICAL (*Gr.* chimaira *a mythical beast*) impractical, visionary; existing only in the imagination.

CLANDESTINE (clandestinus *secret, hidden*) conducted with secrecy, implying deception or evil purpose.

CLAUSTROPHOBIA (claudere *to close* + phobia *fear*) fear of being confined in a small space.

COMPANION (com *with* + panis *bread*) one who shares bread with another will surely accompany him.

CONCISE (com *with* + caedere *to cut*) terse; expressing much in brief form.

CONGREGATION (com *with* + gregis *a flock*) the shepherd and his flock is now the pastor and parishioners.

CONNIVE (com *with* + nictare *to wink*) to encourage a wrong by silence or collusion.

CUE Cue is the letter "Q," thought to be short for the Latin *quando* (when), signaling entrance or speech.

CUMULUS (cumulus *a heap*) clouds with rounded masses heaped one upon another.

CURFEW (*OFr.* courfeu *"cover fire"*) in the Middle Ages, a bell rung at night to rake up the fire and retire; now, generally a time for children to return home.

CYNOSURE (*Gr.* kyon *dog* + oura *tail*) Cynosure formed the dog's tail (in Ursa Minor) as the guiding star to guide ships; now, cynosure is still the object of all eyes.

DANDELION (*Fr.* dent de lion *tooth of the lion*) the obnoxious weed with the jagged teeth (*L.* dent).

DELIBERATE (de *intens.* + librare *to weigh*) to weigh in the mind; to stop and think.

DELIRIUM (de *from* + lira *line, furrow*) a wandering of the mind; a temporary state of mental disturbances caused by fever.

DEPRECATE (de *from* + precari *to pray*) to pray earnestly against.

DERMATITIS (*Gr.* derm *skin* + itis *inflammation*) "inflammation of the skin."

DESUETUDE (desuetudo *disuse*) [des′wētude] discontinuance because of non-use.

DEXTERITY (dexter *right hand*) the original meaning of the "right hand" now applies to skillful use of the hands or body.

DIAGNOSIS (dia *through* + gnoskein *to know*) "a knowing through"; identification of a disease or a problem.

DISCRIMINATE (dis *apart* + crimen *judgment*) to distinguish; to observe the differences.

DISCURSIVE (dis *away* + currere *to run*) "to run away" from one subject to another.

DISMAL (dies *a day* + mal *evil*) "evil days"; and oh! so dreary.

DISPARATE (dis *not* + par *equal*) not alike; radically different.

DUPLICITY (duo *double* + plicare *to fold*) tricky deceitfulness; double-dealing.

DYNASTY (*Gr.* dynasteia *able*) a succession of rulers in one line of a family.

EBULLIENT (ebullire *to boil up*) bubbling of a liquid; bubbling over with enthusiasm.

EFFUSIVE (e *out* + fundere *to pour*) when feelings are "poured out," they are unrestrained.

ELEEMOSYNARY (*Gr.* eleemosyne *alms*) dependent on charity.

ELIMINATE (e *out* + limen *the threshold*) to remove an unneeded or unwanted object.

EMOLUMENT (e *out* + molire *to exert oneself*) remuneration for services done or office held.

ENDEMIC (*Gr.* en *in* + demos *the people*) prevailing among a people or a country.

ENDORSE (in *on* + dorsum *the back*) what is done when the name is written on the back of a document.

ENEMY (in *not* + amicus *a friend*) "not a friend" but a committed antagonist.

ENIGMA (*Gr.* ainigma *a riddle, dark saying*) anything that puzzles; speaking in riddles.

ENTHUSIASM (en *in* + theos *god*) originally, supernatural inspiration; now, zeal or fervent feeling.

EPITAPH (epi *upon* + taph *tomb*) an inscription on a tombstone.
EQUIVOCATE (aequus *equal* + vocis *voice*) speaking "in equal voices" so as to be ambiguous and mislead.
ERADICATE (e *out* + radix *root*) "out by the roots"; to destroy completely.
ESCAPE (ex *from* + cappa *cape*) when you escape, you lose your cape.
EXACERBATE (ex *intens.* + acerbus *bitter*) to irritate, aggravate, exasperate.
EXAGGERATE (ex *out* + aggerare *to heap up*) to overstate the truth.
EXCORIATE (ex *out* + corium *the skin*) "to strip off the skin"; to denounce strongly.
EXEMPLARY (exemplum *a pattern*) serving as a model to be copied.
EXPEDITE (ex *out* + pedis *foot*) to speed or make easy the project's progress.
EXTEMPORANEOUS (ex *out* + tempus *time*) performed offhand with little study or preparation.
EXTRAVAGANT (extra *beyond* + vagari *to wander*) "wandering beyond" a limit; lavish in expenditure.
FACSIMILE (facere *to make* + similis *like*) an exact copy or likeness.
FALLACIOUS (fallere *to deceive*) delusive reasoning; faulty in logic.
FEIGN (fingere *to shape*) to dissimulate, invent; make a false show.
GAUCHE (*Fr.* gauche *crooked or warped*) [gōsh] left-handed; awkward, clumsy, lacking social grace.
GENUFLECT (genu *the knee* + flectere *to bend*) to bend the knee is to worship.
GLADIOLUS (gladiolus *a sword*) gladioli are sword lilies.
GRADUATE (gradi *to step*) one gradually steps up the gradient and graduates, unless he retrogrades and suffers degradation.
GRANITE (granum *a seed, grain*) a very hard rock with distinct grains.
GROTESQUE (grotta) *ludicrous* The word comes from the grottoes discovered in Italy long ago, with curious paintings on their walls.
HETERODOX (*Gr.* hetero *other* + doxa *opinion*) departing from established doctrines, as the Bible.
HIPPOPOTAMUS (*Gr.* hippos *horse* + potamus *river*) a large mammal in Africa that is a "river horse."
HUBRIS (*Gr.* hybris) arrogance formed from excessive pride.
HYPERBOLE (*Gr.* hyper *beyond* + ballein *to throw*) "to throw beyond"; rhetorical overstatement.

IMMOLATE (in *on* + mola *a meal*) the ancient custom was to sprinkle a victim with sacrificial meal; now it is to kill as a sacrificial victim.

IMPEDIMENT (in *not* + pedis *foot*) entangling the foot is now all kinds of obstructions.

IMPOTENT (in *not* + potens *powerful*) powerless; destitute of power or strength.

IMPROVISE (in *not* + providere *foresee, anticipate*) to extemporize on the spur of the moment without previous preparation.

IMPUGN (in *against* + pugnare *to fight*) to contradict; to make insinuations against.

INCOGNITO (in *not* + cognitus *know*) in disguise or under an assumed name.

INCREDULITY (in *not* + credulus *believing*) "not believing" and skeptical.

INDENTURE (in *toward* + dentis *tooth*) the contract binding one to work for a master had jagged tooth marks, showing identical copies.

INDIGNITY (in *not* + dignus *worth*) an offense against personal dignity.

INEXORABLE (in *not* + exorare *to pray*) "cannot be prayed away"; relentless, immovable.

INFANT (in *not* + fantis *to speak*) a very young child—of course!

INFLUENCE (in *in* + fluere *to flow*) originally, the ethereal fluid from stars, thought to affect behavior; now, the power of a person or group to persuade followers by their behavior, position, or ability.

INGENIOUS (in *in* + gignere *to produce*) possessing an inventive faculty.

INGENUOUS (in *in* + gignere *to produce*) frank, open, candid.

INNOCUOUS (in *not* + nocere *to harm*) having no harmful qualities.

INNUENDO (innuere *to nod, to hint*) a hint or indirect remark implying something depreciatory.

INQUISITORIAL (inquirere *to search for*) making a rigorous inquiry.

INSCRUTABLE (in *not* + scrutari *search, examine*) incomprehensible, cannot be understood; unsearchable.

INSECT (in *into* + secare *to cut, divide*) so called, because the bodies of some insects appear cut or divided into segments.

INSTIGATE (in *in* + stigare *to goad on*) to provoke; to incite.

INSTILL (in *into* + stillare *to drop*) qualities and knowledge are attained "drop by drop."

INSULT (in *into* + salire *to leap*) originally, an attack; now, any abuse or contempt or insolence to another person.

INTROSPECTION (intro *within* + spicere *to look*) a looking into one's own mind; a self-examination.

IOTA [*Gr.*] the tiniest letter in the Greek alphabet, corresponding to our "i"; it is a very small quantity.

IRASCIBLE (ira *anger*) easily provoked; inflamed to anger.

IRREPARABLE (in *not* + reparabilis *can be repaired*) "cannot be repaired" or rectified.

KLEPTOMANIA (*Gr.* kleptes *thief* + mania *madness*) an uncontrollable propensity to steal.

LACONIC (*Gr. an inhabitant of Laconia, noted for concise speech*) a brief, pithy expression; expressing much in a few words.

LIBEL (liber *book*) libellus was "a little book"; because early pamphlets reported scurrilously of rivals, libel came to mean defaming.

LUNACY (luna *moon*) intermittent insanity was once thought caused by phases of the moon.

MALEVOLENCE (male *badly* + volens *wish*) "to wish badly"; ill-disposed toward others.

MANDATORY (mandare *to command*) authoritatively ordered; a positive command.

MANIPULATE (manu *hand*) to work with the hands; to control artfully or fraudulently.

MANUFACTURE (manu *hand* + facere *to make*) "make by hand"; now, to produce in quantity.

MATRIX (matrix *the womb*) originally, the womb; now, that from which anything takes form or develops.

MERCURICAL (Mercurius *the god Mercury*) having attributes of Mercury—clever, shrewd; having qualities of mercury—quick, volatile.

MELANCHOLY (*Gr.* melas *black* + chole *bile*) black bile, one of the ancient four humors, was thought to come from the spleen or kidneys, and cause gloominess and depression.

MERETRICIOUS (meretrix *a prostitute*) not to be confused with "merit"; false, tawdry; speciously attractive.

METAPHOR (*Gr.* meta *over* + pherein *to bear*) "giving to one word the sense of another"; a figure of speech where one thing is likened to another.

MICROCOSM (*Gr.* micros *small* + cosmos *world*) "a little world"; studying a sample as a substitute for the whole.

MITIGATE (mitis *mild* + agere *to drive, do*) lessen, assuage; less severe, to render less harsh.

MONOTONOUS (*Gr.* monos *single* + tonos *tone*) no variation; tiresome because the same old thing.

MORTIFY (mors, mortis *death* + facere *to make*) "to make death"; to humiliate.

MOUNTEBANK (*It.* montare *to mount* + banco *bench*) "one who mounts a bench" to attract an audience; a boastful pretender.

MULTIPLICATION (multi *many* + plicare *to fold*) the process of repeating a given number a certain number of times.

MUTABILITY (mutare *to change*) ability to change in form, nature, or essential qualities.

NASTURTIUM (nasus *nose* + torquere *to twist*) the flower's pungent odor is "nose-twisting."

NEBULOUS (nebula *a cloud, mist, vapor*) vague; having its parts confused or mixed.

NEFARIOUS (ne *not* + fas *lawful*) wicked, sinful, detestable, heinous.

NEGLIGENCE (negligentia *carelessness*) failure to exercise the care that the circumstances require.

NOSTALGIA (*Gr.* nostos *a return* + algos *pain, grief*) homesickness; longing for something long ago.

NUANCE (*Fr.* nuer *to shade*; *L.* nubes *a cloud*) a delicate shading of difference perceived by any of the senses (tone, speech, motive).

ORCHESTRA (*Gr.* orcheisthai *to dance*) a semicircular space in the front of the stage for dancing; later, a narrow space, part of and below the stage, was called the orchestra pit. All "orchestras" come from this.

PANACHE (penna *feather*) plume on a helmet; flamboyance of manner.

PANDEMONIUM (*Gr.* pan *all* + daimon *a demon*) home of the demons; any disorderly gathering.

PANIC The ancient god Pan supposedly caused terror among humans.

PEDIGREE (*OFr.* pie de grue *crane's foot*) the genealogical graph of ancestors resembles the crane's foot in its shape.

PEN (penna *feather*) the earliest pens were feathers or quills.

PENCIL (pencillus *a little tail*) early writers wrote with a bunch of hairs or bristles, like a little tail.

PENINSULA (pene *almost* + insula *an isle*) jutting into the water, it is almost an isle.

PERSONIFICATION (persona *a character* + facere *to make*) figuratively endowing things or ideas with personal attributes.

POIGNANT (pungere *to prick*) painful to the feelings, as a tinge of grief.

PORCELAIN (porcella *a little pig*) the upper surface of the Venus shell resembled a pig's back and was probably called "a little pig" for this reason.

PORCUPINE (porcus *a pig* + spina *a thorn*) a thorny pig—beware!

PORPOISE (porcus *a pig* + piscus *a fish*) "a pig fish"; (really, a mammal).

PRECIPITATE (praeceps *headlong*) done without deliberation or care.

PRECOCIOUS (pre *before* + coquere *to cook, mature*) development "before its time"; premature development of a child's capabilities.

PREFIX (pre *before* + figere *to fix*) "to fix before" a syllable to the root, forming a new word.

PRELIMINARY (pre *before* + limen *threshold*) "before the threshold"; this initiatory step is before the main business.

PREMISE (pre *before* + mittere *to send*) a proposition laid down that serves as a ground for an argument.

PREPOSTEROUS (pre *before* + posterus *coming after*) "before-behind-us"; (i.e., cart before the horse); a ridiculous situation.

PREVARICATE (pre *before* + varicus *straddling*) when you straddle, you quibble, evade the truth, and even lie.

PRIVY (privus *private*) privately knowing of a secret transaction.

PROCRASTINATE (pro *forward* + crastinus *of tomorrow*) to put "forward to tomorrow" is to put off to tomorrow.

PROFLIGATE (pro *forward* + fligere *to drive*) immoral, dissolute; recklessly extravagant.

PSEUDONYM (*Gr.* pseudes *false* + onyma *name*) a borrowed name; a pen name.

QUINTESSENCE (quinta essentia *fifth essence*) the four elements were air, fire, water, earth; the fifth (highest) essence was the pure, concentrated essence of anything.

RADICAL (radix *a root*) going to the root of the matter; now, it also means an extreme political position.

RAPTURE (rapere *to carry off by force*) the mind, instead of the body, is now transported to intense excitement.

RECALCITRANT (re *back* + calx, calcis *the heel*) one "who kicks back"; one rebellious of authority.

REMORSE (re *back* + modere *to bite*) "to bite back"; anguish caused by sense of guilt.

REPREHENSIBLE (re *back* + prehendere *to seize*) blamable; censurable.

RETROGRESSION (retro *backward* + gradi *step*) to "step backward" and return to an earlier state.

RHINOCEROS (*Gr.* rhinos *nose* + keras *horn*) a large plant-eating mammal with a horn-on-the-nose.

RIVAL (rivalis *one who uses the same brook;* rivus *a stream*) theory is that rivals were originally people on a same stream, with many disputes.

RUMINATE (ruminare *to ruminate*) to "chew the cud" is to meditate and ponder.

SACRIFICE (sacer *sacred* + facere *to make*) giving up a cherished object in hope of obtaining something better.

SACRILEGE (sacer *sacred* + legere *to gather up*) the intentional desecration of something sacred.

SALACIOUS (salire *to leap*) lustful, lecherous.

SALAD (sal *salt*) a side dish over which salt and vinegar are sprinkled.

SALARY (sal *salt*) Roman soldiers were paid "salt money," or salary, for their services.

SALAMI (sal *salt*) salted sausage.

SARCASM (*Gr.* sarkasmos *a bitter laugh*, from sarkazein *to tear flesh like dogs*) a keenly ironical or caustic utterance.

SARDONIC (*Gr.* sardanios *bitter*) derisive, sneering; unnaturally forced.

SCENE (*Gr.* skene *tent*) the earliest theater was in two tents; later, a canvas was stretched across the rear of the tent and painted. The word for tent was extended to cover this painted background, becoming a "scene."

SCINTILLA (scintillare *to sparkle*) a gleam, a spark; "the least particle," not even a trace.

SCINTILLATE (scintillare *to sparkle*) to emit sparks; intellectual sparkling.

SCION (secare *to cut*) a child or descendant, like a cutting that is grafted and grows again.

SEMESTER (sex *six* + mensis *month*) six months; one of two or three terms in most American schools.

SINISTER (sinister *the left hand*) superstition early associated the left hand with evil, so now sinister is evil or a disaster.

STIGMA (*Gr.* stigma *a prick with a pointed instrument*) a mark cut or burnt on a criminal; now, any sign of moral blemish or mark of disgrace.

SUBJUGATE (sub *under* + jugum *a yoke*) "to place under the yoke"; to subdue completely.

SUBTLE (subtilis *finely woven*) from fabrics "finely woven" has now come behavior and speech, skillful and cunning.

SUBTRACTION (sub *under* + trahere *to draw*) to take away or deduct one quantity from another.

SUCCINCT (sub *under* + cingere *to gird*) clothes "tucked up" now means speech shaped to be terse.

SUPERCILIOUS (super *above* + cilium *eyelid*) "above the eyelid"; eyebrows lifted haughtily, exhibiting contempt or indifference.

SUPERFLUOUS (super *above* + fluere *to flow*) more than is needed; excessive.

SUPERNUMERARY (super *above* + numerus *number*) on the stage, one performer above the necessary number.

SUPPLIANT (sub *under* + plicare *to bend*) "to bend under"; entreating, beseeching.

SURREPTITIOUS (sub *under* + rapere *to seize*) done by secret or improper means; underhanded.

TANTALIZE Tantalus [*Gr.*] son of Zeus was doomed to the lower world, where he could never quite reach food and water.

TITILLATE (titillare *to tickle*) to excite or stimulate pleasurably.

TORRENT (torrere *to burn*) water flowing with great velocity and turbulence.

TORRID (torrere *to burn*) sultry and parched; highly passionate.

TREPIDATION (trepidare *to tremble*) state of terror, fear, dread, tremor.

TRIVIAL (tri *three* + via *road*) when people on three roads meet, trifles (trivia) result.

TRUCULENT (trucis *fierce*) behavior and speech that is threatening and formidable.

UBIQUITOUS (ubique *where*) being a number of places at once.

VANDALISM (Vandals *a barbaric Germanic tribe*) to ruthlessly and maliciously destroy what is beautiful and good.

VEHEMENCE (vehere *to carry* + mens, mentis *mind*) impetuosity of feeling; violent ardor.

VENTRILOQUIST (venter *belly* + loqui *to speak*) speaking from the stomach, so the sound seems to come from another place.

THE MEANING OF AFFIXES

PREFIXES

A PREFIX IS A SYLLABLE placed before a word to change its meaning—slightly or moderately or massively. Thus, prefixes enable one root to express many different shades of meaning.

Prefixes are especially effective in the word building of verbs. If we take the Latin *scribere* "to write" (root SCRI), and use ten prefixes, we can create ten new verbs—which, in turn, create 66 words: ascribe (5), circumscribe (8), conscript (2), describe (8), inscribe (8), prescribe (8), proscribe (8), subscribe (8), superscribe (4), transcribe (7).

Since so many of our words are of Latin origin, almost all of our prefixes are Latin as well. When we borrowed teneo (to make our word "tenant"), we also borrowed abstineo (abstinent), contineo (continent), and pertineo (pertinent).

The Anglo-Saxons used prefixes, but over time most of them lost their vitality. *For* is still in use: forget, forgive. *To, over, under,* and *with* have all but disappeared; *un* still exists.

The fifteen prefixes most often used in this book are: AB *from*, AD (and variants) *to*, CON *together, with*, DE *down, away*, DIS *not*, EX *out*, IN *into, not* PER *throughout*, PRE *before*, PRO *in place of, forward*, RE *back, again*, SUB *under*, TRANS *across, over*, UN *not*.

All are Latin except the last; UN is Anglo-Saxon.

Some words that could qualify as roots are generally classed as prefixes if that is their chief function: *holo*caust, *homo*sexual.

Prefixes are an essential element of work building; a relatively few are used again and again. This makes it both important and feasible to learn their meanings.

All prefixes are Latin unless otherwise designated.

Prefix	Meaning	Examples
A	[Gr] not, without	apathy, apolitical, atheist, anomally, abyss.
A	[A-S] on, in,to	afloat, ahead, arise, asleep, about, amiss.
AB	from, away	abdicate, abhore, absolve, abject, abjure.
A/AN	[Gr] want of, not	abyss, adamant; anarchy, anomaly.
AD	to, toward	adhere, admit, admonish, adjust, adapt.

The following prefixes are variants of AD; for easier pronunciation, the second letter of the prefix becomes the same as the first letter of the root that follows:

Prefix	Meaning	Examples
AC	to, toward	accident, accord, accrue, accumulate.
AF	to, toward	affable, affirmation, affluent, affront, affix.
AG	to, toward	agglomerate, aggrandize, aggregate.
AL	to, toward	allege, alleviate, alliance, alliteration, ally.
AN	to, toward	annex, annihilate, annotate, annoy, annual.
AP	to, toward	applause, approach, appropriate, appeal.
AR	to, toward	arrange, arrest, arrive, arrogate, array.
AS	to, toward	assert, assiduous, assimilate, associate.
AT	to, toward	attach, attend, attire, attraction, attest.
AMBI	[Gr] both	ambidextrous, ambient, ambiguous.
AMPHI	[Gr] on both sides	amphibiology, amphibious, amphitheater.
ANA	[Gr] through, up	analysis, anatomy, anachronism, anagram.
ANTE	before	antecedent, antedate, antediluvial.
ANTI	[Gr] against	antibiotic, anticlimax, antidote, antigen.
APO	[Gr] away from	apoplexy, apostle, apostrophe, apocryphal.
AUTO	[Gr] self	autobiography, automobile, automatic.
BE	[A-S] make, render	behave, belong, besiege, betray, beneath.
BENE	well, good	benediction, benefactor, benefit.
BI	two, twice	biennial, bigamy, bilingual, bifocal.
CATA	[Gr] down	cataclysm, catalepsy, catalogue, catapult.
CAT	[Gr] down	cathedral, catholic, cathartic, catheter.
CIRCUM	around	circumference, circumnavigate.
COM	together, with	commiserate, commotion, community.

		The following prefixes are variants of COM:
CO	*together, with*	cohabitation, coherence, co-operate.
COL	*together, with*	collate, colleague, colloquial, collect.
CON	*together, with*	conceivable, concession, concentration.
COR	*together, with*	correct, correlate, correspond, corrupt.
CONTRA	*against*	contradict, contract, contrary, contravene.
COUNTER	*against*	counteract, countermotion, counterpart.
DE	*down*	declivity, degenerate, denounce, deject.
DE	*away*	deception, deduct, defame, delude, deduce.
DIA	*[Gr] through*	diagnosis, dialect, dialogue, diatribe.
DIS	*not*	discourage, dishonest, displeasing, disable.
DIS	*away, apart*	disinherit, dislocate, dismiss, disband.
E	*out of*	educe, eject, elude, emerge, emit, edict.
EF	*out of*	efface, effervesce, effluent, effulgent.
EX	*out of*	exact, exceed, excess, exclamation, exit.
EN	*[A-S] in, make*	enact, encircle, encourage, endurable.
EM	*[A-S] in, make*	embalm, embargo, embarrass, empower.
EN	*[Gr] in, on*	endemic, energy, enharmonic, encourage.
EM	*[Gr] in, on*	emphasis, empirical, empyesis, employer.
EP	*[Gr] upon*	epilogue, epitaph, epithet, epitome.
EU	*[Gr] good, well*	euphony, eulogy, eugenics, euthanasia.
EXTRA	*beyond*	extradition, extraordinary, extravagant.
FORE	*[A-S] before*	forebode, forehead, fortell, foresee.
HYPER	*[Gr] above*	hyperthyroid, hypercritical, hyberbole.
HYPO	*[Gr] under*	hypothesis, hypothyroid, hypocrite.
INTER	*between*	interlude, intermission, intermediate.
INTRO	*within*	introduce, intromit, introvert, introspect.
IN	*into (vb)*	incline, include, inflict, inhale, incur.
IM	*into (vb)*	immerse, impel, impose, imprison, imply.
IN	*not (adj)*	inactive, inalienable, innocuous, inanimate.
		The following prefixes are variants of IN:
IM	*not (adj)*	immature, immoderate, immoral, impartial.
IL	*not (adj)*	illegal, illegible, illegitimate, illicit.
IR	*not (adj)*	irrational, irreligious, irrelative, irregular.
IM	*[A-S] make*	imbue, impress, improve, impulse, impel.
MAG	*large*	magnanimous, magnificent, magnify.
MAL	*bad*	malediction, malfunction, malevolence.

META	[Gr] *changed*	metamorphosis, metaphor, metaphysics.
MIS	[Gr] *hatred*	misanthrope, misogamist, misogynist.
MIS	[A-S] *wrong, bad*	misbehave, misdeed, misfortune, mistake.
MONO	*one*	monosyllable, monotone, monotonous.
MULT	*many*	multifarious, multiform, multitude.
NE	*not*	nefarious, neglect, negation, neither.
NON	*not*	nonentity, nonconformist, nonessential.
OB	*against*	obdurate, oblige, obverse, object, oblique.
OP	*against*	oppose, oppress, oppugn, opponent.
OUT	[A-S] *beyond*	outbid, outdo, outline, outrage, outside.
OVER	[A-S] *above, much*	overcast, overcome, overreach, overdo.
PARA	[Gr] *beside, like*	paradigm, paradox, paragraph, parameter.
PER	*through*	perennial, perdition, perfume, pervade.
PERI	[Gr] *around*	perimeter, periodic, peripatetic, periscope.
POLY	[Gr] *many*	polygamist, polysyllable, polygram.
POST	*after*	post-bellum, postdate, post-mortem.
PRE	*before*	preamble, preface, precipitate, precede.
PRO	*before*	procedure, procreate, promise, produce.
PRO	*in place; behalf of*	pronoun, proconsul, proponent, propose.
PRO	*forward*	project, promotion, progress, propellant.
RE	*back*	regressions, rebel, recede, reject, recall.
RE	*again*	reimburse, recapitulate, reclamation.
SE	*aside*	secede, seclusion, seduce, sedition.
SUB	*under*	subordinate, subpoena, subjugate, subdue.
SUC	*under, up*	succor, succeed, succumb, succinct.
SUP	*under, up*	supplicant, suppress, suppose, support.
SUS	*under, up*	suspect, suspicion, sustain, suspend.
SUPER	*over*	superficial, superfluous, superstition.
SUR	*above, upon*	surface, surreptitious, surrogate, survey.
SYM	[Gr] *together, with*	symbol, symmetry, sympathy, symbiotic.
SYN	[Gr] *together, with*	synonym, synergistic, syntax, synopsis.
TRANS	*cross, over*	transact, translate, transfer, transmit.
UN	[A-S] *reverse (vb)*	unbind, undo, unfold, unhinge, uncork.
UN	[A-S] *not (adj)*	uncertain, unfair, unjust, untrue, unequal.
UNDER	[A-S] *beneath*	undergo, underrate, understand, underlie.
UNI	*one*	unicameral, uniform, unify, universal.
WITH	[A-S] *against*	withdraw, withhold, without, withstand.

SUFFIXES

Suffixes are added to roots to make nouns, verbs, adjectives, and adverbs. They change the function of a word, enabling it to be one part of speech or another, or more than one.

Thus, from the root MOV, we get move (vb), movement (n), movable (adj), and movably (adv).

NESS is a noun ending; LESS makes adjectives out of nouns; LY makes adverbs out of adjectives.

There are many more suffixes than prefixes; one book lists fifteen hundred suffixes. To illustrate, we can start with the Latin word *mittere*, and root MISS/MIT, which means, "to send." By adding the prefix *per*, we get the verb "permit."

From this, we can form twelve words by using suffixes: permittance, permitee, permiter, permitivity, permissibility, permissible, permissibleness, permissibly, permission, permissive, permissively, permissory.

In addition to creating words, suffixes can also limit the meanings of words. *Er* and *or* (performer, donor) show the person doing the action. *Ee* (donee) shows the person receiving the action. Gender may also be distinguished: act*or*, act*ress*; avia*tor*, avia*trix*.

The Latin word *facere* "to make" appears in various features of our language. The root FAC/FEC/FIC appears as the suffixes FIC, FICATION, IFY, FY—all meaning *to make:* FIC (terrific), FICATION (justification), IFY (verify), FY (liquefy). One root may accept variants of the suffix: certify, certification.

The Greek suffix IZE also means *to make* (utilize, visualize). The Greek suffix IC illustrates a peculiarity of some suffixes: it has different meanings and takes different forms. IC may mean *with* (volcanic), *like* (angelic), *caused by* (symphonic), *made up of* (alcoholic), *chemical* (nitric). It can also be used to form adjectives (biographic). Other forms IC takes may differ somewhat in meaning from the basic IC suffix: ICAL, ICALLY, ICALNESS, ICISM, ICIAN, ICIST, ICALITY, ICLY, ICNESS, ICITY, ICIZE, ICA, ICATE.

Since it is fairly easy to determine the general meaning of a word without studying its suffix, this part of the word has been, regrettably or justifiably, somewhat neglected.

ABLE	*tending to (adj)*	durable, laudable, obtainable, persuadable.
AC	*pertaining to (n)*	demoniac, hypochondriac, bivouac, maniac.
ACIOUS	*tends to be (adj)*	fallacious, loquacious, pugnacious, officious.
ACY	*office, state (n)*	aristocracy, celibacy, privacy, democracy.
ADE	*made of (n)*	lemonade, limeade, marmalade.
AGE	*action of (n)*	damage, postage, steerage, wastage.
AGE	*collective (n)*	average, baggage, mileage, percentage.
AGE	*process (n)*	carnage, marriage, pillage, ravage, dotage.
AL	*relating to (adj)*	argumental, brutal, inimical, natural.
ALLY	*an adverb*	accidentally, incidentally occasionally.
AN	*relating to (n)*	artisan, American, European, veteran.
ANCE	*state of (n)*	annoyance, endurance, abeyance.
ANT	*person who (n)*	appellant, combatant, confidant.
ANT	*state of (adj)*	dominant, indigant, flamboyant, variant.
AR	*relating to (adj)*	articular, jugular, muscular, popular, linear.
AR	*person who (n)*	beggar, liar, registrar, scholar, vicar.
ARD	*person who (n)*	coward, drunkard, dullard, wizard.
ARIAN	*person who (n)*	grammarian, antiquarian, librarian.
ARY	*person, thing (n)*	actuary, adversary, missionary, auxiliary.
ARY	*relating to (adj)*	anniversary, customary, documentary.
ATE	*person who (n)*	advocate, candidate, delegate, legate.
ATE	*having, being (adj)*	desperate, fortunate, obdurate, desolate.
ATE	*cause to be (vb)*	agitate, calculate, castigate, eradicate.
ATION	*state of (n)*	adulation, configuration, exhilaration.
ATION	*process, action (n)*	alteration, altercation, arrogation.

ATOR	*process, action (n)*	incinerator, orator, predator, generator.
ATORY	*process, place (n)*	conservatory, laboratory, oratory, lavatory.
CULE	*small (adj) & (n)*	animalcule, minuscule, molecule, pedicule.
CY	*process of (n)*	advocacy, militancy, truancy, innocency.
DOM	*condition (n)*	boredom, freedom, martyrdom, wisdom.
EE	*recipient (n)*	assignee, donee, selectee, lessee, trustee.
EER	*one who (n)*	auctioneer, engineer, mountaineer, pioneer.
EN	*made of (adj)*	earthen, brazen, waxen, woolen, wooden.
EN	*to make (vb)*	deepen, fasten, gladden, harden, widen.
ENCE	*condition of (n)*	condolence, decadence, eloquence.
ENT	*one who (n)*	agent, client, opponent, student, regent.
ENT	*state of being (adj)*	coherent, effulgent, solvent, potent.
EOUS	*like (adj)*	beauteous, gorgeous, hideous, envious.
ER	*higher degree (adj)*	further, greater, later, tighter, better.
ER	*person doing (n)*	baker, biographer, carpenter, bricklayer.
ER	*action of (n/vb)*	discover, plunger, recover, waiver, murder.
ERY	*place where (n)*	bakery, bindery, brewery, winery, tannery.
ERY	*state of (n)*	drudgery, bravery, savagery, slavery.
ESCENCE	*becoming (n)*	convalescence, obsolescence, adolescence.
ESS	*female doer (n)*	actress, mistress, poetess, songstress.
ETTE	*small (n)*	etiquette, cigarette, kitchenette, statuette.
EUR	*agent (n)*	amateur, entrepreneur, raconteur, auteur.
FIC	*making (adj)*	specific, honorific, scientific, terrific.
FICATION	*process of (n)*	beautification, glorification, edification.
FUL	*full of (adj)*	careful, doubtful, fearful, hopeful, tearful.
FY	*make (vb)*	fortify, magnify, purify, rectify, glorify.
GRAM	*a thing written (n)*	diagram, chronogram, neurogram.
GRAPH	*used in writing (n)*	autograph, phonograph, photograph.
HOOD	*condition of (n)*	boyhood, childhood, adulthood, fatherhood.
IAL	*condition of (adj)*	artificial, official, magisterial, ministerial.
IAN	*one who (n)*	agrarian, Christian, Grecian, historian.
IBLE	*fit, can be (adj)*	divisible, incorrigible, invisible, legible.
IC	*behavior of (adj)*	academic, angelic, heroic, volcanic, erratic.
ICAL	*the nature of (adj)*	comical, historical, physical, poetical.
ICE	*being, thing that (n)*	justice, malice, notice, service, avarice.
ICLE	*small (n)*	article, cuticle, denticle, particle, canticle.
ICS	*science of (n)*	acoustics, ethics, optics, politics, dialectics.

ID	*state of being (adj)*	frigid, splendid, torrid, vivid, livid, lucid.
IDE	*chemical (n)*	bromide, cloride, hydride, iodide, ozonide.
IER	*person who (n)*	bombardier, cashier, clothier, glazier.
ILE	*pertaining to (adj)*	fragile, hostile, juvenile, virile, peurile.
INE	*belonging to (adj)*	canine, divine, feminine, infantine.
INE	*forms a noun*	doctrine, discipline, medicine, quarantine.
INE	*a product (n)*	bromine, iodine, morphine, vasoline.
ING	*present action (n)*	acting, doing, falling, skiing, playing.
ION	*act, state of (n)*	corruption, expansion, inspection.
IOUS	*behaviour of (adj)*	anxious, furious, rebellious, religious.
ISH	*forms verbs*	finish, furnish, furbish, punish, cherish.
ISH	*adjectives*	boyish, foolish, Scottish, Spanish, whitish.
ISM	*state of (n)*	barbarism, fanatacism, heroism.
IST	*person who (n)*	artist, botanist, florist, humanist.
ITE	*from Latin (adj)*	exquisite, opposite, requisite, unite.
ITIS	*inflammation of (n)*	arthritis, bronchitis, meningitis, phrenitis.
ITY	*state of being (n)*	ability, captivity, docility, fertility, acidity.
IVE	*having power (adj)*	adhesive, attractive, corrective, active.
IVE	*person who (n)*	captive, fugitive, native, operative.
IZATION	*state of (n)*	civilization, legalization, realization.
IZE	*to make, to (vb)*	civilize, fertilize, legalize, modernize.
KIN	*small (n)*	catkin, lambkin, manikin, napkin, pumpkin.
LENT	*full of (adj)*	fraudulent, pestilent, succulent, violent.
LESS	*without (adj)*	artless, fruitless, loveless, powerless.
LESS	*negation (adj)*	ageless, ceaseless, dauntless, tireless.
LET	*small (n)*	armlet, bracelet, leaflet, starlet, amulet.
LIKE	*resembling (adj)*	Godlike, homelike, manlike, warlike.
LING	*small (n)*	darling, gosling, seedling, yearling.
LOGY	*science of (n)*	geology, psychology, theology, physiology.
LOGY	*speaking (n)*	eulogy, doxology, homology, tautology.
LY	*adverbial*	cowardly, fatherly, princely, worldly.
LYSIS	*freeing, dissolving (n)*	analysis, dialysis, paralysis.
MAN	*one who does (n)*	craftsman, gasman, motorman.
MENT	*state of result (n)*	acquirement, excitement, retirement.
MENT	*process of (n)*	development, measurement, movement.
MONY	*condition of (n)*	matrimony, sanctimony, testimony.
MOST	*superlative (adj)*	aftermost, foremost, outermost, utmost.

NESS	*state of (n)*	boldness, coolness, fondness, sickness.
OCK	*small (n)*	buttock, haddock, hillock, paddock.
OID	*resembling (n)*	adenoid, celluloid, spheroid, typhoid.
OON	*large (n)*	balloon, bassoon, cartoon, harpoon.
OR	*person who (n)*	collector, executor, imitator, sponsor, juror.
OR	*condition (n)*	error, favor, horror, terror, fervor, rigor.
ORY	*place where (n)*	depository, dormitory, factory, refectory.
ORY	*relating to (adj)*	exploratory, prefatory, satisfactory, factory.
OSE	*full of, like (adj)*	globose, jocose, morose, verbose, comatose.
OSE	*a nutrient (n)*	cellulose, glucose, proteose, sucrose.
OSIS	*a condition (n)*	hypnosis, neurosis, osmosis, psychosis.
OUS	*full of (adj)*	dangerous, gracious, religious, mendacious.
RY	*collection of (n)*	bravery, cookery, slavery, surgery, usury.
SHIP	*state of (n)*	fellowship, friendship, hardship, leadership.
SHIP	*rank, office (n)*	authorship, governorship, partnership.
SOME	*somewhat (adj)*	awesome, lonesome, tiresome.
STER	*who does (n)*	gamester, punster, trickster, youngster.
TRIX	*female doer (n)*	aviatrix, executrix, narratrix.
TUDE	*state of (n)*	fortitude, rectitude, servitude, certitude.
ULAR	*state of being (adj)*	circular, secular, popular, regular.
ULE	*small (n)*	capsule, globule, granule, module, sporule.
ULENT	*full of (adj)*	fraudulent, malevolent, opulent, virulent.
UND	*nature of (adj)*	fecund, jocund, moribund, rotund.
URE	*act of (n)*	censure, composure, enclosure, torture.
WARD	*direction (adj/adv)*	eastward, heavenward, homeward.
WAYS	*adverb form*	always, crossways, endways, sideways.
WISE	*adverb form*	anywise, clockwise, crosswise, lengthwise.
Y	*state of being (n)*	chastity, honesty, mastery, modesty, ability.
Y	*consist of (adj)*	bloody, dewy, fleshy, rocky, muddy, sweaty.

SUFFIXES BY PARTS OF SPEECH

NOUN SUFFIXES DEPICTING *STATE OF, QUALITY OF, RESULT OF*

ACY	accuracy, celibacy, efficacy, lunacy, supremacy.
AGE	average, damage, marriage, parentage, percentage.
ANCE	allowance, ignorance, performance, vigilance, endurance.
ANCY	constancy, occupancy, vacancy, vagrancy, arrogancy.
ENCE	antecedence, audience, diligence, patience, persistence.
ENCY	agency, clemency, decency, emergency, effulgency.
ESCENCE	acquiescence, adolescence, convolescence, effervescence.
EUR	grandeur, hauteur, amateur, raconteur, auteur.
HOOD	brotherhood, childhood, falsehood, manhood.
ICE	armistice, justice, malice, poultice, practice, device.
ICS	mathematics, mechanics, physics, politics, gymnastics.
ISM	despotism, heroism, ostracism, plagarism, Catholicism.
ITY	calamity, felicity, necessity, sincerity, unity, density.
MENT	amazement, puzzlement, punishment, refinement.
MONY	acrimony, alimony, ceremony, testimony, patrimony.
NESS	goodness, kindness, sweetness, sickness, wickedness.
ORY	directory, factory, memory, territory, armory, victory.
RY	bravery, chemistry, imagery, slavery, surgery.
SHIP	censorship, friendship, hardship, worship, leadership.

T	complaint, deceit, gift, joint.
TH	birth, health, truth, warmth, girth, breadth, worth.
TUDE	amplitude, fortitude, gratitude, platitude, servitude.
TY	brevity, capacity, density, novelty, honesty, modesty.
URE	censure, culture, exposure, failure, measure, treasure.
Y	agony, apathy, destiny, inquiry, worthy, healthy, wealthy.

NOUN SUFFIXES DENOTING *DIMINUTIVES*

CLE	corpuscle, article, particle, follicle, icicle, cuticle.
CULE	minuscule, molecule, animalcule, pedicule.
ETTE	(also ET) cigarette, etiquette; locket, bassinet.
IE	birdie, goodie, Goldie, Lassie, dearie, calorie.
KIN	manikin, napkin, catkin, lambkin, pumpkin.
LET	starlet, bracelet, armlet, leaflet, ringlet, streamlet.
LING	seedling, yearling, darling, gosling, hireling, nestling.
OCK	hillock, paddock, buttock, haddock, tussock.
ULE	capsule, globule, granule, module, pustule, spherule.

NOUN SUFFIXES DENOTING *FEMININE*

ESS	actress, poetess, mistress, songstress, conductress.
INE	heroine, Adeline, Clementine, valentine.
TRIX	administratrix, aviatrix, executrix, narratrix, mediatrix.

NOUN SUFFIXES DENOTING *PERSON WHO DOES*

AN	comedian, librarian, optician, veteran, historian, artisan.
ANT	accountant, assistant, pedant, vagrant, confidant, tenant.
AR	beggar, liar, registrar, scholar, vicar.
ARD	dullard, drunkard, coward, wizard, laggard.
ARIAN	antiquarian, grammarian, librarian, libertarian, agrarian.
ARY	adversary, actuary, missionary, notary, votary.
ATE	advocate, candidate, delegate, magistrate.
EE	(*recipient of*) appointee, assignee, donee, lessee, trustee.
EER	auctioneer, engineer, mountaineer, pioneer, mutineer.
ENT	agent, client, opponent, student, president, resident.
ER	baker, biographer, carpenter, philosopher, discerner.
EUR	amateur, entrepreneur, raconteur, saboteur, auteur.
IER	carrier, cashier, financier, clothier, copier.

IST	artist, chemist, pianist, humanist, egotist, oculist.
IVE	captive, fugitive, native, operative.
OR	ancestor, confessor, doctor, executor, orator, predator.
STER	gangster, monster, songster, spinster, mobster, minister.

ADJECTIVE SUFFIXES DENOTING *OF, PERTAINING TO*

AC	demoniac, elegiac, maniac, hypochondriac.
AL	formal, natural, ornamental, hypocritical, nasal, annual.
AN	American, diocesan, republican, veteran, sylvan.
ANT	brilliant, distant, militant, vigilant, abundant, buoyant.
AR	angular, circular, polar, popular, insular, consular.
ARY	customary, literary, momentary, reactionary, military.
ATE	adequate, illiterate, obstinate, temperate, desolate.
EN	earthen, golden, waxen, wooden, silken, oaken.
IC	barbaric, comedic, heroic, volcanic, politic.
ICAL	comical, critical, apolitical, political, inimical.
ID	candid, lucid, morbid, splendid, acrid, humid.
ILE	fragile, docile, versatile, virile, puerile, mobile.
INE	canine, feminine, serpentine, sanguine, genuine, saline.
ORY	cursory, inflammatory, satisfactory, transitory, desultory.

ADJECTIVE SUFFIXES DENOTING *FULL OF, ABOUND IN*

ATE	fortunate, passionate, proportionate, insatiate.
FUL	beautiful, careful, successful, skillful, joyful, painful.
OSE	cellulose, globose, sucrose, verbose, fructose, morose.
OUS	courageous, fabulous, joyous, gracious, sonorous.
SOME	handsome, quarrelsome, troublesome, wholesome.
Y	bony, earthy, rocky, thorny, grassy, muddy, dewy.

ADVECTIVE SUFFIXES DENOTING *THAT MAY, CAN BE*

ABLE	allowable, laudable, obtainable, tolerable, endowable.
IBLE	credible, divisible, eligible, legible, invisible, incredible.
ILE	agile, docile, futile, tractile, fragile, fertile, versatile.

ADJECTIVE SUFFIXES DENOTING *LIKE, RESEMBLING*

ISH	boyish, brutish, feverish, selfish, bookish, clownish, waspish.
LIKE	ball-like, childlike, manlike, warlike, giantlike, saintlike.
LY	brotherly, friendly, lonely, unmanly, homely, boldly.

VERB SUFFIXES DENOTING *TO MAKE*

ATE	agitate, anticipate, communicate, emigrate, elevate.
EN	brighten, lengthen, ripen, weaken, strengthen, fatten.
FY	beautify, clarify, justify, purify, electrify, satisfy, fortify.
ISH	astonish, finish, publish, vanish, banish, ravish, diminish.
IZE	(also ISE) activize, agonize, civilize, advertise, chastise.

ADVERBIAL SUFFIXES

LY	*like*	humanly, meekly, worthily, actually, fairly.
WARD	*direction of*	afterward, homeward, onward, northward.
WISE	*in the manner*	clockwise, likewise, sidewise, otherwise.

THE MEANING OF ROOTS

SIMPLIFIED MAJOR ROOTS

ACT	*drive, do*	active, actor, counteract, enact, react, transact.
ANIMA	*soul, mind*	animal, animate, animosity, equanimity.
BOL	*throw*	bolt, diabolical, embolism, hyperbole, symbol.
CAD/CAS	*fall*	cadaver, cadence, decadence; cascade, casual.
CAP	*take*	capable, capacity, capacious, captivate.
CEP	*take*	accept, concept, deception, except, intercept.
CAP/CIP	*head*	capital, capitulate; precipice, precipitous.
CED	*go, lead*	cede, concede, intercede, proceed, succeed.
CES	*go, lead*	access, excess, incessant, process, success.
CER/CRE	*judge*	concern, discern, discrete, excrete, secret.
CIS	*cut*	concise, decisive, excise, incisive, precise.
CIT	*rouse*	cite, excite, incite, recite, resuscitate.
CLAM	*shout*	clamor, acclamation, declamation, proclamation.
CLI	*slope*	incline, decline, recline, acclivity, proclivity.
CLUD	*shut*	include, conclude, exclude, preclude, seclude.
COGN	*know*	cognition, cognizance, incognito, recognize.
CORP	*body*	corpse, corporation, incorporate, corpuscle.
COR/COU	*heart*	accord, concord, discord; courage, encourage.
CREA	*create*	creativity, creature, procreate, recreation.
CRED	*trust*	credence, credentials, credit, incredible.
CRIM	*crime*	criminal, criminology, discriminate, incriminate.
CUB/CUM	*lie down*	incubate, concubine; incumbent, recumbent.

CUR	*care*	curious, accurate, procure, sinecure, secure.
CUR	*run*	current, concur, discursive, incur, occur.
CUSS	*shake*	concussion, discussion, percussion, repercussion.
DIC	*proclaim*	abdicate, dedicate, indicate, predicate.
DICT	*say*	addict, dictate, contradict, predict, verdict.
DIT	*give*	addition, edit, editor, tradition, perdition.
DIVI	*divide*	dividend, division, subdivide, individualism.
DUC	*lead*	abductor, adducible, conducive, conductor, duct, deduct, educate, induce, produce, reduce, seduce.
DUR	*lasting*	durable, duress, endure, indurate, obdurate.
EQU	*equal*	equality, equate, equator, adequate, equivocal.
ERR	*wander*	aberrance, err, erratic, erroneous, errant.
FAB	*speak*	affable, ineffable, fable, fabulous, confabulate.
FAC	*make*	factor, manufacture, faction, facilitate, facsimile.
FAL	*false*	fallacy, infallible, falter, false, falsetto.
FEND	*keep off*	fend, fender, defend, offend, inoffensive.
FER	*bear*	confer, defer, infer, offer, refer, transfer.
FID	*faith*	fidelity, affidavit, confident, diffident, perfidy.
FIG	*shape*	figure, configuration, prefigure, figment.
FIN	*end*	finish, finale, infinite, confine, define.
FIX	*fix*	fixation, fixture, Crucifix, prefix, suffix.
FLEC	*bend*	flection, circumflect, deflect, inflect, reflect.
FLIC	*strike*	afflict, affliction, conflict, inflict, profligate.
FLU	*flow*	fluent, fluidity, affluent, influential, superfluous.
FORM	*shape*	inform, formula, conform, deform, inform.
FORT	*strong*	forte, fortitude, comfort, effort, reinforce.
FRA	*break*	fraction, infraction, fracture, fragile.
FRONT	*forepart*	front, frontier, frontispiece, affront, confront.
FUG	*flee*	fugitive, fugue, refuge, subterfuge, centrifugal.
FUNCT	*perform*	function, dysfunction, functionary, defunct.
FUS	*pour*	confuse, diffuse, effusive, profuse, refuse.
GAM	*marriage*	bigamy, endogamy, misogamy, monogamy.
GEN	*beget*	gene, genetics, generic, general, generate.
GEST	*carry*	gesture, gestation, congest, digest, suggest.
GRAD	*step*	gradation, gradual, graduation, degrade.
GRAPH	*write*	autograph, biography, choreography, epigraph.
GRAT	*thankful*	grateful, congratulate, ingrate, gratuity.

GRAV	*heavy*	grave, gravitate, gravity, aggravate.
GREG	*flock*	gregarious, aggregate, congregate, egregious.
HAB	*have*	habit, habitual, cohabit, inhabit, rehabilitate.
HER	*stick*	adhere, cohere, coherence, incoherent, inhere.
HUMAN	*man*	humane, humanize, humanistic, humanitarian.
HUM	*lowly*	humble, exhume, inhume, humility, humiliate.
INT	*within*	interior, internal, intestinal, intimate, intrinsic.
JECT	*throw*	object, objective, conjecture, deject, ejection, inject, interject, object, project, reject, subject.
JOIN	*join*	adjoin, conjoin, disjoin, enjoin, rejoin.
JUD	*law*	judgment, prejudice, adjudicate, judicious.
LAT	*carry*	ablation, collate, correlate, dilate, elate, legislate, prelate, relate, relativity, translate.
LEC	*gather*	collect, dialect, eclectic, elect, intellectual, lectern, lecture, neglect, prelect, select.
LEG	*law*	legality, legislate, legitimate, illegitimate.
LEV	*raise*	lever, levitate, alleviate, elevate, relevant.
LIBER	*free*	liberal, illiberal, liberate, libertine, liberty.
LIQU	*liquid*	liquid, liquefy, liquor, liquidate, liquidity.
LOC	*place*	locality, localize, locomotive, allocate, dislocate.
LOG	*reason*	analogy, apology, dialogue, eulogy, logic.
LOQ	*speak*	colloquy, eloquence, loquacious, soliloquy.
LU	*wash*	ablution, affluence, alluvial, dilution, pollution.
LUD	*deceive*	ludicrous, allude, delude, elude, prelude.
MAGN	*great*	magnanimous, magnate, magniloquent.
MAL	*bad*	dismal, malady, malcontent, malice, malign.
MAND	*command*	mandate, command, countermand, demand.
MANU	*hand*	manual, manufacture, manacle, manipulate.
MAT	*mother*	maternal, matricide, matrimony, matron, matrix.
MEDI	*middle*	mediate, mediocre, medium, immediate.
MEM	*memory*	memento, memoir, memorandum, commemorate.
MENT	*mind*	mental, mentality, comment, demented.
MERC	*trade*	merchant, merchandise, mercenary, mercurial.
MERG	*dip*	merge, emerge, emersion, emergency.
METR	*measure*	meter, diameter, diametric, symmetry.
MIN	*small*	minute, minority, diminish, minus, minimum.
MISS	*send*	admission, commission, dismiss, emission,

MITT	*send*	committee, intermittent, omitter, permitter.
MOD	*manner*	mode, model, remodel, moderator, modification.
MON	*warn*	admonition, premonition, monitor, monumental.
MONO	*one*	monocle, monologue, monopolize, monotonous.
MONS	*show*	monster, demonstrate, remonstrate.
MORAL	*manner*	amoral, moral, immoral, demoralize, morose.
MORT	*death*	mortal, morbid, mortify, amortize, mortgage.
MOUNT	*mount*	mountain, amount, dismount, paramount.
MOV	*move*	move, countermove, immovable, remove.
MUN	*gift*	communal, communicate, immune, remunerate.
MUT	*change*	commute, immutable, mutiny, mutation.
NAT	*born*	native, natural, supernatural, innate, pregnate.
NEG	*deny*	abnegate, negative, neglect, negligent, renegade.
NOM	*name*	nomination, nominee, denomination, renominate.
NORM	*rule*	abnormal, enormous, norm, normalization.
NOT	*known*	notable, notary, notify, notorious, annotate.
NOUN	*announce*	announce, denounce, pronounce, mispronounce.
NOV	*new*	novel, novella, novice, novocain, renovate.
ORA	*speak*	exorable, inexorable, oral, oration, oratorio.
ORD	*order*	order, disorder, ordain, ordinary, subordinate.
ORG	*instrument*	organ, inorganic, organize, disorganize.
PAN	*all*	panacea, pandemic, pandemonium, panorama.
PAR	*prepare*	apparatus, parade, compare, prepare, separate.
PART	*share*	partial, particle, particular, partition, partner, participate, apart, counterpart, depart, impart.
PASS	*spread*	compass, passage, impassable, surpass, trespass.
PASS	*bear*	passion, compassion, dispassion, impassion.
PATH	*feeling*	apathy, antipathy, pathos, pathetic, sympathy.
PAT	*father*	paternal, patrician, patron, patriot, compatriot.
PED	*foot*	pedal, impediment, expedite, expedient.
PEL	*drive*	compel, dispel, expel, impel, propel, repel.
PEN	*punish*	penalty, penance, penitence, penitentiary, repent.
PEND	*hang*	depend, expend, impend, pend, spend, suspend.
PENS	*weigh*	compensate, dispense, expense, pension.
PET	*seek*	appetite, compete, incompetence, impetuous.
PLEA	*please*	plea, plead, please, pleasure, displeasure.
PLE	*full*	plethora, complete, deplete, replete, supplement.

PLIC	*fold*	applicable, complicate, duplicity, explicit, implication, pliable, replica, multiplication.
PORT	*carry*	portable, deport, export, import, report.
POS	*put*	pose, superpose, propose, repose, suppose, depose, expose, impose, interpose, oppose.
POT	*able*	potent, impotent, omnipotent, potential.
PREH	*seize*	apprehend, misapprehend, comprehend.
PRESS	*press*	compress, depress, express, impress, oppress.
PROV	*prove*	approve, disprove, improve, provable, reprove.
PUNC	*point*	punch, punctual, puncture, punctuate.
PUR	*cleanse*	purge, expurgate, impure, purify, puritanical.
PUT	*think*	compute, dispute, impute, repute, disreputable.
RECT	*rule*	correct, incorrect, direct, erect, rectify.
ROG	*ask*	abrogate, arrogance, derogate, interrogate.
RUPT	*break*	abrupt, corrupt, disrupt, erupt, interrupt.
SAT	*enough*	satiate, satiety, satisfy, unsatisfactory, saturate.
SCEND	*climb*	ascend, reascend, descend, condescend.
SCI	*know*	science, omniscient, conscience, conscionable.
SCRIB	*write*	scribble, scripture, describe, prescribe.
SECT	*cut*	bisect, dissect, intersect, insect, section.
SEN	*feel*	assent, consent, dissent, resent, sentence, sense, sensation, sensitive, sensual, nonsense.
SEQ	*follow*	consequence, obsequious, sequel, subsequent.
SERT	*join*	assert, desert, exert, insert, reassert.
SERV	*save*	conserve, conservative, observe, preserve.
SERV	*serve*	deserve, disservice, servile, service, subservient.
SESS	*sit*	assess, possess, obsess, dispossess, repossess.
SIGN	*sign*	assign, consign, design, resign, signature.
SIMI	*like*	assimilate, dissimilar, facsimile, simulate, similar.
SIST	*stand*	assist, consist, desist, exist, co-exist, pre-exist, insist, persist, resist, irresistible, subsist.
SOCI	*companion*	social, society, associate, disassociate, unsocial.
SOLV	*solve*	absolve, dissolve, resolve, irresolute, insoluble.
SPEC	*see*	expect, inspect, respect, retrospect, suspect, specify, speculate, spectator, specimen, special.
SPIR	*breathe*	aspire, conspire, expire, perspire, transpire.
SPON	*promise*	correspond, despondency, respond, spontaneous.

STA	*stand*	circumstance, constant, establish, understand, instant, reinstate, stable, statement, statistic.
STIN	*mark*	distinct, indistinct, extinct, instinct.
STRI	*bind*	strict, constrict, restrict, astringent, stricture.
STRU	*build*	construe, misconstrue, structure, construction.
SUA	*advise*	assuage, dissuade, persuade, impersuadable.
SUM	*take*	assume, consume, presume, resume, subsume.
TEMP	*temper*	temporary, tempest, contemporary, temper.
TEN	*hold*	tenable, content, discontent, malcontent.
TIN	*hold*	abstinence, continence, discontinue, pertinent.
TEND	*stretch*	attend, contend, extend, intend, portend, pretend, superintend, tend, tensor, tensile.
TERMIN	*limit*	term, interminable, determine, exterminate.
TEST	*witness*	attest, contest, detest, incontestable, testify.
THES	*placing*	antithesis, hypothesis, parenthesis, synthesis.
TON	*tone*	intonation, baritone, astonish, monotonous.
TORT	*twist*	contort, distort, extort, retort, torture.
TRACT	*draw*	abstract, attract, contract, detract, distract, extract, intractable, protract, retract, traction.
TRIB	*give*	attribute, contribute, distribute, retribution.
TRUD	*thrust*	abstruse, extrude, intrude, obtrude, protrude.
TURB	*turmoil*	disturb, perturb, imperturbable, turbulent.
UNI	*one*	uniform, unify, unique, union, universal.
USE	*use*	useful, abuse, disuse, misuse, peruse, unusual.
VAL	*value*	prevalent, convalescent, equivalent, valid.
VEN	*come*	adventure, convene, event, invent, prevent.
VERS	*turn*	adverse, conversant, inverse, obverse, perverse,
VERT	*turn*	advertise, convertible, divert, introvert, revert.
VEST	*clothe*	divest, devest, investment, reinvest, vest.
VIA	*way*	via, viaduct, deviate, obviate, trivial.
VID	*see*	provide, providence, evident, self-evidence.
VIS	*see*	provision, advise, revise, supervise, visible.
VIV	*life*	convivial, revive, survive, viable, vivacity.
VOC	*call*	advocate, convocation, equivocate, unequivocal, evocative, invocation, provocation, revocable.
VOLV	*roll*	convolve, devolve, evolve, involve, revolve.
VOL	*will*	benevolent, malevolent, volition, voluntary.

ROOTS WITH SELECTED DERIVATIVES

ACT *drive*
action
actuary
actor
counteract
enact
exact
react
transact

CAP *take*
capable
capacity
capacious
capsule
captivate
capture

CED *yield*
cede
accede

antecedent
concede
intercede
precede
proceed
recede
secede
succeed

CIS *cut, kill*
circumcise
concise
decisive
indecisive
excise
incisive
incisor
precise

CLU *shut*
conclude

inconclusive
exclude
include
occlude
preclude
recluse
seclude

CRED *believe*
credo
credulous
incredible
credit
accredited
discredit

CUR *run*
current
curriculum
cursory
concur

discursive
excursion
incursion
occur
precursor
recur

DIC *proclaim*
abdicate
dedicate
indicate
contraindicate
predicament
predicate

DICT *say*
diction
dictate
addict
contradict
edict
indict
interdict
jurisdiction
malediction
predict
valedictory
verdict

DIVI *divide*
dividend
divisible
indivisible
division
divisive
subdivide
individual

DIT *give*
addition
edit
edition
editor
tradition
extradition
perdition

DUC *lead*
abduct
adduce
conducive
conductor
deduction
ductility
educe
induce
introduce
inducement
reduce
produce
reproduce
seduce
subdue
traduce
viaduct
aqueduct

EQU *equal*
equal
equality
equanimity
equate
equator
equilibrium
equity

ERR *wander*
err
erratic
errata
error
erroneous
aberrance
errant

FAL *deceive*
fallacy
fallible
infallible
falter
false
falsetto

FER *bear*
confer
defer
differ
infer
offer
inference
proffer
refer
suffer
transfer
fertile

FID *faith*
fidelity
fiduciary
affidavit
confidant
diffident
perfidy

SELECTED DERIVATIVES | 57

FIG *shape*
figure
disfigure
configuration
prefigure
transfigure
effigy
figment

FIN *end*
affinity
confine
define
definitive
refine
superfine
finale
finance
finish
infinity
infinitesmal

FIX *fix*
fix
fixture
crucifix
affix
infix
prefix
suffix

FLAM *burning*
flame
flamboyant
flamingo
inflammatory
inflammation

FLU *flow*
affluence
confluence
effluence
influence
fluent
mellifluence
superfluous
fluctuate
fluvial
influenza

FORM *shape*
form
formal
informal
formula
conform
deform
inform
misinform
perform
reform
transform
uniform

FORT *strong*
fortify
fortitude
forte
comfort
discomfort
effort

FUG *flee*
fugitive
fugue

refuge
refugee
subterfuge
vermifuge

FUS *pour*
fusion
confusion
diffuse
effusion
infuse
profuse
refuse

GEST *carry*
gesture
gesticulate
congestion
digest
ingest
suggest

GRES *walk*
aggress
congress
degression
digress
egress
ingress
introgression
progress
regress
transgress

GRAT *thankful*
grateful
gratify

gratis
gratitude
gratuity
ingratiate
congratulate

GREG *flock*
gregarious
aggregate
congregate
egregious
segregate

GEN *beget, kind*
gene
genetics
gender
genesis
general
generous
congenial
congenital
ingenious
ingenuous

HAB *have, able*
habit
habitat
cohabit
inhabit
habilitate
rehabilitate

JECT *throw*
abject
adjective
conjecture

deject
eject
inject
interject
object
project
reject
subject
trajectory
ejaculate

JOIN *join*
join
joint
adjoin
conjoin
disjoin
enjoin
rejoin
subjoin

LAT *carry*
collate
correlate
dilate
elate
legislate
prelate
relate
relation
relative
superlative

LECT *gather*
collect
dialect
eclectic

intellect
lecture
select

LOG *reason*
analogy
apology
catalogue
dialogue
epilogue
eulogy
logic
monologue
genealogy

LOQ *speak*
colloquy
eloquence
locution
circumlocution
loquacious
soliloquy
ventriloquist

LUD *deceive*
allude
collude
elude
illusion
ludicrous
interlude
postlude

MAL *bad*
dismal
maladroit
malady

malaria
malcontent
malediction
malefactor
malevolence
malpractice

MAND *command*
mandate
mandatory
command
countermand
demand
remand

MANU *hand*
manual
manacle
manage
manicure
manifest
manufacture
manipulate
maneuver
manuscript
maintenance
manure
emancipate

MEM *memory*
memory
memorial
memorable
memoir
memorandum
commemorate
remember

MERG *to dip*
merge
submerge
emerge
emersion
emergency
immerse

MISS *send*
admission
commission
demission
dismiss
omission
permission
promissory
remission
submission
surmisable

MOD *manner*
accommodate
commodity
mode
model
moderate
immoderate
modern
modest
immodest
modify
modulate

MORT *dead*
mortal
mortgage
mortify
amortize
mortician
mortuary

MOT *move*
motion
commotion
emotion
locomotion
demotion
remotely
motor
motive
promotion

NAT *born*
native
national
international
prenatal
natural
supernatural
unnatural
innate
impregnate

NOT *mark*
notation
note
notable
notary
notify
notion
notorious
annotate
connote
denote

NOV *new*
novel
novice
novitiate
innovate
novocain
renovate

ORD *order, rank*
order
disorder
ordnance
co-ordinate
subordinate
ordinary
extraordinary
inordinate

PARA *prepare*
apparatus
parade
compare
prepare
reparation
separate

PART *share*
part
partial
impartial
particle
particular
partition
partner
participate
compartment
counterpart

depart
impart

PED *foot*
expedite
expedition
expedient
impede
impediment
pedestrian
pedigree
pedicure
biped

PEL *drive*
compel
dispel
expel
impel
propel
repel

PEN *punishment*
penalty
penance
penitence
impenitent
penitentiary
repent

PEND *hang*
pend
pendulous
pendulum
append
appendix
depend

independent
expend
impending
perpendicular
suspend

PET *seek*
appetite
compete
competition
competence
incompetent
impetuous
petition
repetition

PLE *full, plenty*
plenty
plethora
plenipotentiary
complement
complete
deplete
expletive
implement
replete
supplement

PLI *fold*
applicable
apply
complicate
complicity
duplicity
explicit
implicit
implication

multiplication
pliable
replica
supplicant
triplicate

PORT *carry*
port
portable
portage
porter
portfolio
comport
deport
deportment
disport
export
import
important
opportune
purport
rapport
report
sport

POS *put, sit*
pose
position
posture
apropos
compose
decompose
depose
deposit
dispose
disposition
expose

exposition
impose
superimpose
interpose
juxtapose
preposition
impostor
oppose
opponent
propose
purpose
transpose

PREHEND *seize*
apprehend
misapprehend
comprehend
miscomprehend
reprehend
irreprehensible

PRESS *press*
press
pressure
compress
depress
express
impress
impression
oppress
repress
suppress

PROV *prove*
approve
disapprove
prove

improve
reprove

PROPR *one's own*
proper
improper
property
propriety
proprietary
appropriate
expropriate

PUG *fight*
pugilism
pugnacious
impugn
repugnant

PUR *cleanse*
purge
purgatory
expurgate
pure
purify
puritanical
impure

PUT *think, trim*
amputate
compute
deputy
dispute
indisputable
impute
reputable
disrepute
disputant

RECT *rule*
arrect
correct
incorrect
direct
indirect
erect
rectify
rectitude

ROG *ask*
abrogate
arrogate
arrogance
derogatory
interrogate
prerogative
supererogate
surrogate

RUPT *break*
abrupt
bankrupt
corrupt
incorruptible
disrupt
erupt
interrupt
rupture

SCEND *climb*
ascend
condescend
descend
descendant
transcend
reascend

SCRIB *write*
ascribe
circumscribe
conscription
describe
indescribable
inscribe
prescribe
proscribe
perscription
subscription
transcribe
scribble

SECT *cut*
sect
sectarian
section
sector
bisect
trisect
dissect
vivisection
intersect
insect

SENS *feel*
sense
insensible
nonsense
consensus
sensation
sensible
sensitize
desensitize
sensual
sensuous

SEQ *follow*
consequence
inconsequence
obsequious
sequacious
sequel
sequence
subsequent

SERT *join*
assert
reassert
desert
dissertation
exert
insert
reinsert

SERV *save*
conserve
conservation
observe
inobservance
observation
preserve
reserve
reservation
unreserved

SES *sit*
assess
obsess
possess
possessive
dispossess
prepossess
session

SIGN *mark, sign*
assign
assignation
consignment
countersign
design
designate
insignia
resign
sign
ensign
signal
signature
significance
insignificant

SIMI *like*
assimilate
dissimilar
facsimile
simile
similar
simulate
simultaneous
verisimilar

SIST *stand, place*
assist
consist
inconsistent
desist
exist
co-exist
insist
persist
resist
subsist

SOLV *loosen*
absolve
absolute
dissolve
dissolute
resolve
irresolvable
resolute
resolution
irresolute
solvent
insolvent
soluable
insoluable

SON *sound*
assonance
consonance
dissonance
resonance
sonorous
sonic
sonar

SPEC *look*
spectacle
spectacular
aspect
expect
circumspect
inspect
introspect
prospect
respect
irrespective
disrespect
unrespected

retrospect
suspect
unsuspected
spectrum
speculate

SPIR *breathe*
aspire
conspire
expire
inspire
inspiration
perspire
transpire
spirit
spiritual

SPON *promise*
correspond
respond
responsible
irresponsible
sponsor
spontaneous
spouse

STA *stand*
circumstance
constant
inconstant
contrast
distance
equidistant
establish
instance
instant
instate

STA *stand*
reinstate
stand
understand
standard
stable
stamina
stage
state
statesman
station
static
statistics
statue
stature
substantial

STRU *build*
construe
misconstrue
construct
misconstruct
destruct
instrumental
instruct
obstruct
structure
superstructure

TEN(T) *hold*
content
discontent
malcontent
retention
sustenance
tenacious
detention

TEND *stretch*
attend
contend
distend
extend
intend
portend
pretend
superintend
tend
tension
tendon

TEST *a witness*
attest
contest
detest
protest
test
testament
testify
testimony

THES *a placing*
thesis
synthesis
synthetic
synthesize
parenthesis
hypothesis
antithesis
anathema

TOR *twist*
contort
distort
extort
retort
torment
torture
torque

TRAC *draw*
abstract
attract
contract
detract
distract
extract
intractable
protract
retract
subtract
track
tract
traction
tractor

VAL *strong*
ambivalent
convalescent
equivalence
prevalence
valiant
valid
invalid
valor
value

VEN *come*
event
adventure
circumvent
convene

VEN *come*
convenience
circumvent
convention
intervention
inventory
prevent
covenant
revenue

VIV *life*
convivial
revive
survive
vivacity
vivid

VIS *see*
advise
revise
supervise
provision
visible
visual
vista

VOC *call*
vocal
vocation
vocabulary
avocation
advocate
convocation

equivocal
revocable
irrevocable

VOL *roll*
evolve
evolution
revolve
revolt
revolution
revolver
involve
convolution
volume
voluminous
voluble

MAJOR ROOTS

THE ROOT IS THE SINGLE SYLLABLE left after a word has been stripped of all its prefixes and suffixes. It is the heart of the word, giving it its basic meaning. To make some roots more easily recognizable to the student, a letter may be added so as to identify words that should come under this root, and exclude words that have a similar appearance but come from another root.

The reason one can be definitive about word roots and their meanings is that the Latin words borrowed to fill the inadequacies of our Anglo-Saxon language were borrowed from the written classical Latin of the Romans at the peak of their culture, 200 B.C. to 100 A.D.

Latin is a "dead" language, in that its words and meanings have never changed, so Latin words today have the same meanings they had two thousand years ago. We are thus able to trace our families of words with certainty to their original and highly developed (and unchanged) language.

In a number of families of words, there are certain words whose roots appear in variance with the designated root. The simple explanation lies in the development of the English language and the way words were brought in and added to it.

*A small number of Latin words came early into the English language, and, as they changed from the Middle English to Modern English, their spelling and pronunciation changed.

*Our borrowed words may have come from different parts of speech of the Latin. For example, the root CERN/CRET, meaning sift or judge, comes from the conjugation: cerno, cernere, crevi, cretum. From this root we have words such as discern (the second part of speech) and discrete (the fourth part).

*The most common variance within a root is caused by borrowing from the French. While the greatest borrowing was directly from Latin, Old French words were borrowed during domination by the Normans from 1066 to the 1200s, and then a heavy borrowing of the more pure French during the Renaissance of the 1300s to 1500s. Most of these words were original Latin words and retained their meaning, but entailed changes in spelling to accommodate a different speech pattern.

All roots in the following section are Latin unless otherwise noted. The numerals on the first line of each root are the number of derivative words of that root.

ACT
AGI
drive
do

AGERE *to drive,* **ACTUM** *driven;* **AGITARE** *to drive*   **87**

ACT *a thing done; behave, function; a law,* actibility, actable.
ACTION actionable, actionably, actionless.
ACTIVE activate, activation, activator, actively, activeness.
ACTUAL *existing in fact,* actualist, actuality, actualization, actualize, actually, actualness.
ACTUARY *an official statistician,* actuarial.
ACTOR *one who plays a part,* actress.
COUNTERACT *to act directly against,* counteraction, counteractive.
AMBIGUOUS (ambi *about* + agere *to drive) capable of being understood in more than one sense,* ambiguity, ambiguously, ambiguousness.
ENACT *to establish, to accomplish,* enactive, enactment, enactor, enactory.
EXACT *precise, correct,* exacter, exacting, exactingly, exactingness, exaction, exactitude, exactly, exactness, exactor.
REACT *to act in return,* reactance, reactant, reaction, reactive, reactivate, reactively, reactivity.
REACTIONARY *one who wants to undo political progress.*
TRANSACT (trans *through* + agere *to drive*) transaction, transactional, transactor.
AGENT (agere *to act) one who has power to act,* agential, agentive.
COGENT *compelling, convincing,* cogency, cogently.
EXIGENCY (ex *out* + agere to *drive*) *urgency, requiring immediate action,* exigent.
AGILE *nimble, brisk,* agilely, agileness, agility.
AGITATE *to stir violently,* agitatedly, agitation, agitational, agitative.
COGITATE (cogitare *to think) to meditate,* cogitation, cogitative, cogitator.
NAVIGATE (navis *a ship* + agere *to lead*) navigation, navigator.
PRODIGAL (pro *forth* + agere *to drive*) *one who is wasteful,* prodigality, prodigalize, prodigally.

AMA
love
friend

AMARE *to love;* **AMICUS** *a friend*   **25**

AMATEUR *one who pursues an art or sport not professionally,* amateurish, amateurishly, amateurishness, amateurism.
AMATORY *expressing love, often sexually,* amatorial, amatorially.
AMIABLE *friendly, pleasant disposition,* amiableness, amiably.
AMICABLE *promoting good will,* amicability, amicably.
AMITY *friendship, good understanding.*

AMA
love
friend

AMOROUS *ardent in affection and love*, amorously, amorousness.
ENAMOR *inspire to ardent love*, enamorment.
ENEMY (in *not* + amicus *a friend*) *a committed antagonist*.
ENMITY *hostility, antagonism*.
INIMICAL *unfriendly*, inimicality, inimically.

ANIMA
soul
mind

ANIMA *the soul;* ANIMUS *the mind*   38
ANIMADVERT (animus *mind* + ad *to* + vertere *to turn*) *to remark critically*, animadversion, animadversive, animadversiveness.
ANIMAL *any living creature other than man capable of sensation*.
ANIMALISM *the belief that man is a mere animal without a soul*, animalist, animalistic, animality.
ANIMISM *the belief that all life is produced by a spiritual force separate from the physical*.
ANIMATE *to give life to*, animatedly, animating, animatingly, animation, animative, animator.
REANIMATE *to restore to life*, reanimation.
ANIMOSITY *active enmity*, animous, animus.
EQUANIMITY (aequus *even* + animus *mind*) *"eveness of mind,"* equanimous.
INANIMATE (in *not* + anima *life*) *dead, dull, spiritless*, inanimateness, inanimation.
MAGNANIMOUS (magnus *great* + animus *mind*) *elevated in soul*, magnanimity, magnanimously.
PUSILLANIMOUS *faint-hearted, cowardly*, pusillanimity, pusillanimously, pusillanimousness.
UNANIMOUS *united in opinion*, unanimity, unanimously, unanimousness.

BOL
throw

BALLEIN [*Gr*] *to throw*   43
BOLT [*A-S* bolt] *to make a sudden flight*.
DIABOLICAL *like the devil*, diabolically, diabolicalness, diabolify, diabolism, diabolist.
EMBLEM (en *in* + ballein *to throw*) *a figurative representation or symbol*, emblematic, emblematical, emblematically, emblematist, emblematize.
EMBOLISM *in medicine, a blood clot carried in a vein or artery*, embolismic, embolus.
HYPERBOLE (hyper *beyond* + ballein *to throw*) *exaggeration for effect*, hyperbolism, hyperbolist, hyperbolize.

BOL
throw

PARABLE (para *beside* + ballein *to throw*) *a religious allegory or short story with a moral*, parabolist, parabolize.

PARABOLA *a plane curve that remains equal distant from a point*, parabolic, parabolical, parabolically.

PROBLEM (pro *forward* + ballein *to throw*) *a question proposed for consideration*, problematical, problematically, problematize.

SYMBOL (syn *together* + ballein *to throw*) *something that represents something else*, symbolic, symbolically, symbolicalness, symbolics, symbolism, symbolist, symbolistic, symbolistical, symbolization, symbolize, symbolizer.

CAD CAS CID
fall

CADERE *to fall,* CASUM *fallen down*   53

CADAVER *a corpse*, cadaveric, cadaverous, cadaverously, cadaverousness.

CADENCE *rhythmic pitch in reading or singing*, cadenced.

CADENZA *a brilliant musical solo passage, sometimes improvised.*

DECADENCE *a decline in force or quality*, decadent.

DECAY (de *down* + cadere *to fall*) *to deteriorate.*

CASE *an event; an example; facts involving a question for discussion.*

CASCADE *a small, steep waterfall, especially one of a series.*

CASUAL *happening by chance*, casualism, casualist, casually, casualness.

CASUALTY *a bodily injury or death.*

CASUIST *one who studies questions of right or wrong situationally.*

OCCASION *a happening, a particular event*, occasionable, occasional, occasionalism, occasionalist, occasionality, occasionally, occasioner.

ACCIDENT (ad *to* + cadere *to fall*) *something that takes place without it being expected*, accidental, accidentalism, accidentality, accidentally, accidentalness.

COINCIDE (co *together* + in *upon* + cadere *to fall*) *to occur simultaneously*, coincidence, coincident, coincidental, coincidentally, coincidently.

INCIDENT *a subordinate event part of a larger endeavor*, incidental, incidentally, incidentalness.

OCCIDENT (ob *before* + cadere *to fall*) [*before sun falls?*] *Western Hemisphere*, Occidental, Occidentalism, Occidentalist, Occidentalize, occidentally.

RECIDIVISM (re *back* + cadere *to fall*) *tendency to return to crime*, recidivation, recidivist, recidivous.

CALC

CALX, CALCIS *lime;* CALCULUS *a pebble*   22

CALCIUM *a soft metallic chemical element found in limestone and chalk,*

CALC
pebble

calciferous, calcific, calcification, calciform, calcify, calcimine, calcinator.
CALCULUS *a pebble; a method of higher mathematics.*
CALCULATE *to count by pebbles; to determine by reasoning,* calculating, calculative, calculation, calculator, calculatory.
INCALCULABLE *unpredictable,* incalculability, incalculableness, incalculably.
MISCALCULATE *misjudge,* miscalculation.

CAND
white

CANDEO **I shine;** CANDIDUS **white;** CANDELA ***a candle***   9
CANDID *open, frank, sincere,* candidly, candidness.
CANDOR *frankness in expressing oneself.*
CANDIDATE (candidus *white*) *those who sought office in Rome wore white gowns,* candidacy.
CANDLE *a round body of tallow with a wick.*
CHANDELIER *a branching fixture for lights.*
INCANDESCENT *glowing with intense heat,* incandesce, incandescence.

CANT
CENT
sing

CANERE *to sing;* CANTARE *to sing*   35
CANT *the jargon or phraseology peculiar to a profession.*
RECANT *to renounce former beliefs or statements in a formal manner,* recantation, recanter.
CANTATA *a musical composition.*
CANTO *a division of a long poem; in music, the highest part.*
INCANTATION (in *in* + cantare *to chant*) *the chanting of magical words to cast a spell,* incanatory.
CHANT (cantus *a song*) *a singsong mode of singing or speaking,* chanter, chantress.
ENCHANT *to cast a spell over,* enchanted, enchanter, enchantress, enchanting, enchantingly, enchantment.
CHANTICLEER *a rooster in Reynard the Fox; called a chanticleer because of its crowing.*
CHARM *a fascinating or alluring quality,* charmer, charming, charmingly, charmingness, charmless.
AC'CENT (ad *to* + canere *to sing*) (n) *a particular stress of voice on a certain syllable or word,* accentless.
ACCENT' (v) *to emphasize or stress,* accentual, accentuality, accentually, accentuate, accentuation.
INCENTIVE *influencing to action,* incentively.

CAP
CEPT
CEI
CIP

take
seize

CAPIO, CAPERE *to take,* CAPTUM **205**

CAPABLE *adequate ability to do or understand,* capableness, capably.

INCAPABLE *lacking the necessary ability,* incapability, incapably.

CAPACITY *the ability to receive or contain.*

INCAPACITY *lack of capacity or fitness,* incapacitate, incapacitation.

CAPACIOUS *capable of containing much,* capaciously, capaciousness; incapacious, incapaciousness.

CAPSULE *a small vessel or shell or cap or seal,* capsulize.

CAPTION *the heading of a chapter, page, or subtitle.*

CAPTIOUS *hypercritical, faultfinding, objection,* captiously, captiousness.

CAPTIVATE *capture the attention by charm,* captivating, captivatingly, captivation.

CAPTURE *to take by force or surprise,* captive, captivity, captor.

CATCH *to seize,* catchable, catcher, catching, catchy.

CATER *to provide food; to give what is wanted,* caterer.

CHASE *to pursue quickly,* chaseable, chaser.

ACCEPT *to take what is offered,* acceptability, acceptable, acceptableness, acceptably, acceptance, acceptancy, acceptant, acceptation, accepter or acceptor; unacceptable.

CONCEPT *combining elements into the idea of one or a class of objects.*

CONCEPTION *the act of conceiving; a mental impression,* conceptional, conceptionalist, conceptive, conceptual, conceptualize, conceptualist.

DECEPTION *the act of misleading,* deceptibility, deceptible, deceptive, deceptively, deceptiveness.

EXCEPT *to exclude,* exceptant, excepting, exception, exceptionable, exceptionableness, exceptionably, exceptional, exceptionalism, exceptionality, exceptionally, exceptionalness, exceptionless.

INCEPT *to take in,* inception *the beginning,* inceptive, inceptively, inceptor.

INTERCEPT *to interrupt the course of,* intercepter or interceptor, interception, interceptive.

PERCEPT *awareness,* perceptibility, perceptible, perceptibleness, perceptibly, perception, perceptional, perceptive, perceptivity.

IMPERCEPTION *not distinct to the senses,* imperceptible, imperceptibility, imperceptibleness, imperceptibly, imperceptive.

RECEPTACLE *that which contains things.*

RECEPTION *the act of receiving,* receptionist, receptive, receptiveness, receptivity, receptor.

CAP
CEPT
CEI
CIP
take
seize

SUSCEPTIBLE (sub *under* + capere *to take*) *yielding readily*, susceptibility, susceptibleness, susceptibly, susceptive, susceptivity; unsusceptible.

CONCEIT *over-weaning self-esteem*, conceitedly, conceitedness, conceitless.

CONCEIVE *become pregnant; form a mental image*, conceivability, conceivable, conceivableness, conceivably.

INCONCEIVABLE *not imagined*, inconceivability, inconceivableness, inconceivably.

PRECONCEIVE *to form an opinion beforehand*, preconception.

DECEIVE (de *from* + capere *to take*) *to mislead, to delude*, deceivable, deceiver.

DECEIT *lying, a trick*, deceitful, deceitfully, deceitfulness.

PERCEIVE *to comprehend*, perceivable, perceivably, perceiver.

RECEIVE (re *back* + capere *to take*) receivable, receivability, receivableness, receiver, receivership; unreceived.

RECEIPT *the written acknowledgement of something received*, receiptable, receipter.

ANTICIPATE (ante *before* + capere *to take*) *to foresee an act*, anticipant, anticipation, anticipative, anticipatively, anticipator, anticipatorily, anticipatory.

EMANCIPATE (manus *hand* + capere *to take*) *to liberate*, emancipation, emancipationist, emancipator, emancipatory.

MUNICIPAL (munia *functions* + capere *to take*) *pertaining to a local government*, municipalism, municipalist, municipality, municipalization, municipalize, municipally.

OCCUPY *take possession of*, occupant, occupancy, occupier.

PARTICIPATE (partis *a part* + capere *to take*) *to take a part*, participance, participant, participantly, participation, participative, participator.

PARTICIPLE *the form of a verb enabling it to be both a verb and adjective.*

PRINCIPAL *chief, highest in rank*, principality, principally, principalness, principalship.

PRINCIPLE *a general truth or proposition; the essence;* unprincipled, unprincipledness.

INCIPIENT *the beginning*, incipiently, incipiency.

PERCIPIENT *the power of perceiving*, percipience, percipiency; impercipient.

RECIPIENT *one who receives anything sent*, recipience.

RECIPE *a medical prescription; list of ingredients and directions in food preparation.*

CAPIT
CIPIT
head
cap

CAPUT, CAPITIS *the head*   **44**

CAP *a cover without a brim for the male head.*
CAPARISON *a decorative trapping for the saddle of a horse.*
CAPE *a garment without sleeves; land jutting out of the coast.*
CAPITOL *house for Congress or a Statehouse.*
CAPITAL *wealth available for production; seat of government of state or nation.*
CAPITALISM *an economic system of privately owned industry run for profit,* capitalist, capitalistic, capitalistically, capitalization, capitalize; recapitalize.
CAPILLARY *fine tubes, like hair,* capillariness, capilliform.
CAPITATION *the act of counting individuals; tax or payment per head.*
CAPITULATE *to give up,* capitulation, capitulator.
RECAPITULATE *to summarise; to repeat what has been said before,* recapitulation, recapitulative, recapitulator, recapitulatory.
DECAPITATE *to cut off the head,* decapitation, decapitator.
CAPTAIN *one who is the head of others.*
CHAPTER *a division of a book or club.*
PRECIPICE *a vertical cliff.*
PRECIPITOUS *very steep,* precipitously, precipitousness.
PRECIPITATE *moving hurriedly; rushing headlong,* precipitability, precipitable, precipitance, precipitancy, precipitant, precipitantly, precipitantness, precipitately, precipitator.
PRECIPITATION *a rushing down with violence; rain, snow, sleet.*

CARN
flesh

CARO, CARNIS *flesh*   **21**

CARNAL *pertaining to the bodily appetites; worldly, sexual,* carnalism, carnality, carnaling, carnally.
CARNAGE *slaughter, massacre in battle.*
CARNATE *having flesh.*
INCARNATE *cause to assume a living bodily form; embodiment of a quality,* incarnant, incarnation.
REINCARNATE *rebirth of the soul in another body,* reincarnation.
CARNATION *formerly a flesh colored flower; now deep red colored.*
CARNIVAL (carnis *flesh* + vale *farewell*) *last meat feast before Lent; commercial entertainment including rides.*
CHARNEL *containing dead bodies,* charnel house.
CARNIVOROUS *a flesh-eating animal,* carnivora, carnivore.
CARNOSITY *an abnormal growth of flesh anywhere on the body.*

flesh   CARRION *decaying flesh of a dead body.*
CHILE CON CARNE *"chile with meat" Mexican dish of red pepper, spices, and meat.*

CAUS
cause

CAUSA *a cause*   37
CAUSE *anything producing a result; a reason,* causeful, causeless, causelessly, causelessness, causer.
CAUSAL *relating to cause and effect,* causable, causality, causally.
CAUSATION *anything producing an effect or result,* causationist, causative, causatively, causator.
ACCUSE (ad *to* + causa *a reason*) *to charge, to blame,* accusable, accusal, accusant, accusation, accusatively, accusatorial, accusatorially, accusatory, accusement, accuser.
EXCUSE *to try to free a person of blame,* excusable, excusableness, excusably, excusatory, excuseless, excuser.
INEXCUSABLE *unjustified,* inexcusability, inexcusableness, inexcusably.

CAUT
beware

CAVEO, CAVERE *to beware,* CAUTUM   17
CAUTION *prudence in avoiding injury or misfortune,* cautionary, cautioner, cautious, cautiously, cautiousness.
INCAUTION *not circumspect,* incautious, incautiously, incautiousness.
PRECAUTION (pre *before* + cavere *to beware*) *"care taken beforehand,"* precautional, precautionary, precautious, precautiously, precautiousness.
CAVEAT *"let him beware," a warning or admonition.*

CAV
hollow

CAVUS *hollow*   16
CAVE *a natural cavity beneath the surface of the earth.*
CAVERN *large cave,* cavernous.
CAVIL *to raise hollow objections,* caviller, cavilling, cavillingly.
CAVITY *a hollow place.*
CONCAVE *hollow and curved spherically,* concaved, concaveness, concavity, concavously.
EXCAVATE (ex *out* + cavea *a hollow place*) *to dig out,* excavation, excavator.

CED
go

CEDO *I go,* CEDERE *to yield,* CESSO *I leave off*   96
ACCEDE *give one's consent to another,* acceder.
ANTECEDE *to go before,* antecedence, antecedent, antecedently, antecessor.

CED
CES
go
yield

CEDE *to yield,* cedent *an assignor in a lawsuit.*

CONCEDE *to yield to demand; to acknowledge; to admit as true or just,* concession, concessionist, concessive.

DECEASE *to die.*

DECEDENT *in law, the deceased.*

EXCEED *to go beyond; to surpass,* exceedable, exceeder, exceeding, exceedingly, exceedingness.

INTERCEDE *to mediate; to intervene,* intercedent, intercession, intercessional, intercessor, intercessorial, intercessory.

PRECEDE *to go before in time, place or order,* preceding.

PRECEDENT *any act or statement that serves as an example for a later one,* precedence, precedial; unprecedented.

PROCEED *to move from one point to another,* proceeder, proceeding.

PROCEDURE *a particular course of action or way of doing something,* procedural.

RECEDE *to move back, to retreat,* recess, recessional.

SECEDE *to withdraw from a group,* seceder, secession, secessional, secessionism, secessionist.

SUCCEED *to follow; to accomplish something attempted,* succeeder; unsucceeded.

ABCESS *an inflamed part of the body in which pus gathers.*

ACCESS *an approach or admittance,* accessible, accession; unaccessible.

INACCESSIBLE *impossible to reach,* inaccessibility, inaccessibleness, inaccessibly.

ACCESSORY *in law, helping in an unlawful act; an article of clothing or equipment.*

CEASE *to end, to stop.*

CEASELESS *incessant, continual,* ceaselessly.

CESSATION *discontinuance.*

CESSION *a yielding; in law, the voluntary surrender of one's property or rights to avoid imprisonment.*

EXCESS *in amount greater than necessary,* excessive, excessively, excessiveness.

INCESSANT *continual,* incessantly.

PROCESS *progressive course,* processal, processive.

PROCESSION *movement forward in an orderly manner,* processional, processionally, processionary, processioner, processionist.

CES
go
yield

RECESSIVE *in genetics, a latent factor.*
SUCCESS *a favorite outcome or result,* successful, successfully, sucessfulness; unsuccess, unsuccessful.
SUCCESSIVE *following in order,* successively, successiveness, successor, successorship, successory; unsuccessive.

CENT
hundred

CENTUM *a hundred*   **11**
CENT *a hundredth part of a dollar.*
CENTENARIAN *a person at least a hundred years old.*
CENTENNIAL *a hundred years after the event,* centennary.
CENTIGRADE (centum *hundred* + gradus *a degree*) *a 100 degrees between water freezing and boiling.*
CENTIPEDE *any wormlike animals with a pair of legs for each body segment.*
CENTURY *a hundred years.*
PER CENT *a given rate in every hundred,* percentage, percentile, percentum.

CENTR
middle

CENTRUM *the middlepoint*   **33**
CENTER *the middlepoint of anything,* centered, centering.
CENTRAL *main; near the center,* centralism, centralist, centrality, centralization, centralize, centrally.
CENTRIC *near the center,* centrical, centrically, centricalness, centricity.
CENTRIFUGAL *tending to move away from the center,* centrifugalize, centrifuge, centrifugence.
CENTRIPETAL *tending to move toward the center,* centripetence.
CONCENTRATE *to direct toward a common center,* concentration, concentrative, concentrativeness, concentrator.
CONCENTRIC *having a common center,* concentrically, concentricity.
ECCENTRIC *"off center"; anyone or anything that operates in an unconventional manner,* eccentrical, eccentrically, eccentricity.

CERN
CRET
sift

CERNO, CERNERE *to separate,* CRETUM *sift, see, judge*   **64**
CONCERN *interest and importance to,* concernedly, concerning, concernment.
UNCONCERN *free from anxiety,* unconcerned, unconcernedly, unconcernment.
DISCERN (dis *apart* + cernere *to separate*) *to see as distinct from other objects,* discernance, discerner, discernible, discernibleness.

CERN / CRET
sift judge

INDISCERNIBLE *imperceptible*, indiscernibleness, indiscernibly, indiscernibility.
UNDISCERNED *not seen*, undiscernible, undiscernibly, undiscerning.
DECREE (de *from* + cernere *to judge*) *an edict; an official order by an authority as to what is to be done in a certain matter*, decreeable, decreer.
DISCREET *careful about what one does or says*, discreetness.
INDISCREET *imprudent*, indiscreetly, indiscreetness, indiscretion.
DISCRETE *made up of distinct parts*, discretely; indiscrete.
DISCRETION *distinctive, separation; cautious and wise judgment*, discretional, discretionally, discretionary, discretive, discretively.
EXCRETE *to separate and eliminate from the body*, excreta, excretion, excretive, excretory.
EXCREMENT *matter excreted and ejected*, excremental, excrementitious.
RECREMENT *superfluous or useless matter*, recremental, recremential, recrementitious.
SECRET *kept from other's knowledge*, secrecy, secretive, secretiveness, secretly, secretness; unsecret.
SECRETE *to hide or conceal*.
SECRETION *the substance secreted by animal or plant*.
SECRETARY *one who keeps records and correspondence*, secretarial, secretariat, secretaryship.

CHART
paper

CHARTA *paper*   8
CHART *a marine map; a sheet giving information in the form of graphs*.
CHARTER *a franchise or grant conferring special rights and privileges*.
CARTOON *a caricature, often satirical, showing some person or situation*.
CARTE BLANCHE *"white paper"; authorizing anything you want*.
CARTRIDGE *paper case enclosing gun charge*.
CARD *a thin pasteboard fulfilling many functions*.
DISCARD *to throw away*.
MAGNA CARTA *the great English charter*.

CIRC
ring around

CIRCUS *a circular line*   20
CIRCUS *an oval arena, under tent, for acts of acrobats, clowns and animals*.
CIRCLE *all points equally distant from the center*.
ENCIRCLE *enclosed in a circle*.
SEMICIRCLE *a half circle*.

CIRC
*ring
around*

CIRCULATE *to keep moving around.*
CIRCULAR *moving in a circle,* circulable, circularity, circularize, circularizer, circularly.
CIRCUIT *the passage taken in performance of duties.*
CIRCUITOUS *not direct, but purposely roundabout,* circuitously, circuitousness, circuity.
CIRCUMFERENCE *the distance around any circle or globe,* circumferential, circumferentially, circumferentor.

CIS CID
*cut
kill*

CAEDO, CAEDERE *to cut, kill,* CAESUM   48
CIRCUMCISE *to cut off the foreskin of males,* circumciser, circumcision.
UNCIRCUMCISED uncircumcision.
CONCISE *brief and to the point,* concisely, conciseness.
DECISIVE *the power to settle a dispute conclusively,* decision, decisively, decisiveness, decisory.
INDECISIVE *inability to decide,* indecision, indecisively, indecisiveness.
EXCISE (ex *off* + caedere *to cut*) "*to cut away,*" excission.
INCISE *to cut into with a sharp tool,* incised, incision, incisure.
INCISIVE *sharp, keen, piercing, acute.*
INCISOR *any of the front teeth of either jaw between the canines,* incisorial.
PRECISE *strictly defined; accurately stated,* precisely, preciseness, precision, precisionist, overprecise; precisian, precisianism, precisianist.
DECIDE *to bring to an end; to determine a question,* decidedly, decidedness, decider, decidingly; undecidable.
HOMICIDE *murder of a man,* fratricide *of a brother,* infanticide *of a child,* matricide *of a mother,* patricide *of a father,* regicide *of a king,* suicide *of oneself,* genocide *of a whole people.*
CAESARIAN *Surgical operation for delivery by cutting through abdominal and uterine wall. Word probably from caesum cut or caesim with cutting. Folklore attributes word to the supposed manner of birth of Julius Caesar.*

CIT
*rouse
call*

CITO, CITARE *to arouse, to call*   38
CITE *to quote a passage; to give legal notice to,* citation, citator, citatory, citer; miscitation.
EXCITE *to arouse the feelings,* excitability, excitable, excitement, excitant, excitation, excitative, excitor, excitory, excitedly, excitement, exciter, exciting, excitingly, excitive.

CIT
rouse
call

INCITE *to move to action; to arouse*, incitant, incitation, incitement, inciter, incitingly.
RECITE (re *again* + citare *to call*) reciter.
RECITAL *telling of the facts; a musical ensemble.*
RECITATION *an account; delivering something memorized.*
RECITATIVE *a type of declamatory singing.*
SUSCITATE *to excite*, suscitation.
RESUSCITATE *to bring back to life*, resuscitation, resuscitative, resuscitator.

CIV
CIT
citizen

CIVIS *a citizen;* CIVITAS *a state*   16
CIVIC *behavior of a citizen for his country*, civicism, civics.
CIVIL *private rights of citizens*, civilly.
CIVILIAN *anyone not in the military.*
CIVILITY *good breeding; courtesy.*
CIVILIZE *to better the habits and manners*, civilizer; uncivilized.
CIVILIZATION *social organization of a high order.*
CITY *a large, important town.*
CITIZEN *a member of a state or nation*, citizenry, citizenship.
CITADEL *a high fortress for defense of a city.*

CLAIM
CLAM
shout

CLAMO *I cry out*   41
ACCLAIM *to applaud or cry aloud*, acclaimer, acclamation, acclamatory.
CLAIM *to call for; to assert as a fact*, claimable.
DECLAIM *to make a formal speech*, declaimer, declamation, declamatory.
DISCLAIM *to deny or relinquish all claims to*, disclaimer, disclamation.
EXCLAIM *to cry out abruptly*, exclaimer, exclamation, exclamative, exclamatively, exclamatorily, exclamatory.
PROCLAIM *to announce officially*, proclaimer, proclamation; unproclaimed.
RECLAIM *to bring back to a former condition*, reclaimable, reclaimant, reclaimer, reclamation, reclaimless.
IRRECLAIMABLE irreclaimability, irreclaimably.
UNRECLAIMED unreclaimable.
CLAMOR *a great outcry*, clamorer, clamorous, clamorously, clamorousness.

CLAR

CLARUS *clear*   23
CLARET *a clear, dark red Bordeaux wine.*

CLAR
clear

CLARIFY (clarus *clear* + facere *to make*) *to make easier to understand*, clarification, clarifier; unclarified.

CLARION *clear, sharp, shrill.*

CLARINET *a woodwind instrument with a single reed.*

DECLARE *to announce openly*, declaredly, declaredness, declarer.

DECLARATION *a formal statement of facts*, declarative, declaratively, declaratorily, declaratory.

CLEAR (clarus *clear*) *easily seen or comprehended*, clearage, clearer, clearing, clearly, clearness.

CLIN
CLIV
bend
slope

CLINO *bend, lean;* CLINICUS *bedridden person;* CLIVUS *a slope*   31

CLINIC *the teaching of medicine by treating patients before students*, clinical, clinically, clinician.

INCLINE *to have some wish or desire; sloping*, inclinable, inclined, incliner, inclining.

INCLINATION *a tendency; bent of the mind; slant*, inclinatory.

DISINCLINE *to make unwilling*, disinclination.

DECLINE *to lessen in force, value, health*, decliner; undeclined, undeclinable.

RECLINE *to lie back or down*, reclination, recliner.

DECLINATION *refusal; sloping downward*, declinator, declinatory, declinature.

DECLENSION *falling lower; inflection of nouns, etc.*, declensional, declinable.

ACCLIVITY *a slope upward*, acclivous, acclivitous.

DECLIVITY *a slope downward*, declivitous.

PROCLIVITY (pro *before* + clivus *slope*) *a natural disposition or tendency.*

CLU
CLO
close
shut

CLAUDO, CLAUDERE *to close,* CLAUSUM *shut*   61

CONCLUDE *to arrive at by reasoning*, concluder, concluding, concludingly, conclusion, conclusional, conclusive, conclusively, conclusiveness; unconcluded.

INCONCLUSIVE *not decisive*, inconclusively, inconclusiveness.

EXCLUDE *to shut out*, excluder, exclusion, exclusionary, exclusioner, exclusivism, exclusivist, exclusory.

INCLUDE *to enclose; to contain; to take into account*, includable, inclusion, inclusive, inclusively.

OCCLUDE *to shut out*, occludent, occlusion, occlusive, occlusor.

PRECLUDE *to prevent by prior action*, preclusion, preclusive.

RECLUSE *one who lives a solitary life*, reclusely, recluseness, reclusion, reclusive, reclusory.

CLU / CLO
close shut

SECLUDE *to make hidden*, secludedly, secludedness, seclusion, seclusive.
CLOSE *to shut; to end; to complete*, closely, closure.
DISCLOSE (dis *apart* + claudere *to close*) *to make known*, discloser, disclosure.
INCLOSE *to confine on all sides; to put into something*, incloser, inclosure.
CLAUSE (clausum *shut*) *a group of words containing a subject and verb, part of a sentence.*
CLAUSTROPHOBIA *abnormal fear of being confined.*
CLOISTER (claudere *to close*) *where one leads a sheltered life*, cloistered, cloisterer, cloistral; incloister.

COGN
know

COGNOSCERE *to know*   21

COGNITION (cognoscere *to know*) *the process of knowing and perceiving*, cognitive, cognizable, cognizably, cognizance, cognizant, cognize.
CONNOISSEUR (cognoscere *to know*) *one who has expert knowledge or discrimination in some field.*
INCOGNITO *one in disguise in person or character.*
INCOGNIZABLE *cannot be recognized or distinguished*, incognizant, incognizance, incognoscibility.
RECOGNIZE *to identify as known before*, recognition, recognizability, recognizable, recognizant.
RECOGNIZANCE *acknowledgement of a person or thing; in law, an obligation or bond to do or not to do something.*
RECONNAISSANCE/RECONNOITER (cognoscere *to know*) *the act of obtaining information of an enemy position, or survey of an area.*

CORP
body

CORPUS, CORPORIS *a body*   26

CORPORAL *relating to the body, as corporal punishment.*
CORPORATE *united into a legal body*, corporately, corporateness, corporation.
INCORPORATE *formed into one body or unit*, incorporation, incorporative, incorporator.
CORPOREAL *consisting of material nature and physical substance*, corporealism, corporeality, corporeity.
INCORPOREAL *not having a material body; immaterial*, incorporealism, incorporealist, incorporeality, incorporeity.
CORPS *a body of persons associated in a common enterprise; an army unit.*
CORPSE *a person's dead body.*
CORPULENT *a fat body.*

CORP
body

CORPUSCLE *a very small particle*, corpuscular.
CORSAGE *a bodice or bouquet worn by a woman.*
CORSET *a woman's close-fitting undergarment.*
CORSELET *a knight's protecting armor; a woman's lightweight corset.*

CORD
COUR
heart

COR, CORDIS *the heart*   **43**

CORE *the heart of anything.*
ACCORD *harmony of minds*, accordable, accordance, accordantly, accorder, according, accordingly.
CONCORD *agreement between persons or things*, concordance, concordant, concordantly.
CORDIAL *warm-hearted*, cordiality, cordialize, cordially.
CONCORDAT *a covenant or formal agreement*, concordist.
DISCORD (dis *apart* + cordis *the heart*) *lack of harmony*, discordance, discordancy, discordant, discordantly, discordantness.
RECORD *to preserve, as in writing*, recordation, recorder, recording.
COURAGE (cor heart) *to show calmness and firmness in the face of danger and opposition*, courageous, courageously, courageousness.
ENCOURAGE *to inspire and help*, encouragement, encourager, encouraging, encouragingly.
DISCOURAGE *to dishearten*, discourageable, discouragement, discourager, discouraging, discouragingly.

CRE
grow

CRESCERE *to grow, to come forth*   **41**

ACCREMENTION *growth by addition of new cells*, accrementitial.
ACCRESCIMENTO *in music, a dot behind a note to indicate half its length in time.*
ACCRETION *growth in size*, accrete, accretive, accrescence, accrescent.
CREW *a group of persons associating together.*
CRESCENT *the moon in its first or last quarter*, crescentric.
CRESCENDO *in music, to gradually increase loudness.*
CONCRETE (com *together* + crescere *to grow*) *formed into a solid mass*, concretely, concreteness, concretion, concretional, concretionary, concretive, concretively, concretize.
EXCRESCENCE *a normal outgrowth, such as hair; a disfiguring outgrowth*, excrescency, excrescent, excrescential.
INCREMENT *increase, growth, gain*, incremental.

CRE
grow

INCREASE *to become greater in size, value, etc.*, increaseful, increaser.
DECREASE (de *from* + crescere *to grow*) *to lessen or make smaller*, decreasing.
ACCRUE (ad *to* + crescere *to increase*) *to come as a natural advantage*, accruer, accrument.
RECRUIT (re *again* + crescere *to increase*) *to enlist any new members to an organization*, recruital.

CREA
create

CREO, CREARE *to create,* **CREATUM**   26

CREATE *to bring into existence*, creation, creational, creationism, creationist, creator, creatrix, Creator; miscreate.
CREATIVE *inventive*, creativeness, creativity.
CREATURE *anything created; a living being*, creaturely.
PROCREATE (pro *before* + creare *to create*) *to bring into existence*, procreant, procreation, procreative, procreativeness, procreator.
RECREATE *to revive or refresh; to create anew*.
RECREATION *refreshment in body and mind*, recreational, recreative, recreatively, recreativeness.

CRED
trust
believe

CREDO, CREDERE *to trust, believe*   30

CREDO *a creed.*
CREDENCE *belief in the reports and testimony of others.*
CREDENTIALS *letter or certificate entitling a person to certain rights.*
CREDULOUS *act of believing on slight evidence*, credulity, credulousness.
INCREDULOUS *not believing*, incredulously, incredulousness, incredulity.
CREDIBLE *worthy of belief or trust*, credibly, credibleness, credibility.
INCREDIBLE *that cannot be believed*, incredibly, incredibleness.
CREDIT *belief, faith, favorable reputation; one's integrity in financial matters*, creditable, creditably; uncredited.
CREDITOR *one to whom money is due.*
ACCREDITED *to bring into credit or favor or trust*, accreditation.
DISCREDIT *to disbelieve; to damage the reputation of*, discreditable, discreditably.
MISCREANT *an evil person.*
RECREANT *one who yields in combat and begs for mercy.* recreance, recreancy.
CREED (credo *I believe*) *a statement of beliefs or principles, especially religious.*

CRIM
crime
accuse

CRIMEN, CRIMINIS *a crime* **43**

CRIME *an extreme violation of the law,* crimeless.
CRIMINAL *one committing an offense punishable by law,* criminalist, criminality, criminally.
CRIMINOLOGY *scientific study of crime and criminals,* criminological, criminologically, criminologist.
CRIMINATE *to charge with a crime,* crimination, criminative, criminatory.
DISCRIMINATE *to distinguish; to select from others,* discriminant, discriminately, discriminateness, discriminating, discriminatingly, discrimination, discriminative, discriminatively, discriminator, discriminatory; undiscriminating.
INDISCRIMINATE *not making any distinction,* indiscriminately, indiscriminating, indiscriminatingly, indiscrimination, indiscriminative.
INCRIMINATE *to charge with a crime,* incrimination, incriminator, incriminatory.
RECRIMINATE *to repel one accusation with another,* recriminating, recrimination, recriminative, recriminator, recriminatory.

CRUC
cross

CRUX, CRUCIS *a cross* **21**

CROSS *the emblem of Christianity; anything that perplexes,* crossing, crossroad, crosswalk.
CRUCIAL *of supreme importance.*
CRUCIBLE *a vessel tempered to resist extreme heat (formerly marked by a cross).*
CRUCIFY *to put to death on a cross,* crucifix, crucifier, crucifixion, cruciform.
CRUISE *to sail or wander from place to place or crosswise,* cruiser, cruising.
CRUSADE *religious wars from 1086 to 1271,* crusader, crusading.
EXCRUCIATE *to inflict intense bodily pain,* excruciating, excruciatingly, excruciation.

CUB
CUM
lie down

CUBO, CUBARE *to lie,* **CUBITUM** **23**

CUBICLE *a small sleeping compartment; any small compartment.*
CUBIT *an old measure of the elbow to the tip of the middle finger, used because feasters reclined on their elbows when eating: about 18 to 20 inches.*
INCUBATE *to sit on to hatch eggs; to hatch ideas,* incubation, incubational, incubative, incubator, incubatory.
CONCUBINE *a secondary wife in some societies,* concubinage, concubinal, concubinarian, concubinary.

CUB / CUM — lie down

SUCCUBUS (sub *under* + cubare *to lie*) *in folklore, a female demon thought to have sexual relations with a sleeping man.*
INCUBUS *a nightmare; in medieval times, a demon thought to lie on sleeping women.*
ACCUMBENT *to recline on a couch, as the ancients at their meals.*
INCUMBENT *now in office; pressed or emphatically urged,* incumbency, imcumbently.
RECUMBENT *reclining,* recumbency, recumbently.
SUCCUMB *to yield or permit.*

CUL / COL — care for

COLO, CULTUM *cultivate, till, care for*   18
CULTIVATE *to till and prepare the soil,* cultivable, cultivatable, cultivation, cultivator.
CULTURE *improvement of plants; training of manner; all the concepts, instruments, and skills of a given people at a given time,* cultureless, culturist.
AGRICULTURE *tilling of the fields.*
HORTICULTURE *care of gardens.*
COLONY *a group that settle in a distant land, but remain under the jurisdiction of their native land.*
COLONIAL *inhabitants of a colony,* colonialism, colonist, colonization, colonizationist, colonize, colonizer.

CUR / SUR — care

CURA *care;* **SECURUS** *safe*   71
CURE *a healing; a remedy; to preserve meats,* cureless, curer, curative.
CURATE *a clergyman who assists the vicar.*
CURATOR *one who superintends a library or museum; a guardian of a minor,* curatorship, curatrix.
CURIOUS *strongly desirous of learning,* curiosa, curioso, curiosity, curiously, curiousness.
ACCURATE *exact conformity to the truth,* accurately, accurateness.
INACCURATE *erroneous,* inaccuracy, inaccurately.
PROCURE *to obtain; to obtain girls for prostitution,* procurement, procurer, procuress.
PROCURATION *management of another's affairs,* procuracy, procurance, procurator, procuratorial, procuratorship, procuratory.
SINECURE *a position which pays without requiring much work,* sinecural, sinecurism, sinecurist.

CUR
SUR
care

SECURE (se *free from* + cura *care*) *free from fear or anxiety,* securable, securely, secureness, securer.
INSECURE *unreliable; feeling undue anxiety,* insecurely, insecurement, insecurity.
SURE (securus) *that can be relied upon,* surely, sureness, surety.
ASSURE *to give confidence by a declaration,* assurance, assuredly, assuredness, assurer.
REASSURE *to restore confidence,* reassurer, reassuring, reassurance.
INSURE or ENSURE *to guarantee; to make safe and secure,* ensurer.
INSURANCE *a system of payment against loss,* insurability, insurable, insurant, insured, insurer.
PROCTOR (procurator) *one employed to manage the affairs of another,* proctorage, proctorial, proctorship.
PROXY *the authority to act for another.*

CUR
COUR
run

CURRERE *to run,* **CURSUM** 44
CURRENT *now in progress; generally received,* currently, currentness.
CURRENCY *what is passed in exchange in transactions.*
CURRICULUM *a specific course of study in schools,* curricular, extracurricular.
CURSORY *hasty, superficial, careless,* cursorily, cursoriness.
CONCUR (com *together* + currere *to run*) *to be in accord,* concurrence, concurrency, concurrent, concurrently, concurrentness, concurring.
DISCURSIVE *skimming over many unrelated topics,* discursion, discursively, discursiveness.
EXCURSION *a short, round trip; a longer trip at a lower rate and fixed conditions.*
INCUR *things or problems one brings on one's self.*
INCURSION *an unfriendly entry or raid.*
OCCUR *to take place; to come to mind,* occurrence.
PRECURSOR *a forerunner; that which goes before,* precursorship, precursory.
RECUR *to come up again for consideration,* recurrence, recurrent, recurrently.
COURIER (currere *to run*) *a messenger sent with important correspondence; one who helps travellers.*
COURSE (cursus *a running*) *the direction of motion; plan of study; gradual progress of anything.*
CONCOURSE *a place where crowds gather.*

CUR
COUR
run

DISCOURSE *expression of ideas, conversation; a treatise*, discourser.
INTERCOURSE *interchange of thought, products, services; sexual relations.*
RECOURSE *that to which one turns seeking aid.*
SUCCOR (sub *under* + currere *to run*) *to help when in difficulty or distress*, succorable, succorer, succorless.

CUSS
shake

QUATERE *to shake*, QUASSUM   16
CONCUSSION (com *together* + quatere *to shake*) *a shock from an impact*, concussive.
DISCUSS (dis *apart* + quatere *to shake*) *to take up in a conversation*, discusser, discussible, discussion, discussional, discussive.
PERCUSSION *the impact of one body on another; impact of sound waves on the ear; a group of musical instruments sounded by striking*, percussive.
REPERCUSSION *a rebound, a recoil*, repercussive.
SUCCUSS *to shake forcibly*, succussation, succussion, succussive.

DAMN
DEMN
harm

DAMNUM *harm, loss*   25
DAMN *to criticize adversely*, damning.
DAMNABLE *execrable; worthy of punishment*, damnableness, damnably, damnation, damnify, damningness.
DAMAGE *any hurt or harm to one's person or property*, damageable.
ENDAMAGE *to bring loss; to prejudice*, endameageable, endamagement.
CONDEMN *to pass an adverse judgment on*, condemnable, condemnation, condemnatory, condemner; uncondemned.
INDEMNITY *protection or insurance against damage; reimbursement for loss*, indemnification, indemnifier, indemnify, indemnitee, indemnitor.

DEBT
DU
owe

DEBEO, DEBERE *to owe*, DEBITUM   18
DEBT *that which is due from one person to another; an obligation*, debtee, debtor, debtless.
INDEBTED (in *in* + debitum *debt*) *in debt; gratitude due for favor received*, indebtedness, indebtment.
DUE (debere *to owe*) *owed, proper, suitable; enough, adequate*, due bill, due date.
UNDUE *not just or lawful; not appropriate; excessive.*
DUTY *the moral or legal obligation to follow certain conduct; tax, toll, customs.*

owe DUTIFUL *obedient, respectful,* dutifully, dutifulness, duteous, duteously, duteousness.

DEC
comely

DECENS *becoming;* DECORIS *comeliness*   21
DECENT *conforming to standards of propriety,* decently, decentness.
INDECENT *not fitting, immodest; obscene,* indecency, indecently.
DECORUM *behavior, dress and speech that is suitable and proper;* indecorum.
DECOR *the decorative scheme of a room, stage, etc.*
DECORUS *showing good taste and propriety,* decorously, decorousness.
INDECOROUS *unbecoming, unseemly,* indecorously, indecorousness.
DECORATE *to make more attractive,* decorative, decorativeness, decorator.
DECORATION *that which decorates or adorns.*

DEMO
people

DEMOCRATIA [*Gr*] *democracy*   20
DEMOCRACY (demos *the people* + kratein *to rule*) *rule by the people; government directly by the people or through elected representatives.*
DEMOCRATIC *upholding democracy; considering others as one's equal,* democrat, Democrat, democratical, democratically, democratization, democratize.
DEMOGRAPHY *the science of vital statistics of populations; births, deaths, marriages.*
DEMAGOGUE *one who appeals to people's baser emotions to become a leader,* demagogic, demagogical, demagogically, demagogism, demagoguery, demagogy.
ENDEMIC (en *in* + demos *the people*) *indigenous; prevalent in a particular region,* endemically.
EPIDEMIC *affecting many people, widespread; a disease prevalent in a locality.*
PANDEMIC *universal; disease prevalent over a whole area.*

DENT
tooth

DENS, DENTIS *a tooth*   18
DENTAL *pertaining to the teeth,* dentary, dentality.
DENTIST *one whose profession is care of the teeth.*
DENTICLE *a small tooth or toothlike projection.*
DENTRIFICE *anything used to clean the teeth.*
DENTITION *the period of cutting the teeth.*
DENT *a toothlike projection, as a comb, gear, or lock.*

DENT
tooth

INDENT (in *in* + dentis *a tooth*) *to cut toothlike points in an edge; the beginning of a paragraph,* indentation, indentedly, indenting, indention.

DENTURE *in dentistry, a partial or complete set of teeth.*

INDENTURE *in law, a deed or agreement between parties (originally cut in a teeth-like line, so they were exact copies).*

INDENTURES *contracts binding apprentices to masters, or immigrants to serve in a colony.*

DANDELION ([Fr] dent de lion *tooth of the lion*) *the jagged edged perennial weed.*

TRIDENT *a spear with three prongs (teeth) carried by Neptune; U.S. submarine inferring Neptune's supremacy.*

DEI DIV
god

DEUS; DIVUS *a god*   23

DEISM *belief that God created the world but had no further responsibility,* deistic, deistical, deistically, deisticalness.

DEITY *a god; divine nature.*

DEIFY *to exalt to the rank of a god,* deific, deifical, deification, deifier.

DIVINE *godlike; sacred; extraordinary,* divining, diviningly, divineness, diviner, diviness.

DIVINATION *practice of foretelling future events; clever conjecture,* divinator, divinatory.

DIVINITY *a god; supreme virtue; theology,* divinization, divinize.

DIA
day

DIES *day;* DIURNUS *daily*   13

DIAL *face of a watch; disk of telephone; sundial.*

DIARY *a personal daily written record.*

MERIDIAN (medius *middle* + dies *day*) *height of the sun at noon; metaphorically, the highest point of prosperity or the middle point of one's life.*

ANTEMERIDIAN *pertaining to the forenoon; between midnight and noon.*

POSTMERIDIAN *occurring in the afternoon.*

PER DIEM *employee daily expense allowance.*

SINE DIE *meeting adjourned without date set for next meeting.*

DIURNAL (diurnis *daily*) *daily; in 24 hours; only in daytime,* diurnalist, diurnally, diurnalness, diurnation.

DISMAL (dies *day* + mali *evil*) *depressing, gloomy.*

DIC
proclaim

DICARE *to declare;* **DICATUM** 31

ABDICATE *to formally relinquish or renounce an office or right*, abdicator, abdication, abdicable, abdicative.

DEDICATE *to set apart for a special purpose, such as religious; naming and honoring a person for an artistic production; naming a public building for someone*, dedicator, dedicatee, dedication, dedicatory.

INDICATE *to point out*, indication, indicative, indicator, indicatory.

CONTRAINDICATE *in medicine, to make the expected treatment inadvisable*, contraindicant, contraindication.

PREDICABLE *capable of being affirmed*.

PREDICAMENT *an unpleasant and embarrassing position*, predicamental.

PREDICATE *a statement contingent on something; verb in a sentence makes a statement about its subject noun*, predication, predicative, predicatory.

INDEX (in *in* + dicare *to declare*) *that which points out; a title*, indexer, indexical.

PREACH (pre *before* + dicare *to proclaim*) *to urge with earnestness*, preacher, preaching.

DICT
say

DICERE *to say;* **DICTUM** *something said* 60

ADDICT *to apply habitually*, addiction, addictedness.

BENEDICTION *the act of blessing*, benedictive, benedictional, benedictionary.

CONDITION *something essential to the existence or occurrence of something else*, conditional, conditionally, conditionality; recondition.

CONTRADICT *to deny a statement directly*.

CONTRADICTION *a statement in opposition to another or that contradicts itself*, contradictor, contradictional, contradictive.

DICTATE *to deliver orally to another to write down; expressly command*, dictation.

DICTATOR *a ruler with absolute authority*, dictatorial, dictatorialness, dictatorship.

DICTION *choice of words or manner of speaking*.

DICTIONARY *alphabetical arrangement of words of the language with definitions*.

DICTUM (s), DICTA (pl) *in law, a judge's opinion on matters not vital to the main issue*.

EDICT *an official proclamation*, edictal.

INDICT *to charge with a commission of a crime*, indictable, indictee, indicter, indictment.

DICT
say

INTERDICT *to prohibit with authority,* interdiction, interdictive, interdictory.
JURIDIC *acts of judges,* juridical, juridically.
JURISDICTION *legal authority to hear and decide cases,* jurisdictional.
MALEDICTION *speaking of evil about someone,* maledictory.
PREDICT *to foretell, to prognosticate,* prediction, predictional, predictively, predictor.
VALEDICTION *a farewell utterance.*
VALEDICTORY *an address delivered at school graduation,* valedictorian.
VINDICATE *to clear from criticism,* vindication, vindicative, vindicator, vindicatory.
VERDICT (vere dictum *truly said*) *answer of a jury to the court on the matter put to it.*
VENDETTA (vindicta *vengeance*) *a blood feud in which relatives of the murdered person try to kill the murderer or his family.*
VENGEANCE (vindicare) *the return of an injury for an injury; the avenging of an insult or injury.*

DIGN
worthy

DIGNUS **worthy**   18

DIGNIFY *to make worthy; to invest with honor,* dignification, dignified; undignified.
DIGNITY *calm self-possession,* dignitary; indignity.
INDIGNATION *mingled emotions of anger and scorn and contempt,* indignant, indignantly.
CONDIGN *deserved; adequate punishment for wrongdoing,* condignity, condignness.
DEIGN (dignari *to be worthy*) *doing something consistent with one's dignity; to grant with condescension.*
DISDAIN (dis *not* + dignari *deem worthy*) *to reject as unworthy of oneself,* disdainful, disdainfully, disdainfulness.

DIT
DAT
give

DO, DARE *to give,* DATUM   43

ADDITION (ad *to* + dare *to give*) *a thing added; an increase,* additional, additionally, additive.
ADDENDUM *something added; a supplement in writing,* addenda.
EDIT (e *out* + dare *to give*) *to revise a manuscript for publication.*

DIT
DAT
give

EDITION *the size and number of a book printing.*
EDITOR *one who edits; a writer of editorials.*
EDITORIAL *an article specifically stating the opinions of the writer or publisher,* editorialize, editorially.
TRADITION *oral communications of opinions and practices from generation to generation,* traditional, traditionalism, traditionalist, traditionalistic, traditionally, traditionary, traditionist, traditioner.
EXTRADITION *delivery of a wanted person from one state or nation to another,* extradite, extraditable.
PERDITION *irreparable loss or ruin; loss of soul.*
DONATE *to contribute,* donation, donative, donator, donatory, donee, donor.
DATA *facts from which conclusions can be inferred,* datum (sing), datamation.
DATE *the time at which a thing happens: day, month, year,* datable, dated, dateless, dater.
POSTDATE *dated afterward.*
ANTEDATE *a prior date.*
MANDATE (manus *hand* + dare *to give*) *a written authoritative order,* mandater.
MANDATORY *obligatory; authoritatively required.*
MANDAMUS *in law, a writ by a higher to a lower court that a specified thing be done.*

DIVI
divide

DIVIDERE *to divide*   40
DIVIDE *to part or separate into pieces or groups,* dividable, dividedly, divider, dividual; undivided.
DIVIDEND *the number or quantity to be divided; the amount to be divided among stockholders, etc.; the insurance fund paid from the year's surplus profit.*
DIVISIBLE *that can be divided,* divisibility, divisibleness, divisibly.
DIVISION *separation, distribution; a difference of opinion; in voting, a separation of groups,* divisional, divisionally, divisionary.
DIVISION *mathematically, the finding of the quotient, which is the number of times that the divisor is contained in the dividend.*
DIVISIVE *causing or showing division,* divisively, divisiveness.
SUBDIVIDE *to divide further after previous division,* subdivision, subdivisible.
INDIVIDUAL *existing as a single, separate thing; originally not separable; distinguishable from others by special characteristics,* individuate, individuator, individuation.
INDIVIDUALISM *the leading of one's life in one's own way without regard for*

DIVI
divide

others, individualist, individualistic.
INDIVIDUALITY *the sum of the characteristics or qualities that set one person apart from others*, individualizer, individualize, individualization, individually.
INDIVISIBLE *that cannot be divided, separated, or broken*, indivisibleness, indivisibly, indivision.
DEVICE *a plan or scheme formed by design; a trick, invention, or anything fancifully conceived.*
DEVISE *to invent, contrive, or plan a new combination of ideas or principles*, divisee, deviser.
DEVISOR *in law, a person devising: the testator.*

DOC
teach

DOCERE *to teach*, DOCTUM   25
DOCILE *tractable; easily instructed*, docible, docibility, docibleness, docility.
INDOCILE *not easy to teach or discipline*, indocility.
DOCTOR *a teacher or physician*, doctoral, doctorally, doctorate, doctorly.
DOCTRINE *principles or tenets of a religion or a political party.*
DOCTRINAIRE *a visionary theorist*, doctrinarian, doctrinarianism.
DOCTRINAL *pertaining to the doctrine taught*, doctrinally.
INDOCTRINATE *to instruct in theories and beliefs*, indoctrination, indoctrinator.
DOCUMENT *to provide references to support position*, documental, documentation.
DOCUMENTARY *a motion picture showing actual not fictional events.*

DOG
DOX
belief

DOGMA [Gr] *an opinion;* DOXA *a notion*   28
DOGMA *a doctrine; an arrogant assertion of opinion.*
DOGMATIC *asserted without proof, arrogantly*, dogmatical, dogmatically, dogmaticalness, dogmatics, dogmatism, dogmatist, dogmatize, dogmatizer.
DOXOLOGY *hymns of praise to God*, doxological, doxologize.
ORTHODOX (orthos *correct* + doxa *opinion*) *conforming to the usual beliefs or doctrines*, orthodoxical, orthodoxly, orthodoxness, orthodoxy; unorthodox.
HETERODOX *departing from established doctrines, unorthodox*, heterodoxly, heterodoxness, heterodoxy.
PARADOX *a statement that appears contradictory but may be true*, paradoxer, paradoxical, paradoxically, paradoxicalness.

DU *two* — DUO, DUALIS *two*   44

DUAL *consisting of two*, dualism, dualist, dualistic, dualistically, duality.

DUEL *a formal fight between two persons with weapons*, dueling, duelist.

DUET *music composed for two performers*, duetino.

DEUCE *a die with two dots, or throw of the dice totaling two; a playing card with two dots.*

DUBIOUS (duo *two*) *skeptical; ambiguous; causing doubt*, dubiously, dubiousness; indubious.

DUBITABLE *susceptible to doubt*, dubitably, dubitative, dubitatively.

INDUBITABLE *unquestionable; evident*, indubitableness, indubitably.

DUPLICATE *to make another, corresponding exactly to the first*, duplicable, duplication, duplicative, duplicator.

REDUPLICATE reduplication.

DUPLICITY *hypocritical cunning or deception; double-dealing.*

DOUBLE (duplus *double*) *to multiply by two; adding an equal sum*, doubleness, doubler, doubly.

DOUBLET *a couple; a second garment worn by men centuries ago.*

DOUBT *to hold as questionable*, doubtable, doubter, doubtful, doubtfully, doubtfulness, doubting, doubtingly.

DUC *lead* — DUCERE *to lead*, DUCTUM   150

ABDUCE (ab *from* + ducere *to lead*) *"to lead away"; to kidnap*, abduct, abduction, abductor.

ADDUCE (ad *to* + ducere *to lead*) *"to lead to"; to offer as reason or proof; an example*, adducent, adducer, adducible, adduct, adduction, adductive, adductor.

CIRCUMDUCT *to revolve around an axis*, circumduction.

CONDUCE (con *together* + ducere *to lead*) *"to bring together"; to contribute to as a result*, conducent, conductibility, conducible, conducibleness, conducibly, conducive, conduciveness.

CON'DUCT (n) *personal behavior.*

CONDUCT' (v) *to guide, to escort*, conductance, conductibility, conductible, conduction, conductive, conductivity, conductor, conductress.

DEDUCE (de *from* + ducere *to lead*) *"to draw from"; to conclude from what precedes*, deducement, deductibility, deductible, deductibleness, deducibly, deducive.

DEDUCTION *reasoning from the known to the unknown; from the general to the specific*, deduct, deductible, deductive, deductively.

DUC
lead

DUCTILE *can be stretched without breaking*, ductilely, ductileness, ductility.

INDUCTILE *not easily molded*, inductility.

EDUCE (e *out* + ducere *to lead*) *"to draw out"; to evolve; to infer from the data*, educible, educt, eduction, eductor.

EDUCATE *to give knowledge and training to*, educability, educable, education, educational, educationally, educative, educator, educatress.

INDUCE *to lead by persuasion; to prevail on*, induced, inducement, inducer, inducible.

INTRODUCE (intro *within* + ducere *to lead*) *to bring or conduct a person in; to add a new feature*, introducement, introducer, introduction, introductive, introductively, introductor, introductorily, introductory, introductress.

INDUCT *to lead in; to initiate*, inductance, inductee, inductor, induction, inductinal.

INDUCTIVE *reasoning from individual facts to arrive at general principles; electrical and magnetic induction*, inductively, inductivity.

MANUDUCTION (manu *hand* + ducere *to lead*) *"leading by the hand,"* manuductor, manuductory.

PRODUCE (pro *forward* + ducere *to lead*) *"to lead forward"; to bring to view; to generate*, produced, producer, productibility, producible, producibleness, product, productibility, productile, production, productive, productively, productiveness, productivity, productress; unproduced.

REPRODUCE *to bring into existence again*, reproducer, reproducible, reproduction, reproductive, reproductiveness, reproductory.

REDUCE *to diminish; to classify; to degrade*, reduceable, reduced, reducent, reducer, reducibility, reducible, reducibleness, reducibly; unreduced, unreducible.

SEDUCE (se *apart* + ducere *to lead*) *"to lead astray"; to persuade to do wrong*, seduceable, seducement, seducer, seducible, seducingly, seduction, seductive, seductively, seductress; unseduced, unseductive.

SUBDUCE (sub *under* + ducere *to lead*) *to bring into subjection*, subduable, subdual, subduct, subduction, subdue, subduer.

TRADUCE *to slander, to vilify*, traducement, traducent, traducer, traducingly.

DUCT *a tube or canal by which anything is transported*, ductless. *Also:* duke, duchess, dukedom, duchy, ducal, ducat; aqueduct, viaduct, conduit.

DUR
hard

DURUS *hard*   27

DURABLE *lasting in spite of frequent use*, durability, durableness, durably.

DURATION *length of existence*.

DUR
hard
lasting

DURESS *restraint of liberty; coercion.*
ENDURE *undergo; tolerate,* endurable, endurableness, endurably, endurance, endurant, endurer, enduring, enduringly, enduringness.
INDURATE *to make hard; callous,* induration, indurative.
OBDURATE *stubborn; not easily moved to pity,* obduracy, obdurately, obdurateness, obduration.
PERDURABLE *continuing long,* perdurability, perdurably.

DYNA
power

DYNAMIKOS [Gr] ***powerful, strong***   9
DYNE *the unit of force in the metric system.*
DYNAMIC *energetic; causing energy, action, or change.*
DYNAMICS *the motive and controlling forces, physical and moral.*
DYNAMISM *the quality of being vigorous; the theory that energy, not motion, is basic to all phenomena.*
DYNAMITE *an explosive of an absorbent saturated with nitroglycerine.*
DYNAMO *a device for converting mechanical energy to electrical energy.*
DYNASTY *a succession of rulers from the same family.*
HYDRODYNAMICS *the branch of physics of the motion and action of water and other liquids.*
THERMODYNAMICS *the science of the relationship of heat and mechanical energy and the conversion of one into the other.*

EGO
I

EGO *I*   12
EGO *the self; the individual as aware of himself.*
EGOCENTRIC *dwelling on one's interests to the exclusion of everything else,* egocentricity.
EGOISM *selfishness; conceit,* egoist, egoistic, egoistical, egoistically.
EGOMANIA *abnormally excessive egotism,* egomaniac.
SUPEREGO *the conscience of the unconscious.*
EGOTISM *excessive reference to oneself in speaking and writing.*

EMPT
buy
take

EMERE *to take, buy,* EMPTUM   32
CAVEAT EMPTOR *"let the buyer beware."*
EXEMPT (ex *out* + emere *to take*) *excused; free from rule,* exemptible, exemption; unexempt.
COEMPT *to gain control by taking the whole quantity,* coemption.

EMPT
buy
take

PEREMPTORY *an order that cannot be denied; in law, barring further action,* peremptorily, peremptoriness.

PRE-EMPT *the act of buying something in preference to others,* pre-emption, pre-emptioner, pre-emptive, pre-emptor, pre-emptory.

REDEEM *to recover, to rescue,* redeemability, redeemable, redeemableness, redeemer, Redeemer.

REDEMPTION *by repurchasing, to obtain something previously held; the deliverance of sinners from the bondage of sin,* redemptioner, redemptionist, redemptive, redemptory.

PROMPT (pro *forth* + emere *to take*) *quick to act,* prompter, promptitude, promptly, promptness; unprompted.

ENT
EST
to be

ESSE *to be*   63

ABSENT (ab *away* + esse *to be*) absentation, absentee, absenteeism, absenter, absently, absentness.

ABSENCE *not present; the time of being away.*

ESSENCE *the fundamental nature of something; a perfume.*

QUINTESSENCE *"the fifth essence," the most perfect embodiment of a quality,* quintessential.

ESSENTIAL *the intrinsic nature of something,* essentiality, essentially, essentialness; unessential.

CO-ESSENTIAL *having one and the same essence,* co-essentiality, co-essentially.

INESSENTIAL *not really important.*

ENTITY *anything real in itself.*

NONENTITY *something without existence; a person of little importance.*

PRES'ENT (n)(a) *at hand; happening now.*

PRESENT' (v) *to offer for consideration,* presentability, presentable, presentably, presentative, presentee, presenter.

PRESENTATION *something presented before a group, as a play or gift,* presentational.

OMNIPRESENT *ubiquitous; present elsewhere at the same time,* omnipresence.

PRESENTIMENT *a foreboding that something disastrous will happen,* presentient.

REPRESENT *to present a picture to the mind,* representability, representable.

REPRESENTATION *any exhibition of the form of a thing,* representational,

ENT
EST
to be

representationary.

REPRESENTATIVE *picturing or portraying on behalf of another*, representatively, representativeness, representer.

MISREPRESENT *to give false or erroneous representation*, misrepresentation, misrepresentative, misrepresenter.

INTEREST (inter *between* + esse *to be*) *anything in which one participates or has a share*, interested, interestedly, interestedness, interesting, interestingly.

DISINTEREST *not influenced by personal interest or selfish motives*, disinterested, disinterestedly, disinterestedness, disinteresting.

UNINTERESTING *not personally concerned*, uninterested.

EQU
equal

AEQUALIS *even;* AEQUUS *equal, even*   **67**

ADEQUATE *equal to the occasion*, adequacy, adequately, adequateness, adequation; inadequate.

EQUAL *of the same size, ability, etc.*, equability, equable, equableness, equably; unequal.

INEQUAL inequality.

COEQUAL *equal with another person or thing*, coequality, coequally.

EQUALITY *likeness in values, qualities, etc.*, equalitarian, equalization, equalize, equalizer, equally; inequality.

EQUANIMITY *composure; eveness of mind*, equanimous.

EQUATE *to treat or express as equivalent*, equation, equational; inequable.

EQUATOR *an imaginary line around the earth equidistant from North and South Pole*, equatorial, equatorially.

EQUILIBRIUM (aequus *even* + libra *balance*) *a state of balance between opposing forces*, equilibrant, equilibrate, equilibration, equilibrator, equilibrious, equilibriously.

EQUINOX (aequus *equal* + nox *night*) *the precise time when the sun crosses the equator, making day and night everywhere of equal length*, equinoctial, equinoctially.

EQUIPONDERATE *to be equal in weight*, equiponderant, equiponderance.

EQUIPOISE *equal distribution of weight*.

EQUITY *justice; to give each man his due*, equitable, equitableness, equitably, inequity, inequitable.

EQUIVALENCE *equal in value, effect, meaning, etc.*, equivalency, equivalent, equivalently.

EQUIVOCATE *"having equal voices"; capable of more than one interpretation*,

equal   equivocal, equivocally, equivocalness, equivocation, equivocator, equivocatory.
UNEQUIVOCAL *straightforward,* unequivocally, unequivocalness.

ERR
wander

ERRARE *to wander*   **26**
ABERRANCE (ab *from* + errare *to wander*) *deviation; departure from what is right,* aberrancy, aberrant, aberrate, aberration, aberrational.
ERR *to deviate from the true course,* errable, errableness, errancy; unerring.
ERRATA *(pl) mistakes in writing and printing,* erratum *(s)*.
ERRATIC *deviating from the true course; irregular,* erratically, erraticalness.
ERROR *a mistake in judgment; something incorrectly done,* errorful, errorist.
ERRONEOUS *based on error; liable to mislead,* erroneously, erroneousness.
ERRANT *wandering, deviating from the regular course,* errantry.
ARRANT (a variant of *errant*) *notorious, infamous,* arrantly.

EXEM
copy

EXEMPLUM *a copy*   **13**
EXEMPLAR *anything regarded as worthy of imitation,* exemplarily, exemplariness, exemplary.
EXEMPLIFY *to illustrate by example,* exemplifiable, exemplification, exemplifier; unexemplified.
SAMPLE *a part representative of a whole group.*
SAMPLER *one who prepares samples; an embroidered cloth showing skill.*
EXAMPLE *a sample or specimen; a person worthy of imitation;* unexampled.

EXPER
try

EXPERIOR *I try,* **EXPERTUS**   **22**
EXPERIENCE *anything observed or lived through,* experienced; inexperience, inexperienced.
EXPERIENTIAL *the theory that experience is the origin and test of all knowledge,* experientialism, experientialist, experientially.
EXPERIMENT *a test to discover something,* experimental, experimentalism, experimentalist, experimentalize, experimently, experimentation, experimentative, experimentor, experimentist.
EXPERT *a person skilled or trained in some special field,* expertise, expertly, expertness.

EXTR

EXTER *outward;* **EXTRA** *without;* **EXTRANEUS** *external*   **27**
EXTERIOR *on the outside,* exteriority, exteriorly.

EXTR
outward

EXTERNAL *outward*, externalism, externalistic, externality, externalization, externalize, externally.

EXTRANEOUS *foreign; not essential to a thing*, extraneously.

EXTREME *outermost; excessive, immoderate*, extremeless, extremely, extremism, extremist, extremity.

EXTRINSIC (exter *without* + secus *otherwise*) *not inherent to the real nature.*

STRANGE (OFr. estrange; L. extraneus *external*) *not previously known; unusual; causing surprise*, strangely, strangeness, stranger.

ESTRANGE *to keep at a distance; to alienate*, estrangedness, estrangement, estranger.

FAC FEC FIC
make, do
easy
face

FACERE *to make;* **FACIES** *the face;* **FACILIS** *easy*   148

Because the concept "to make" is so very important, a group of suffixes made from the root "facere" to make, and meaning the same, have wide use, totaling maybe a thousand words. The suffixes are FIABLE, FIC, FICAL, FICATION, FICATIVE, FIER, AND FY. An example is amplification (amplus large + facere to make), amplificative, amplificatory, amplifier, and amplify. There is the Greek suffix IZE, also meaning "to make," as in legalize and propagandize.

FACE (facies *visage*) *the viewing side, front part of head*, facial, facially.

DEFACE *to mar the surface; to disfigure*, defacement, defacer.

EFFACE *to make disappear; to remove from the mind*, effaceable, effacement.

FACADE *the elevation of the face of a building; the front part of anything covering something inferior.*

FACET *surface of a cut gem; an aspect of personality.*

FACETIOUS *lightly joking, sometimes inappropriately*, facetiously, facetiousness.

FACT (factum *a deed*) *reality, the state of things as they are.*

FACTION *a group within an organization having a common end*, factional, factionalism, factionist.

FACTIOUS *tending to produce dissension*, factiously, factiousness.

FACTITIOUS *forced or artificial; not genuine*, factitiously, factitiousness.

FACILE *easy to perform*, facilely, facileness.

FACILITY *to make easier*, facilitate, facilitation.

FACSIMILE (facere *to make* + similis *like*) *an exact likeness.*

FACULTY *ability to do a particular thing; all the teachers of a school.*

FACTOTUM *a handy man; a "do all."*

FACTOR *one who carries on business with others; conditions bringing about a*

FAC
FEC
FIC
make, do
easy
face

result; mathematical unit.

FACTORY *an establishment for manufacturing goods.*

MANUFACTURE (manu *hand* + facere *to make*) *formerly, making of articles by hand; large scale production by machinery,* manufacturer, manufacturing.

AFFECT *to produce an effect, to stir the emotions,* affectation, affectedly, affecter or affector, affectedness, affectible, affecting, affectingly, affection, affectionate, affectionately, affectionateness, affective, affectively, affectivity.

DEFECT *shortcoming, imperfection, flaw,* defectible, defection, defectionist, defective, defectively, defectiveness.

EFFECT (ex *out* + facere *to do*) *the consequences produced by a cause,* effecter, effectible, effection, effective, effectively, effectiveness, effector, effectless.

EFFECTUAL *producing the effect desired,* effectually, effectualness, effectuate, effectuation; ineffectual, ineffectuality, ineffectually, ineffectualness.

INFECT *to cause to become diseased; to affect in a harmful way,* infecter or infector, infectible, infection, infectious, infectiously, infectiousness, infective.

PER'FECT (*a*) *without defect or omission,* perfectly (*adv*).

PER'FECT (*n*) *perfect tense.*

PERFECT' (*v*) *to finish or complete, to make more perfect,* perfecter, perfectability, perfectible, perfection, perfectionism, perfectionist, perfective, perfectively, perfectness.

PREFECT *head of departments in France; monitor in some schools in England,* prefectship, prefecture, prefectural.

CONFECTION *anything preserved with sugar,* confectioner, confectionary or confectionery.

REFECTION *refreshment, a light meal,* refectioner, refectory.

COUNTERFEIT (contra *against, opposite* + facere *to make*) *forged, made to defraud,* counterfeiter, counterfeitly.

FORFEIT *lose the right to possess,* forfeitable, forfeiter, forfeiture.

SURFEIT (super *above* + facere *to make*) *excess in amount; overindulgence, discomfort,* surfeiter.

EFFICIENT *ability to produce the desired effect with the minimum of effort and expense,* efficiently, efficiency.

EFFICACIOUS *producing the result desired,* efficaciously, efficaciousness.

PROFICIENT (pro *forward* + facere *to make*) *highly competent,* proficiently, proficience, proficiency.

PROFIT *advantage; financial gain,* profitable, profitableness, profitably, profiteer, profitless.

FAC
make

SUFFICE *to be sufficient or adequate*, sufficiency, sufficient, sufficiently, sufficing, sufficingly, sufficingness.
BENEFIT (bene *good* + facere *to make*) benefactor, beneficial, etc.
CONFIT *a sweetmeat; any fruit preserved by sugar*.

FAL
deceive

FALLERE *to deceive*, FALSUM   33
FALLACY *a false or mistaken idea*, fallacious, fallaciously, fallaciousness.
FALLIBLE *likely to be inaccurate or deceived*, fallibility, fallibly.
INFALLIBLE *not likely to fail; never wrong*, infallibility, infallibleness, infallibly.
FALTER *to act hesitantly; show uncertainty*, falteringly.
FALSE *untruthful; mistaken*, falsely, falseness.
FALSIFY *to give an untrue or misleading account*, falsifiable, falsification, falsificator.
FALSETTO *a "false" way of singing with the voice in too high a register*.
FAIL (fallere *to deceive*) *not to produce the effect*, failing, failure.
FAULT (fallere *to deceive*) *failure to do what is required*, faultful, faultily, faultiness, faultlessly, faultlessness, faulty.
DEFAULT *failure to do a required act*, defaulter

FAT
FAB
speak

FARI *to speak*, FATUS; FABULA *a story*   40
FATE *something inevitable; power to determine the outcome of future events*, fated, fateful, fatefully, fatefulness.
FATAL *decisive, disastrous, deadly*, fatalism, fatalist, fatalistic, fatalistically.
FATALITY *an event resulting in death*, fatally, fatalness.
INFANT (in *not* + fari *to speak*) *a very young child*.
INFANTILE *acting childlike*, infantilism.
MULTIFARIOUS *composed of differing parts*, multifariously, multifariousness.
PREFACE (pre *before* + fari *to speak*) *a preliminary statement to an article or book*, prefacer, prefatorial, prefatorily, prefatory.
AFFABLE *courteous; easy to talk to*, affability, affableness, affably.
INEFFABLE *inexpressible; too overwhelming*, ineffability, ineffableness, ineffably.
FABLE *a fictitious story to teach a moral truth*, fabled, fabler, fabulist.
FABULOUS *incredible; beyond belief*, fabulously, fabulousness.
CONFABULATE *talk together; to prattle*, confabulation.

FEND
strike
keep off

FENDO, FENDERE *to strike,* **FENSUM** 31

FEND *to keep off, to resist.*
FENDER *any mechanical device that protects.*
FENCE *a structure to hold in or prevent passage.*
FENCING *skilled use of the sword in defense or attack.*
DEFEND *to guard from attack,* defendable, defendant, defender; undefended.
DEFENSE *to keep from harm; an argument to justify,* defenseless, defenselessness, defensibility, defensible, defenseness, defensive, defensively; undefensible.
OFFEND *to displease; to insult,* offender.
UNOFFENDED *doing no injury or harm,* unoffending.
OFFENSE *a transgression: socially, morally, legally,* offenseless, offensive, offensively, offensiveness; unoffensive.
INOFFENSIVE *no provocation,* inoffensively, inoffensiveness.

FER
bear
carry

FERRE *to bear* 87

CONFER *to discuss; to bestow,* conference, conferential, conferment, conferrable.
DEFER (de *down* + ferre *to carry*) *to put off; to yield with courtesy,* deference, deferent, deferential, deferentially, deferment, deferred, deferer.
DIFFER *to be unlike; to disagree,* difference, different, differential, differentially, differentiate, differentiation, differentiator; indifferent.
INFER *to draw a conclusion,* inferable, inference, inferential, inferentially.
OFFER (ob *toward* + ferre *to bear*) *to present for acceptance or rejection,* offerable, offerer, offering.
PROFFER *to offer for acceptance,* profferer.
REFER *to direct attention; to submit for determination,* referable, referer, reference, referendary, referendum, referent, referential, referentially, referral, referrer.
SUFFER (sub *under* + ferre *to bear*) *to undergo something unpleasant; to endure,* sufferable, sufferableness, sufferable, sufferance, sufferer, suffering, sufferingly.
TRANSFER *to convey from one person to another,* transferability, transferable, transferee, transference, transferential, transferor; untransferred, untransferable.
CIRCUMFERENCE *the line bounding a circle,* circumferential, circumferentially.

FER
bear
carry

FERTILE *producing in abundance*, fertilely, fertileness, fertility, fertilizable, fertilization, fertilize, fertilizer; infertile; unfertile.
CONIFEROUS (conus *a cone* + ferre *to bear*) *a tree bearing cone*.
FLORIFEROUS *a plant bearing flowers*.
FRUCTIFEROUS *a plant bearing fruit*.
PESTIFEROUS *carrying disease; dangerous to the welfare of society*.
VOCIFEROUS *shouting noisily*, vociferously, vociferance, vociferant, vociferate, vociferation, vociferator, vociferously, vociferousness.

FERV
boil

FERVEO boil, FERVERE to boil; FERMENTUM leaven   19
FERVID *burning; impassioned*, fervidly, fervidness.
FERVENT *showing great warmth of feeling*, fervently.
FERVOR *intense heat; intense feeling*.
FERMENT *state of excitement; to cause fermentation*, fermentability, fermentable, fermentation, fermentative, fermently, fermentness.
EFFERVESCE *to bubble; to be vivacious*, effervescence, effervescency, effervescent, effervescible, effervescive.

FESS
acknow-
ledge

FATERI to avow, acknowledge, FASSUS   22
CONFESS *to acknowledge*, confessant, confessedly, confesser, confession, confessional, confessionalism, confessionalist, confessor.
PROFESS (pro *before* + fateri *to avow*) *to avow publicly*, professedly.
PROFESSION *a vocation requiring advanced training in an art or science*.
PROFESSIONAL *worthy of high standards; one who plays for money*, professionalism, professionally.
PROFESSOR *a college teacher of the highest rank*, professorate, professorial, professorialism, professorially, professoriate, professorally.

FID
faith

FIDES *faith;* FIDERE *to trust;* FIDELIS *trusty*   38
FIDELITY *faithfulness; firm adherence to a person or party*.
INFIDELITY *lack of faith, trust, or loyalty*.
INFIDEL *one who does not believe in a certain or prevailing religion*.
FIDUCIAL *based on faith*, fiducially.
FIDUCIARY *one who holds something in trust for another*.
AFFIANCE *to pledge; to betroth*, affianced, affiancer.
AFFIDAVIT *a declaration upon oath*, affiant.

FID — *faith*

CONFIDE *to trust; to share secrets; give into keeping.*
CONFIDANT *one to whom secrets are told.*
CONFIDENT *assurance in mind of the trustworthiness of another,* confidence, confidential, confidentially, confidently, confidentness.
DEFY (dis *from* + fidus *faithful*) *to dare someone; to resist; to foil,* defiance, defiant, defiantly, defiantness.
DIFFIDENCE *lack of self-confidence,* diffident, diffidently.
PERFIDY *the deliberate violation of faith,* perfidious, pefidiously, perfidiousness.
FAITH (fides *faith*) *unquestioned belief,* faithful, faithfully, faithfulness, faithless, faithlessly, faithlessness.
FEALTY (fides *faith*) *fidelity owed by a vassal or tenant to his feudal lord.*

FIG — *shape*

FIGURA *a shape;* FINGERE *to touch;* FICTUM *feigned*   35
FIGURE *form, outline, shape, likeness,* figurated, figurately, figuration, figurative, figuratively, figurativeness.
DISFIGURE *to deform, mar, deface,* disfiguration, disfigurment, disfigurer.
CONFIGURATION *external form resulting from the dispositon of its parts; in astronomy, the position of the stars to each other.*
PREFIGURE *to foreshadow; to imagine beforehand,* prefiguration, prefigurative, prefigurement.
TRANSFIGURE *transform; to idealize,* transfiguration.
EFFIGY *an image of a person, often a stuffed likeness hanged or burned in public.*
FIGMENT *an invention; something imagined,* figmental.
FICTION *that which is feigned, invented or imagined,* fictional, fictionalize, fictionist, fictitious, fictitiously, fictitiousness, fictive.
FEIGN (fingere *to touch*) *to pretend, invent, or fabricate,* feignedly, feignedness, feigner, feigningly.
FEINT *a deceptive movement, a pretended attack to get an opponent off his guard.*

FIL — *thread*

FILUM *a thread*   12
FILE *to arrange papers in order; to smooth out.*
FILAMENT *a fine, threadlike wire; a thread,* filamentary, filamentiferous.
FILATURE *a drawing out into threads.*
FILIGREE *delicate, lacelike ornamental work of wire or precious metals.*
DEFILE *to polute or tarnish,* defilement, defiler.

FIL
thread

ENFILADE (en *in* + filum *a thread*) *gunfire directed along the entire length of troops.*

PROFILE (pre *before* + filum *outline*) *side view of a face; short biography*, profilist.

FIN
end

FINIS *an end*   68

AFFINITY (ad *to* + finis *end*) *close relationship; resemblance*, affined, affinitative, affinitatively, affinitive.

CONFINE *to restrain within limits*, confineless, confinement, confiner.

DEFINE (de *from* + finis *a boundary*) *to describe exactly*, definable, definably, definement, definer; undefinable, undefinably.

DEFINITE *bounded with precision*, definitely, definiteness.

DEFINITION *an explanation of what something means*, definitional, definitive, definitively, definitiveness.

INDEFINITE *having no exact limits*, indefinitely, indefiniteness.

REFINE *to bring to a pure state*, refinedly, refinedness, refinement, refiner, refinery; unrefined.

SUPERFINE *extra fine; excessively subtle*, superfineness.

FINANCE *the money resources of a person, organization, nation*, financial, financially, financier.

FINE *perfected, pecuniary penalty*, fineable, finely, fineness.

FINAL *conclusive*, finalist, finality, finalize, finally.

FINALE *the concluding movement or passage.*

FINIS *the end.*

FINISH *to complete, to accomplish*, finished, finisher, finishing.

FINITE *having definable limits*, finitely, finiteness, finitude.

INFINITE *without limits*, infinitely, infiniteness, infinitude, infinity.

INFINITIVE *a simple form of the verb, preceeded by "to,"* infinitively.

INFINITESIMAL *too small to be measured*, infinitesimally.

FIRM
strong
stable

FIRMUS *strong, stable*   32

AFFIRM *to assert positively*, affirmable affirmably, affirmance, affirmant, affirmation, affirmer.

AFFIRMATIVE *confirmative; ratifying*, affirmatively, affirmatory.

CONFIRM *to make certain, to verify*, confirmable, confirmance, confirmation, confirmative, confirmatively, confirmatory, confirmedly, confirmedness, confirmee,

FIRM
strong
stable

confirmer, confirmingly.
FIRM *compact; steady; resolute,* firmly, firmness.
INFIRM *weak, feeble; irresolute,* infirmity, infirmly, infirmness.
INFIRMARY *an institutional place where the sick or injured are treated.*
FIRMAMENT *the sky viewed poetically as a solid arch,* firmamental.

FIX
fix

FINGERE *to fix, fasten,* FIXUM   22
FIX *to make secure; set firmly in the mind; to mind,* fixable, fixative, fixedly, fixedness, fixer, fixing, fixity.
FIXATE *directing the attention particularly to,* fixation.
FIXTURE *something firmly in place; a fitting in the house or store.*
CRUCIFIX *a religious symbol consisting of a cross.*
CRUCIFY *to put to death by suspending to the cross; to mortify,* crucifixion.
AFFIX *any syllable added to a root or word,* affixation, affixture.
INFIX *a syllable placed within the body of a word to change its meaning.*
PREFIX *a syllable placed before a word or root to change its meaning or create a new word.*
POSTFIX *a letter, syllable or word added to the end of a word (a suffix).*
SUFFIX *a syllable at the end of a root, for definition or to form verbs, nouns, adjectives or adverbs.*
TRANSFIX *to make motionless; to pierce through with something pointed.*

FLAM
FLAG
fire

FLAMMA *a stream of fire;* FLAGRARE *to burn*   26
FLAME *burning with a blaze of light,* flameless, flamelet, flaming, flamingly.
FLAMBEAU *a flaming torch.*
FLAMBOYANT *flowery, bombastic,* flamboyance, flamboyancy.
FLAMINGO *a tropical wading bird of red color.*
INFLAME *to set on fire; to exite intensely,* inflamer, inflammability, inflammable, inflammableness, inflammably.
INFLAMMATORY *the rousing of listeners to violence, as from a speech.*
INFLAMMATION *in medicine, the redness or swelling of some part of the body, from injury or infection.*
CONFLAGRATE *to burn up utterly,* conflagrant, conflagration, conflagrative.
FLAGRANT *flaming into notice; outrageous,* flagrance, flagrancy, flagrantly.
FLAGRANTE DELICTO *"the blazing of the crime"; caught red-handed.*

FLEC / FLEX — bend

FLECTO, FLECTERE *to bend,* **FLEXUM**   **48**

FLECTION *the art of bending,* flectional.

CIRCUMFLECT *to bend around,* circumflection, circumflex, circumflexion.

DEFLECT *to swerve,* deflectable, deflection, deflectionization, deflectionize, deflective.

INFLECT *to bend; to vary the voice pitch,* inflected, inflection, inflectional, inflectionless, inflective.

REFLECT *to bend or throw back; to think seriously,* reflectible, reflecting, reflectingly, reflectiveness, reflectivity, reflector.

FLEX *to bend (an arm); to contract (a muscle).*

FLEXUOUS, *winding, wavering,* flexuose, flexuosity, flexuously.

FLEXOR *a muscle that bends the limb or other part of the body.*

FLEXIBLE *bent, pliant, yielding,* flexibility, flexibleness, flexibly.

INFLEXIBLE *unbending; firm in mind or purpose,* inflexibility, inflexibleness, inflexibly.

REFLEX *turned, bent, reflected back,* reflexibility, reflexible, reflexion, reflexive, reflexively, reflexiveness, reflexivity, reflexly.

FLIC — strike

FLIGO, FLIGERE *to destroy;* **FLICTUS** *striking*   **20**

AFFLICT *to cause pain or suffering,* afflicter, afflicting, affliction, afflictionless, afflictive, afflictively.

CONFLICT′ (v) *be in opposition,* conflicting, confliction, conflictive.

CON′FLICT (n) *sharp disagreement; emotional disturbance resulting from clash.*

INFLICT *to cause pain; to impose punishment,* inflicter, infliction, inflictive.

PROFLIGATE (pro *forward* + fligere *to drive*) *abandoned to vice; extremely wasteful,* profligacy, profligately, profligateness.

FLOR — flower

FLOS, FLORIS *a flower*   **27**

FLORA *goddess of flowers.*

FLORAL *made of or made like flowers.*

FLORID *ruddy complexion; gaudy or showy,* floridity, floridly, floridness.

FLORICULTURE *the culture of flowers.*

FLORIFEROUS *blooming abundantly.*

FLORIN *an ancient coin stamped with a lily, first coined in Florence.*

FLORIST *one who cultivates and sells flowers.*

FLOWER *a plant cultivated for its blossoms; the best part of a person or thing,*

FLOR *flower*

floweret, flowering, flowerless, flowerlessness.

FLOWERLY *abounding with blossoms; a highly embellished language*, flowerily, floweriness.

FLOUR *"flower of the meal"; wheat or other grains finely ground*, floury.

FLOURISH *to grow luxuriantly; to speak or write in an ornamental style*, flourisher, flourishingly.

EFFLORESCE *to blossom out; to change to a powdery state*, efflorescence, efflorescency, efflorescent.

FLU *flow*

FLUO, FLUERE *to flow*, FLUXUM   61

AFFLUENCE *flowing freely; wealthy*, affluent, affluently, affluentness.

CONFLUENCE *flowing together so as to form one*, confluent, confluently.

EFFLUENCE *a flowing out*, effluent.

INFLUENCE (originally, *a flowing from the stars to affect people*), *the power of people to affect others*, influencer.

FLUENT *flowing; speaking and writing with facility and smoothness*, fluency, fluently, fluentness.

CONFLUX *flowing together so as to form one*, confluxible, confluxibleness.

EFFLUX *a flowing out*, effluxion.

INFLUX *an inpouring of persons or things.*

FLUX *the act of flowing; anything in continued succession; a substance used in the fusion of minerals*, fluxation, fluxibility, fluxible, fluxibleness, fluxion, fluxional, fluxionary, fluxionist.

SUPERFLUX *more than in needed.*

MELLIFLUENCE *sweetly flowing, as with honey, as a voice*, mellifluent, mellifluently, mellifluous.

SUPERFLUOUS *overflowing; more than is needed*, superfluity, superfluously, superfluousness.

FLUCTUATE *varying in an irregular way*, fluctuability, fluctuant, fluctuation, fluctuous.

FLUE *a pipe or shaft for gas or air.*

FLUID *that can flow*, fluidal, fluidic, fluidify, fluidity, fluidize, fluidness.

FLUME *a narrow gorge or artificial channel*, fluminous.

FLUSH (fluxus) *a hand of cards all in the same suit.*

FLUVIAL *what is found in or produced by rivers*, fluvialist, fluviatic, fluviatile; effluvium *to flow out.*

INFLUENZA *a contagious, infectious disease.*

FORM *shape*

FORMA *shape* **80**
FORM *the shape or outline of anything*, formable.
FORMLESS *shapeless*, formlessly, formlessness.
FORMAL *according to fixed customs or ceremonies*, formally, formality, formalize, formalization.
INFORMAL *casual, unceremonious, relaxed*, informally, informality.
UNFORMAL unformalized, unformalated.
FORMALISM *excessive attention to forms and customs*, formalistic.
FORMAT *make-up of a book, etc.*, formative, formation.
FORMULA *a method of repeatedly doing something; a medical prescription*, formulate, formular, formulary, formulation, formularization, formulator.
CONFORM *to bring into harmony or agreement*, conformance, conformation, conformity, conformable, conformability, conformableness, conformer, conformist; nonconformist, nonconformity.
DEFORM *to injure the form or shape of*, deformable, deformation, deformer, deformity.
INFORM *to give form or vitality; to communicate knowledge of facts*, informant, informer, information, informational, informative.
MISINFORM *supply with false information*, misinformant, misinformation.
MULTIFORM *having many forms or shapes*, multiformity.
PERFORM *to accomplish, to complete, to execute*, performable, performance, peformer; unperformed.
REFORM *to make better by removing faults and defects*, reformable, reformation, reformative, reformer, reformist; unreformed, unreformable.
REFORMATORY *institution for young offenders*.
TRANSFORM *to change the form, nature, condition*, transformable, transformation, transformative, transformational, transformer, transformist.
UNIFORM *always the same; not changing in any degree*, uniformity, uniformize, uniformness.

FORT *strong*

FORTIS *strong* **31**
FORT *army post; a fortified building for defense*, fortress.
FORTIFY *to strengthen physically or with arguments*, fortifiable, fortification, fortifier.
FORTITUDE *patient endurance of misfortune*, fortitudinous.
FORTE *the thing a person does particularly well; loud music*.
COMFORT *(vb) to ease the misery or grief; (n) state of quiet enjoyment*,

FORT
strong

comfortable, comfortableness, comfortably, comforter, comfortful, comforting, comfortless, comfortlessly, comfortlessness.
DISCOMFORT *uneasiness; distress.*
EFFORT *the use of energy to get something done,* effortless.
ENFORCE *to strengthen, to compel,* enforceable, enforcedly, enforcement, enforcer, enforcible.
REINFORCE *to make stronger or compelling,* reinforcement, reinforcer.

FRACT FRANG
break

FRANGO, FRANGERE *to break,* FRACTUM   52
FRACTIOUS *unruly, rebellious,* fractiously, fractiousness.
FRACTURE *a break in the bone or other substance,* fractural.
FRACTION *a small portion of the whole,* fractional, fractionally, fractionary, fractionate, fractionation, fractionize.
INFRACTION *a violation of an agreement, treaty or law,* infract, infractor.
REFRACT (re *again* + frangere *to break*) *to bend, as a ray passes through one medium to another,* refractable, refracting, refraction, refractional, refractive, refractiveness, refractivity.
REFRAIN *to stop; a verse or musical phrase repeated,* refrainer.
INFRINGE *to violate; to transgress,* infringement, infringer.
FRAGILE *easily broken,* fragilely, fragility.
FRAGMENT *a part broken off,* fragmental, fragmentarily, fragmentariness, fragmentary, fragmentation, fragmented, fragmentize.
FRAIL *delicate, weak,* frailly, frailness, frailty.
FRANGIBLE *easily broken,* frangibility.
INFRANGIBLE *that cannot be violated or broken,* infrangibility, infrangible, infrangibleness.
REFRANGIBLE *capable of being turned from a direct course passing from one medium to another,* refrangibility, refrangibleness.

FRONT
forepart

FRONS, FRONTIS *forehead*   14
AFFRONT *to insult openly,* affronter, affrontingly.
CONFRONT *to face boldly, to oppose,* confrontation, confronter.
EFFRONTERY (ex *out* + frons *the forehead*) *impudence; shameless boldness.*
FRONT *countenance; disposition; beginning,* frontage, frontal, frontingly.
FRONTIER *the border of a country adjoining another.*
FRONTISPIECE *title page; illustration thereof; preface.*
FRONTLET *a brow band.*

FRU
enjoy

FRUOR, FRUI *to enjoy,* **FRUCTUS** 27

FRUIT (fructus *enjoyment*) *edible part of plant or tree substance,* fruitage, fruiter, fruitful, fruitfully, fruitfulness, fruitiness, fruiting, fruitless, fruitlessly, fruitlessness, fruity.

FRUITION *coming to fulfillment; pleasure derived from use,* fruitive,

FRUCTIFY (fructus *fruit* + facere *to make*) *to make fruitful,* fructiferous, fructification.

FRUGAL *economical, saving,* frugality, frugally, frugalness.

FRUGIFEROUS *producing fruit or grain.*

FRUGIVOROUS *feeding on fruits.*

FRUCTUOUS *fruitful; productive,* fructuously, fructuousness.

FRUCTOSE *a crystalline sugar, found in sweet fruits and honey.*

FUG
flee

FUGERE *to flee,* **FUGITUM** 19

FUGITIVE *one who flees from danger, justice, etc.; anything hard to catch,* fugitively, fugitiveness.

FUGACIOUS *transitory, fleeting,* fugaciousness, fugacity.

FUGUE *a piece where the parts regularly "chase each other";* fuguist.

REFUGE *a place of safety; action taken to escape consequences.*

REFUGEE *one who flees to a place of safety.*

SUBTERFUGE (sub *under* + fugere *to flee*) *an artifice used to escape censure.*

VERMIFUGE *to expel worms and parasites from the intestinal tract,* vermifugal.

FEBRIFUGE *a substance used for reducing or removing fever,* febrifugal.

CENTRIFUGE *a machine used to separate particles of varying density (cream from milk),* centrifugal, centrifugalize, centrifugence.

FULG
flash

FULGEO, FULGERE *to shine* 22

FULMINATE *to explode with violence,* fulminant, fulminating, fulmination, fulminator, fulminatory, fulminic, fulminous.

FULGENT *dazzlingly bright,* fulgently, fulgency.

FULGID *glittering.*

FULGURANT *like lightning,* fulgurate, fulgurating, fulguration, fulgurite, fulgurous.

EFFULGENT *great brightness,* effulge, effulgence, effulgency.

FUNCT
perform

FUNGOR, FUNGI *to perform*, **FUNCTUS**   **15**

FUNCTION *the normal action of anything*, functional, functionalism, functionalize, functionally, functionary, functionless.

FUNCTIONARY *one who holds an office or trust*, functionate.

DEFUNCT (de *from, off* + fungi *to perform*) *no longer existing*.

DYSFUNCTION *in medicine, an abnormal or impaired function of an organ*.

MALFUNCTION *to fail to function as it should*.

PERFUNCTORY *done without care*, perfunctorily, perfunctoriness.

FUND
FOUND
bottom

FUNDUS *the bottom;* **FUNDARE** *to found*   **14**

FUND *a sum of money for a purpose*.

REFUND *make payment*, refunder, refundment.

FUNDAMENT *a basic principle which serves as the groundwork*, fundamental.

PROFUNDITY *of great depth; a profound thought*.

PROFOUND *marked by intellectual depth; intensely felt*, profoundly.

FOUND (fundare *to found*) *lay the basic of; to begin to raise*.

FOUNDATION *establishment; establishment of institutional upkeep; endowment*.

FOUNDER *one who establishes an institution; one who casts metal; horse lameness; ship sinking*.

REFOUND *to re-establish; to put on a new basis*.

UNFOUNDED *baseless; not founded on fact*.

FUS
FUT
pour

FUNDERE *to pour*, **FUSUM**   **79**

FUSE *to melt, to liquefy by heat*, fusible, fusibility.

FUSEE *a colored railroad flare*.

FUSION *the blending of different interests into a coalition; a process of generating atomic energy*, fusionism, fusionist.

CONFUSE (com *together* + fundere *to pour*) *to bring disorder, to mix up the mind*, confusably, confusability, confusedly, confusedness, confusely, confusion, confusional, confusionive.

DIFFUSE *spread widely*, diffusively, diffusiveness, diffusely, diffuseness, diffuser or diffusor, diffusibility, diffusible, diffusibleness, diffusion, diffusive, diffusively, diffusiveness.

EFFUSE (ex *out* + fundere *to pour*) *to pour out*.

EFFUSION *emotional expression, overflowing kindness*, effusive, effusively, effusiveness.

FUS FUT *pour*

INFUSE *to pour into; to instill qualities*, infuser, infusibility, infusible, infusibleness, infusion, infusionism, infusive.

PROFUSE *a pouring forth; a spending with liberality*, profusely, profuseness, profusion, profusive.

REFUSE *to decline to accept*, refusal, refusable, refuser, refusion.

REFUTE *to prove a person or idea to be wrong*, refutability, refutable, refutably, refutal, refutation, refutatory, refuter.

CONFUTE *argument and evidence that shows a falsity*, confutable, confutant, confutation, confutive, confutment, confuter.

FUTILE *ineffectual, trifling*, futilely, futilitarian, futility.

CONFOUND (com *together* + fundere *to pour*) *to throw into disorder or consternation*, confounded, confoundedly, confoundedness, confounder.

REFUND *to reimburse or make repayment*, refunder, refundment.

GEN *kind beget*

GIGNO, GIGNERE *to beget,* GENITUM; GENS *a nation;* GENUS *a kind* 110

GENE *any elements enabling hereditary characteristics to be transmitted.*

GENETICS *the branch of biology that deals with heredity in animals and plants.*

EUGENICS *the science of hereditary improvement.*

GENUS *subordinate classifications of plants and animals with common characteristics determining species.*

GENDER *sex.*

ENGENDER *to bring about; to cause to exist*, engenderer.

GENERIC *a general class or kind, as contrasted to specific.*

GENESIS *origin, creation; way in which something is formed.*

GENERAL *all the whole, not the particular*, generality, generalizable, generalization, generalize, generalizer, generally, generalness.

GENERAL *top officer of the military*, generalcy, generalship, generalissimo.

GENERATE *to originate, to beget, to produce*, generation, generationism, generative, generator, generatrix; ungenerated.

DEGENERATE *having sunk below a former condition; deteriorate*, degeneracy, degenerateness, degeneration, degenerationist, degenerative.

REGENERATE *spiritually reborn; bring into existence again.*

UNREGENERATE unregeneracy.

GENEROUS *willing to give and share*, generosity, generously, generousness.

GENIAL *kindly warmth of disposition*, geniality, genially, genialness; ungenial.

GEN
kind
beget

CONGENIAL *friendly; having the same tastes and temperament*, congeniality, congenially, congenialness.
GENITAL *pertaining to the act or organs of generation*, genitalia, genitals.
CONGENITAL *belonging to an individual from birth*, congenitally.
GENIUS *the innate ability and mental capacity with which an individual is endowed*.
INGENIOUS *clever, original, inventive*, ingeniously, ingeniousness, ingenuity.
INGENUOUS *frank, candid, simple, naive*, ingenuously, ingenuousness.
DISINGENUOUS *insincere*, disingenuously, disingenuousness.
GENTLE *having qualities appropriate of good birth; easily handled*, gentleness, gentility; ungentle, ungently.
GENTLEMAN *a man of good breeding and refinement*, gentlemanlike, gentlemanliness, gentlemanly; ungentlemanly.
GENTEEL *pretentiously well-bred*, genteelish, genteely, genteelness; ungenteel.
GENTILE *any person not a Jew*.
GENUINE *really being what it is said to be*, genuinely, genuineness; ungenuine.
GENEALOGY (genea *race* + logos *a discourse*) *history of the descent of a person or family from an ancestor*, genealogic, genealogically, genealogist.
GENOCIDE *the systematic killing of a whole people (by the Nazis)*.
GENRE [zhon'r] *a kind or class of works of art or literature*.
BENIGN *kind, favorable, generous*, benignancy, benignant, benignantly, benignity, benignly.
MALIGN (male *badly* + genus *a kind*) *very harmful*, malignancy, malignant, malignantly.
HOMOGENIOUS *essentially alike; of the same nature*.
HOMOGENIZE *make uniform throughout by blending the particles*.
HYDROGEN *named because the combustion of hydrogen generated water* (H_2O).
PROGENITOR *a forefather*.
PRIMOGENITURE *first born of the same parents*, primogenitor.
PROGENY *offspring, descendants collectively*.

GEO
earth

GE [Gr] *earth*   20
GEOLOGY *science of the earth's crust*, geologic, geological, geologically, geologist, geologize.
GEOGRAPHY *study of the countries and their natural resources*, geographer, geographic, geographical, geographically.

GEO
earth

GEOMETRY *the measurement of lines and planes in space (originally, measurement of the earth)*, geometric, geometrically, geometrician, geometrize.

GEOCENTRIC *viewed from the center of earth; regarding earth as the center.*

GEODESIC *designating the shortest distance between two points on a (curved) surface.*

APOGEE *apex; highest or furtherest point (in the heavens).*

PERIGEE *orbit of the moon when it is at the least distance from the earth.*

GEST
carry

GERO, GERERE *to carry,* **GESTUM** **52**

GESTURE *motion of the arms or legs or body to express ideas or emotions,* gestural, gestureless.

GESTICULATE *use of many energetic gestures,* gesticular, gesticulation, gesticulative, gesticulator, gesticulatory.

GESTATE *development of the young in the womb; development of an idea,* gestation.

CONGEST *collect in a mass,* congested, congestion, congestive.

CONGERIES (com *together* + gerere *to carry*) *a collection of things brought together in a mass.*

DIGEST (dis *apart* + gerere *to carry*) *to arrange systematically; changing of food in the stomach so it can be absorbed by the body,* digest, digestedly, digester or digestor, digestibility, digestible, digestion, digestive.

INGEST *to put food or pills in the stomach for digestion,* ingestion.

INDIGESTED *not prepared for nourishing the body, not ordered in the mind,* indigestedness, indigestibility, indigestible, indigestibleness, indigestibly, indigestion, indigestive.

SUGGEST *to bring a thought to the mind for consideration,* suggester, suggestibility, suggestible, suggestion, suggestive, suggestively, suggestiveness.

REGISTER (re *again* + gerere *to carry*) *a record of events and items; exact matching in printing and photography; range of the voice,* registered, registering, registership, registrant, registrar, registration, registry.

GNOS
know

GIGNOSKEIN [Gr] *to know* **28**

DIAGNOSIS *a careful investigation of the facts to determine the true nature,* diagnose, diagnostic, diagnostically, diagnosticate, diagnostician, diagnostics.

PROGNOSIS *a judgment in advance of the probable course of the disease and the chances of recovery,* prognosticable, prognostical, prognosticate, prognostication, prognosticative, prognosticator.

GNOS
know

PHYSIOGNOMY *the specious practice of judging character by facial features,* physiognomist, physiognomically.

GNOME *wise, pithy saying (gnomes or dwarfs were believed to know of hidden treasures),* gnomic, gnomology.

GNOSIS *superior wisdom such as mystically acquired by the Gnostics.*

NOBLE ([g]noscere *to know) illustrious; exalted in rank,* nobly, nobleness.

ENNOBLE *to make noble.*

IGNOBLE *of low birth, mean,* ignobly, ignobleness.

GRAD
GRESS
walk
step

GRADIOR, GRADI *to walk,* GRESSUS   **66**

AGGRADE *building up the slope by depositing sediment, often in streams,* aggradation.

GRADE *degree on a scale according to rank; the degree of a rise or descent on a slope; rating on an examination.*

GRADATION *a gradual change of step or degree, tone or shape; ascending or descending chords,* gradational, gradatory.

GRADIENT *moving by steps; rising or descending by regular degrees of inclination.*

GRADUAL *proceeding by steps or degrees,* graduality, gradually, gradualness.

GRADUATE *receiving a degree or diploma for completion of study at a school,* graduation, graduator.

DEGRADE *to lower in rank or status; to bring into dishonor,* degradingly, degradation.

RETROGRADE (retro *backward* + gradi *to walk*) *"to go backwards"; to become worse, to deteriorate,* retrogradingly, retrogress, retrogression, retrogressional, retrogressive, retrogressively.

AGGRESS *to commit the first act of hostility,* aggressor, aggression, aggressive, aggresssiveness.

CONGRESS *a coming together, social intercourse; the institution,* congressman, congressional, congressionalist.

DEGREE (de *down* + gradi *to walk*) *a step upward or downward toward an end.*

DEGRESSION *a degree or rank of anything,* degressive.

DIGRESS *"to step from the way"; to depart temporarily from the subject, to ramble,* digressive, digressively, digression, digressional.

EGRESS *"to go out"; to leave or exit,* egression.

INGRESS *"to step into"; the act or right to enter,* ingression.

GRAD / GRESS — *walk, step*

INGREDIENT *"to go into"; a constituent of a mixture.*
INTROGRESSION *entrance.*
PROGRESS *to continue toward completion,* progression, progressional, progressionalist, progressive, progressively, progressiveness, progressor.
REGRESS *"to move backward,"* regression, regressive, regressively, regressor.
TRANSGRESS *"to pass over or beyond"; to break some prescribed rule,* transgression, transgressional, transgressive, transgressively, transgressor.

GRAN — *grain*

GRANUM *a grain of corn* 12
GRANARY *a storehouse for grain.*
GRANIVOROUS *feeding on grain.*
GRANULE *a fibre grain,* granular, granulate.
GRANITE *a very hard rock composed of distinct grains,* granitic.
GRAIN (granum *a grain) a small, hard seed.*
INGRAINED *worked into the grain or fibre; firmly established.*
GRENADE (granatus *having seeds) filled with grains of exploding powder.*
GRENADIER *originally a tall soldier who threw grenades.*
POMEGRANATE *a fruit with many seeds.*

GRAPH / GRAM — *write*

GRAPHEIN [Gr] *to write* 143
AUTOBIOGRAPHY (auto *self* + bios *life* + graphein *to write) the writing of one's own life,* autobiographer, autobiographic, autobiographical, autobiographically.
AUTOGRAPH *to write one's own signature,* autographic, autographical, autography.
BIBLIOGRAPHY *list of an author's writings or literature on a specific subject,* bibliographer, bibliographic, bibliographical, bibliographically.
BIOGRAPHY *writing of another's life,* biographer, biographic, biographical, biographically.
CALLIGRAPHY (kalos *beautiful* + graphein *to write) beautiful handwriting,* calligrapher, calligraphic, calligraphical, calligraphist.
CHOREOGRAPH *the design of the movements of a ballet,* choreographer, choreography.
COSMOGRAPHY *the science of the whole universe and its related parts,* cosmographer, cosmographic, cosmographical, cosmographically.
CRYPTOGRAPHY *cipher, and the deciphering of secret characters,* cryp-

GRAPH
GRAM
write

tographer, cryptographic, cryptographical, cryptographically.

EPIGRAPH *inscription on tomb, statue or building*, epigrapher, epigraphic, epigraphical, epigraphics, epigraphist.

ETHNOGRAPHY *study of primitive peoples*, ethnographist.

GEOGRAPHY *science of the surface of the earth*, geographer, geographic, geographical, geographically.

GRAPHIC *describing in realistic and vivid detail*, graphical, graphically, graphicalness, graphics.

HIEROGRAPHIC *pertaining to sacred writing*, hierographer.

HYDROGRAPHY *science of the seas, lakes and rivers and their commercial use*, hydrographer, hydrographic, hydrographical.

LITHOGRAPHY *process of printing from a flat stone or metal plate*, lithograph, lithographer, lithgraphic, lithographical, lithographically.

MONOGRAPH *an article or paper written about a single subject*, monographer, monographic, monographically, monographist.

ORTHOGRAPHY *correct spelling*, orthographer, orthographist, orthographic, orthographical, orthographically, orthographize.

PARAGRAPH *a distinct subdivision of a chapter on a particular point*, paragrapher, paragraphic, paragraphical, paragraphically.

PHONOGRAPH *an instrument producing sounds from a record*, phonographic, phonographical, phonographically.

PHOTOGRAPH *picture taken by a camera*, photographer, photographic, photographical, photographically.

STENOGRAPHY *the taking of dication in shorthand*, stenograph, stenographer, stenographic, stenographical, stenographically, stenographist.

TELEGRAPH *a system of sending messages over the wire by dots and dashes*, telegrapher, telegraphese, telegraphic, telegraphical, telegraphically, telegraphist.

TOPOGRAPHY *science of maps and charts of a region*, topographer, topographic, topographical, topographically, topographist.

ANAGRAM *a word or phrase made by reassembling its own letters*, anagrammatic, anagrammatical, anagrammatically, anagrammatism, anagrammatist, anagrammatize.

DIAGRAM *a sketch, plan, chart or graph to explain*, diagrammatic, diagrammatical, diagrammatically.

EPIGRAM *any witty, pointed statement, often antithetical*, epigrammatic, epigrammatical, epigrammatically, epigrammatism, epigrammatize, epigram-

GRAPH / GRAM — *write*

matizer.

GRAMMAR *word structure of a given language at a given time*, grammarian, grammarianism, grammatic, grammatical, grammatically, grammaticalness, grammaticize, grammatist.

MONOGRAM *a character or the initials of a name put on paper or clothes*, monographic.

PARALLELOGRAM *a four-sided figure with opposite sides equal and parallel.*

GRAT / GRAC — *thankful*

GRATUS *thankful*   63

GRATEFUL *thankful, appreciative*, gratefully, gratefulness.

INGRATE *an ungrateful person*, ingrateful, ingratefully, ingratefulness.

UNGRATEFUL *not showing thanks for favors*, ungratefully, ungratefulness.

GRATIFY *to give pleasure to*, gratification, gratified, gratifier; ungratified.

GRATIS *for nothing, free.*

GRATITUDE *a feeling of appreciation for benefits received;* ingratitude.

GRATUITY *something given in return for service; a tip or gift*, gratuitous, gratuitously.

INGRATIATE *to bring oneself into another's good graces*, ingratiation, ingratiatory.

CONGRATULATE *to compliment a person on a happy event*, congratulant, congratulation, congratulator, congratulatory.

GRACE *beauty of form; elegance, decency*, graceful, gracefully, gracefulness, graceless, gracelessly, gracelessness; ungraced, ungraceful.

GRACIOUS *showing kindness, courtesy, charm*, graciously, graciousness.

DISGRACE (dis *not* + gratia *favor*) *loss of respect*, disgraceful, disgracefully, disgracefulness, disgracer.

UNGRACIOUS *rude, discourteous*, ungraciously; ingraciousness.

AGREE *to be of one mind*, agreeable, agreeableness, agreeably, agreeingly, agreement, agreed.

DISAGREE *to differ in opinion*, disagreeable, disagreeably, disagreement, disagreer, disagreeableness, disagreeability.

GRAV / GRIE — *heavy*

GRAVIS *heavy;* **GRAVITAS** *weight*   23

GRAVE *serious thought, threatening nature.*

GRAVITATE *to tend to move toward something or somebody.*

GRAVITY *tendency to pull all bodies toward the earth's center*, gravitation, gravitational, gravitationally.

GRAV / GRIE
heavy

AGGRAVATE *to make worse*, aggravating, aggravatingly, aggravation, aggravative.
GRIEVE *to give pain of mind to*, grievingly.
GRIEVANCE *a condition thought unjust and the basis for complaint*, grievancer.
GRIEF *intense, emotional suffering*, grieful, grief-stricken, griefless.
GRIEVIOUS *hard to bear*, grieviously, grieviousness.
AGGRIEVE *to give pain or sorrow to*, aggrieved.

GREG
flock

GREX, GREGIS *a flock* 22
GREGARIOUS *living in herds; fond of the company of others*, gregarian, gregariously, gregariousness.
AGGREGATE *to bring together; to collect in a sum or mass*, aggregation, aggregately, aggregative, aggregator, aggregatory.
CONGREGATE *to gather into a mass or crowd*, congregation, congregational, congregationalism, Congregationist *one who believes in Congregationism*.
EGREGIOUS [egrejus] *outstanding for undesirable qualities*, egregiously, egregiousness.
SEGREGATE (se *apart* + gregis *flock*) *to set apart from others*, segregation, segregative.

HAB / HIB
have suitable

HABERE *to have*, HABITUM; HABILIS *suitable* 57
HABIT *a particular costume; characteristic condition of mind or body; a thing often done; a tendency to behave in a certain way.*
HABITANT *a dweller, a resident*, habitation, habitable, habitability, habitableness, habitably, habitancy.
HABITAT *natural abode for plants and animals.*
HABITUAL *acquired by habit*, habitually, habitualness, habituation.
HABITUDE *characteristic condition of mind or body.*
HABITUE' *a frequenter of anyplace, such as a club.*
COHABIT *to dwell together*, cohabitant, cohabitation, cohabiter.
INHABIT *to dwell in*, inhabitant, inhabitable, inhabitability, inhabitancy, inhabitation.
HABILITATE *to clothe or furnish with equipment*, habilitation, habilitator.
REHABILITATE *to reinstate in good repute*, rehabilitation.
ADHIBIT *to admit; to use; to administer.*
COHIBIT *to restrain*, cohibition.

HAB
HIB
have
suitable

EXHIBIT *to present to public view,* exhibitor, exhibition.
EXHIBITIONISM *tendency to call attention to oneself,* exhibitionist.
INHIBIT (in *in* + habere *to have*) *to prohibit or forbid,* inhibition, inhibitive, inhibitor, inhibitory.
PROHIBIT *to forbid, as by law,* prohibiter, prohibition, prohibitive, prohibitory.
REDHIBITION *a legal recourse to purchase of an article damaged,* redhibitory.
ABLE (habere *to have*) *having sufficient strength or power or competency,* ableness; unable.
DISABLE *to make unfit; to deprive of mental or physical power,* disablement, disability.
ENABLE *to provide with means, opportunity or authority to do something.*

HEIR
HER
heir

HERES, HEREDIS *an heir or heiress*   22
HEIR *one who inherits,* heiress, heirless.
HEIR-APPARENT *one entitled to succeed to a position.*
HEIRLOOM *a family relic.*
INHERIT *to receive property; to receive certain characteristics,* inheritability, inheritable, inheritably, inheritance, inheritor, inheritory; disinherit.
HEREDITY *the transmission of certain characteristics to offspring,* hereditability, hereditable, hereditably, hereditament, hereditarian, hereditarily, hereditariness, hereditist.

HER
HES
stick

HAEREO, HAERERE *to stick,* HAESUM   40
ADHERE (ad *to* + haerere *to stick*) *to hold fast,* adherence, adherent, adherently, adherer.
COHERE *to cleave; to be united,* coherence, coherency, coherent, coherently.
INCOHERENT *not logically connected,* incoherence, incoherency, incoherently.
INHERE *an inseparable part of something,* inherence, inherency, inherent, inherently.
ADHESION *the state of sticking,* adhesive, adhesively, adhesiveness.
COHESION *tendency to stick together,* cohesibility, cohesible, cohesive, cohesively, cohesiveness.
INHESION *inherent.*
HESITATE *to pause, respecting decision or action,* hesitancy, hesitant, hesitantly, hesitater, hesitatingly, hesitation, hesitative, hesitatory; unhesitating.

HOM / HUM — *man*

HOMO *a man;* **HUMANUS** *belonging to a man*   25

HOMOGENEOUS *of the same character and nature.*

HOMAGE *to pay respect by some apparent action,* homager.

HOMICIDE *the killing of one human by another,* homicidal.

HUMAN *having the form and nature of a person,* humanly, humaness.

HUMANE *being kind and considerate; the best qualities of mankind,* humanely, humaneness, humanization, humanize, humanizer.

HUMANISM *human nature; any system of thought or action concerned with the interest and ideals of people,* humanist, humanistic, humanistically.

HUMANITARIAN *one devoted to promoting the welfare of humanity; philanthropic,* humanitarianism.

HUMANITY *the desirable qualities of man, by which he is distinguished from other beings;* inhumanity.

INHUMAN *unfeeling; cruel; barbarous,* inhumanly.

HOST / HOSP — *host*

HOSPES, HOSPITIS *host or guest*   14

HOST *one who entertains in his house; one who presides over any social gathering,* hostess.

HOSTLER *a groom who cares for horses.*

HOSTEL *a lodging place, especially for youths.*

HOSPICE *a home for the sick.*

HOSPITAL *an institution for complete medical, surgical, psychiatric care,* hospitalization, hospitalize.

HOSPITABLE *receiving guests in a friendly, generous manner,* hospitableness, hospitably, hospitality; inhospitable.

HOTEL *a building with a number of rooms for the complete accommodation of travelers.*

HUM — *lowly earth*

HUMUS *the earth;* **HUMILIS** *lowly*   11

EXHUME *to unearth; to disclose,* exhumation.

INHUME (in *in* + humus *earth*) *to bury in the earth.*

POSTHUMOUS *after the death (work of author; son of a father).*

HUMBLE *not proud; modest; unpretentious,* humbleness, humbly.

HUMBLER *one who degrades another.*

HUMILIATE *to hurt the feelings of another person,* humiliation, humiliatory.

HUMILITY *absence of pride or self-assertion.*

HYDRO
water

HYDOR [Gr] *water*   11

HYDRANT *fire plug; where water may be discharged from the water main.*
HYDRAULIC *operated by the force of liquids,* hydraulically, hydraulics.
HYDROELECTRIC *production of electricity by water power or water and steam.*
HYDROGEN *the lightest known substance; hydrogen and oxygen (H_2O) is water.*
HYDROGRAPHY *the science of mapping of all seas and rivers, especially for navigation and commerce.*
HYDROPATHY *the attempt to treat all diseases by the external and internal use of much water.*
HYDROPHOBIA (hydro *water* + phobos *fear*) *an abnormal fear of water; rabies (in humans).*
HYDROPSY (dropsy) *collection of water in the body.*
HYDROXIDE *the compound OH from hydro and oxide.*

IMP EMP
command

IMPERARE *to command,* **IMPERATUM; IMPERIUM** *rule*   18

IMPERATIVE *absolutely necessary,* imperatively, imperativeness.
IMPERATOR *in ancient Rome, title of the victorious general,* imperatorial.
IMPERIOUS *haughty; overbearing; arrogant,* imperiously, imperiousness.
IMPERIAL *a country having control of other colonies or countries,* imperialism, imperialist, imperialistically, imperialize, imperially.
EMPIRE *supreme power in governing; territories under this jurisdiction.*
EMPEROR *supreme monarch of an empire;* empery, empress.

INT
within

INTUS *within;* **INTERIOR** *inner*   18

INTERIOR *internal; being within,* interiority, interiorly.
INTERNAL *on the inside; inner nature,* internity, internally.
INTESTINAL *of the intestines; pluck,* intestine, intestinally.
INTIMATE *closely acquainted; very familiar,* intimacy, intimately.
INTIMATION *an indirect suggestion; a hint; a proclamation.*
INTRINSIC *belonging to the actual nature of a thing,* intrinsical, intrinsicality, intrinsically, intrinsicalness.

JECT
throw

JACERE *to throw*   92

ABJECT *sunk to a low condition,* abjectedness, abjection, abjectly, abjectness.
ADJECTIVE *in grammer, to define or describe a noun's implication,* adjectival, adjectivally, adjectivizer.

JECT
throw

CONJECTURE *guesswork, theorizing*, conjectural, conjecturally, conjecturer.
DEJECT *to depress the spirits of*, dejected, dejectedly, dejectedness, dejecter, dejection.
EJECT (e *out* + jacere *to throw*) *to cast or drive out*, ejection, ejective, ejectment, ejector.
INJECT *to throw in a remark; to force a fluid into a cavity*, injection, injective.
INTERJECT *to interrupt with; to insert*, interjection, interjectional, interjectionally, interjectionary, interjector, interjectory.
OB'JECT (*n*) *the aim, the ultimate purpose.*
OBJECT' (v) *to oppose*, objectification, objectify, objection, objectionable, objectionably, objector, objectless; unobjectionable.
OBJECTIVE *a known or perceived object*, objectively, objectiveness, objectivism, objectivity, objectivize.
PROJ'ECT (*n*) *a design or proposal for something intended.*
PROJECT' (v) *to hurl forward; to protrude*, projectile, projection, projectionist, projective, projector.
REJECT (re *back* + jacere *to throw*) *to refuse to take, to throw away*, rejectable, rejecter, rejection.
SUB'JECT (*n*) *that which is treated or handled in discussion, study, writing, etc.; one under control of another*, subjectless (*a*).
SUBJECT' (v) *to bring under control of*, subjection, subjectionist, subjective, subjectively, subjectiveness, subjectivism, subjectivist, subjectivistic, subjectivity; unsubjected.
TRAJECT *to throw through space*, trajection, trajectory.
EJACULATE *to exclaim suddenly; ejection of a seminal fluid*, ejaculation, ejaculative, ejaculator, ejaculatory; interjaculate.
INTERJACENT *being between; intervening*, interjacence, interjacency.
JET (jacere *to throw*) *a stream of liquid or gas; jet propulsion.*
JETSAM or JETSOM *cargo thrown overboard to lighten a ship in danger.*
JETTISON *to throw something away that is a burden.*
JETTY *landing pier.*

JUNC JOIN
join

JUNGERE *to join*, JUNCTUM **69**
JUNCTION *the act or place of joining.*
JUNCTURE *the line or point or time at which two bodies are joined.*
JUNTA (juncto) *group of political intriguers, especially military men.*

JUNC JOIN *join*

ADJUNCT *something added to another thing*, adjunction, adjunctive, adjunctively, adjunctly.

CONJUNCT *association; combination*, conjunction, conjunctional.

CONJUNCTIVE *connecting both elements of a sentence, such as "and,"* conjunctively, conjunctiveness, conjuncture.

CONJUGATE *a pair joined together; in grammar, of the same base*, conjugation, conjugational, conjugative, conjugator.

CONJUGAL (com *together* + jungere *to join*) *relation between husband and wife*, conjugality, conjugally.

DISJUNCT *separated; disjoined*, disjunction, disjunctive, disjunctively, disjuncture.

SUBJUGATE *subdue, bring under the yoke of a superior force*, subjugation, subjugator.

SUBJUNCTIVE *in grammar, not stating an actual fact (indicative), but a possibility, etc.*

JOIN (jungere *to bind together*) *to enter into association with, to participate, to bring together*, joinder, joinery.

JOINT *the place where two parts are joined; united in action*, jointed, jointedly, jointer, jointing, jointless, jointly, jointress, jointure, jointureless, jointress.

ADJOIN *to put in addition; to be next to*, adjoining.

CONJOIN *to join together*, conjoined, conjoint, conjointly, conjointness.

DISJOIN *to separate; to prevent the joining of*, disjoint, disjointed, disjointedly, disjointedness, disjointly.

ENJOIN *to order; in law, to forbid*, enjoiner, enjoinment.

REJOIN *to unite after separation*.

REJOINT *reunite the joints of*, rejointing.

REJOINER *an answer to a reply; the defendant's answer to the plaintiff*.

SUBJOIN *to add after something has been said or written*, subjoiner.

JUD JUR JUS *right law*

JUDICO, JUDICARE *to judge;* JUSTUS *lawful* **64**

JUDGE *one who legally passes judgment; to form an opinion*, judger, judgment; unjudged.

JUDICIOUS *administering justice; fair, unbiased*, judicable, judicative, judicatory, judicature, judicial, judicially, judiciary, judiciously, judiciousness; unjudicial.

ADJUDICATE *to hear and decide (a case)*, adjudication, adjudicative, adjudicator, adjudication.

JUD
JUR
JUS
right
law

INJUDICIOUS *to not use sound judgment*, injudiciously, injudiciousness.
PREJUDGE *to judge in advance*, prejudgment.
PREJUDICE *a preconceived idea before the facts are known*, prejudicial, prejudicially, prejudicialness.
JURIDICAL *acting in the distribution of justice*, juridically.
JURISDICTION *the limit within which power can be exercised*, jurisdictional.
JURISPRUDENCE *the philosophy of law*, jurisprudential.
JURIST *scholar or writer on law*, juristic, juristical, juristically.
INJURE *to harm or damage*, injurer, injurious, injuriously, injuriousness, injury.
JUST (justus *lawful*) *equitable, impartial*, justness.
INJUST injustice.
JUSTICE *righteous, fair*.
JUSTIFY *to prove to be just*, justifiable, justifiability, justifiableness, justifiably, justification, justificative, justificator, justificatory, justifier.
JUSTICIARY *judge of a superior court*.
INJUSTICE *unfair, wrong*.
UNJUSTIFIABLE unjustifiably, unjustified.

JUR
swear

JURO, JURARE *to swear*   **19**
JURY *in law, persons empaneled to give a decision on the evidence*.
JUROR *one who serves on a jury; a juryman*.
ABJURE *to renounce with solemnity*, abjuration, abjuratory, abjurer.
ADJURE *to entreat earnestly; to charge under penalty*, adjuration, adjuratory, adjurer.
CONJURE *to entreat solemnly; to cause to appear*, conjuration, conjurator, conjurement, conjuror.
PERJURY *in law, the willful telling of a lie under oath*, perjure, prejured, prejurer.

LAT
carry
bear

FERO, FERRE *to carry, bear,* **LATUM** *borne*   **64**
ABLATION *a carrying away*, ablatitious, ablative *linguistically, a taking away*.
COLLATE (com *together* + ferre *to carry*) *to compare carefully, point by point*, collateral, collaterally, collateralness, collation, collative, collator.
CORRELATE *to have a reciprocal relationship*, correlatable, correlation, correlative, correlatively, correlativeness, correlativity.
DILATE *to cause to expand or swell*, dilatedly, dilater, dilation, dilative.
ELATE (ex *out* + ferre *to bear*) *to swell within the mind or spirits*, elatedly,

LAT
carry
bear

elatedness, elater or elator.

LEGISLATE (leg *law* + latio *a bringing*) *to enact laws*, legislation, legislative, legislatively, legislator, legislatress, legislatorial, legislature.

OBLATION *an offering of a sacrifice*, oblatory.

PRELATE *a dignitary of the church*.

PROLATE *a design elongated at the poles*, prolation.

RELATE *to tell the story of; to ally by connection*, relatedness, relater, relation, relational; unrelated.

RELATIVE *involving or expressing relations*, relatively, relativeness, relativism, relativist.

RELATIVITY *the close dependence of one occurrence to another; Einstein's theory*.

SUPERLATIVE *excelling all others*, superlatively, superlativeness.

TRANSLATE *to change from one language to another; to change to another medium*, translatable, translation, translational, translator, translatress; mistranslate, mistranslation; untranslated.

LECT
LEG
gather

LEGO, LEGERE *to gather, read, choose,* LECTUM   130

COLLECT *to gather together,* collectable, collectedly, collectedness, collection, collective, collectively, collectiveness, collectivism, collectivist, collectivistic, collectivity, collectivize, collector, collectorate, collectorship.

DIALECT *all of an individual's characteristics of speech*, dialectal, diatectally.

DIALECTIC *examining ideas logically, by questions and answers*, dialectical, dialectically, dialectician, dialecticism, dialector; dialectic materialism *official doctrine of Communism*.

ECLECTIC *selecting discriminatingly from various systems*, eclectically, electicism.

ELECT *to select from two or more*, election, electioneer, electioneerer; elective, electively; elector, electoral, electorate, electorial, electorship; re-elect, re-election.

INTELLECT *the ability to reason, perceive, or understand*, intellection, intellective.

INTELLECTUAL *appealing to the intellect*, intellectualism, intellectualist, intellectuality, intellectualize, intellectually.

INTELLIGENCE *capacity to learn or understand from experience; to reason in solving problems*, intelligencer, intelligent, intelligential, intelligently, in-

LECT
LEG
gather

telligentsia, intelligibility, intelligible, intelligibleness, intelligibly.
UNINTELLIGIBLE unintelligibly, unintelligibility.
LECTION *a reading in a particular text*, lectionary, lector, lectress.
LECTERN *a speaker's desk at social, business or church gatherings.*
LECTURE *a prepared talk before a class or audience*, lecturer, lectureship.
NEGLECT (nec *not* + legere *to gather*) *to ignore or disregard or not care for*, neglector, neglectedness, neglectful, neglectfully, neglectfulness, neglective.
NEGLIGENCE *habitual failure to do the required thing*, negligent, negligently, negligibility, negligible, negligibly.
PREDILECTION *a preconceived liking, a preference.*
PRELECT (pre *before* + legere *to read*) *to give lectures*, prelection.
SELECT *choose in preference to others*, selectedly, selectee, selection, selective, selectivity, selectively, selector.
ELEGANCE *richness and grace in manner, language and dress*, elegancy, elegant, elegantly.
INELEGANCE inelegancy, inelegant, inelegantly.
ELIGIBLE *legally qualified; worthy of choice*, eligibility, eligibleness, eligibly.
INELIGIBLE ineligibility, ineligibly.
LEGIBLE *that can be read or deciphered*, legibility, legibleness, legibly.
ILLEGIBLE *incapable of being read*, illegibility, illegibleness, illegibly.
LEGEND *a story that is handed down by generations, though not verifiable*, legendary.
LEGION *a great number*, legionary.
SACRILEGE *defaming what is consecrated*, sacrilegious, sacrilegiously, sacrilegiousness.
LEXICON *a dictionary of a special vocabulary, etc.*
LESSON *something to be learned.*

LEG
law
ambas-
sador

LEX, LEGIS *law;* LEGATUS *ambassador* 64
LEGAL *based on laws; in conformity with positive rules*, legalism, legalist, legalistic, legality, legalization, legalize, legally; delegalize.
ILLEGAL *unlawful; not authorized or sanctioned*, illegality, illegalize, illegally.
LEGITIMATE *sanctioned by law or custom*, legitimacy, legitimately, legitimateness, legitimation, legitimatist, legitimatize, legitime, legitimism, legitimist, legitimization, legitimize.
ILLEGITIMATE *a bastard child; unlawful; not logical*, illegitimacy, illegitimately, illegitimation, illegitimatize.

LEG
law
ambas-
sador

LEGISLATE *to make or enact laws*, legislation, legislative, legislatively, legislator, legislatorial, legislatorship, legislatress, legislature.

LEGATE *an ambassador or envoy*, legatee, legateship, legation.

LEGACY *anything handed from a will, or from a predecessor (i.e. power)*.

ALLEGE *to give an argument without proof*, allegation, allegeable, allegedly, alleger; misallege.

DELEGATE *a deputy; one acting as another's agent*, delegacy, delegation.

RELEGATE (re *back* + legare *to send*) *to assign inferiorly or in a certain order*, relegation.

PRIVILEGE *a right or advantage, granted by a person or body, not enjoyed by others*, privileged.

COLLEAGUE *a fellow worker in the same profession*, colleagueship.

COLLEGE *collection of scholars formed into a corporation*, collegial, collegialism, collegian, collegiate, collegium.

LEV
raise
light

LEVO, LEVARE *to raise;* LEVIS *light*   33

LEAVEN *in baking, to produce fermentation to make light*, leavening, leavenous.

LEVEE *a quay; a raised river bank to prevent flooding*.

LEVER *a bar placed on a fulcrum so that a heavy weight can be lifted*, leverage.

LEVY *a compulsory tax or other payment*, leviable.

LEVITATE *to float in the air because of lightness and bouyancy*, levitation.

LEVITY *lack of seriousness; tendency to trifle*.

ALLEVIATE *to make easier to be endured*, alleviation, alleviative, alleviator, alleviatory.

ELEVATE (e *out* + levare *to raise*) *to raise to a higher place*, elevatedness, elevation.

ELEVATOR *that which lifts or raises anything*.

RELEVANT *bearing upon the matter at hand*, relevance, relevancy, relevantly.

IRRELEVANT *not applicable or pertinent*, irrelevance, irrelevancy, irrelevantly.

RELIEVE (re *again* + levare *to raise*) *to ease, give aid, set free*, reliever, relievable, relieving.

LIBER
free

LIBERO, LIBERARE *to set free*   30

LIBERAL *a generous giver; favoring reform or progress*, liberalism, liberalist, liberalistic, liberality, liberalization, liberalize, liberalizer, liberally.

ILLIBERAL *intolerant, bigoted*, illiberalism, illiberality, illiberalize, illiberally.

LIBERATE *to set at liberty*, liberation, liberationist, liberator, liberatory.

LIBER
free

LIBERTINE *a rake; one who indulges desires without restraint*, libertinism.
LIBERTARIAN *one who advocates free will or full civil liberties*, libertarianism.
LIBERTY *all the rights of a people in a community.*
DELIVER *to free; transfer; to utter; distribute*, deliverable, deliverance, deliverer, deliveress, delivery.

LIG
bind

LIGARE *to bind*   46

ALLEGIANCE *obligation of a citizen to his government or other organization*, allegiant.
ALLIGATION *arithmetic rule for finding the value of compounds of different ingredients of different values.*
ALLIANCE *union between families; treaty between nations*, alliable, Allies, allied.
ALLY (ad *to* + ligare *to bind*) *to form a treaty relationship between nations or families.*
LEAGUE *a compact between individuals or nations to promote common interests.*
LIABLE *legally bound to make good any damages*, liability, liableness.
LIEGE *bound to be faithful to a superior.*
LIGAMENT *a band of tough tissue connecting one bone to another*, ligamental, ligamentous, ligamentary.
LIGATURE *anything that binds.*
OBLIGE (ob *before, against* + ligare *to bind*) *to make indebted for a kindness done*, obligee, obliger, obliging, obligingly, obligingness.
OBLIGATE *to bind by a sense of duty*, obligant, obligation, obligatorily, obligatoriness, obligatory.
RALLY *to bring order after a rout*, rallyingly.
RELIGION (re *back* + ligare *to bind together*) *belief in the worshiping of divine powers*, religionism, religionist, religionize, religiosity, religious, religiously, religiousness, religiousless.
IRRELIGION *indifferent or hostile to religion*, irreligionist, irreligious, irreligiously, irreligiousness.

LINE
line

LINEA *a linen thread, a line*   19

LINE *a long thin mark made by a pen or scribe; wires connecting stations by phone, etc.*, lineament.
LINEAL *a direct line from an ancestor*, lineage, lineality, lineally.

LINE / line

LINEAR *a design made of lines, sometimes having length only*, linearity, linearly, lineate, lineation.
LINEN *thread or yarn made of flax.*
DELINEATE *to trace a sketch; to describe something with words*, delineable, delineament, delineation, delineative, delineator, delineatory.

LIQU / liquid

LIQUEO, LIQUERE *to melt;* **LIQUIDUS** *flowing*   27
LIQUID *flowing smoothly; agreeable to the ear*, liquidize, liquidness.
LIQUATE *heating metals so fusible substances will separate*, liquation.
LIQUEFY *to make liquid*, liquefacient, liquefaction, liquefiable, liquefied.
LIQUESCENT *becoming liquid*, liquescence, liquescency.
LIQUOR *any alcoholic drink made by distilling.*
LIQUIDATE *to settle by legal process during a debt or bankruptcy*, liquidation, liquidator.
LIQUIDITY *being smooth and agreeable; financially flexible*, liquidly, liquidness.
DELIQUESE *to melt away*, deliquescence, deliquescent.
PROLIX (pro *forth* + liquere *to flow*) *long and wordy; to flow*, prolixity, prolixly, prolixness.

LITERA / letter

LITTERA *a letter*   20
LITERAL *based on the actual words in their ordinary meaning*, literalism, literalist, literalistic, literalistical, literality, literalization, literalize, literalizer, literally.
LITERATE *educated and showing experience and culture.*
LITERATI *scholarly or learned people.*
LITERARY *skilled in learning and literature.*
LITERATURE *writings in prose and verse showing imagination and critical character.*
ALLITERATION *the same sound being used at the beginning of two or more successive words*, alliterate, alliterative, alliteratively, alliterativeness, alliterator.

LOC / a place

LOCUS *a place*   21
LOCAL *confined to a particular place*, locale, localism, locality, localizable, localization, localize.
LOCATE *to establish in a particular spot*, location, locative, locator.
INTERLOCATION *a placing between.*

LOC
a place

TRANSLOCATE *to cause to change location in position*, translocation.
ALLOCATE *to set apart for a specific purpose*, allocable, allocation.
DISLOCATE *to put out of its proper place*, dislocation.
LOCOMOTION *act and power of moving from place to place.*
LOCOMOTIVE *an engine that can move by its own power.*

LOG
reason

LOGOS [*Gr*] *reason, a word, a speech*   43
ANALOGY *a likeness between things which are different in all other respects*, analogous, analogously, analogousness.
APOLOGY *expressing regret for a fault committed*, apologist, apologize, apologizer.
CATALOGUE *a list of names and articles arranged in order (often alphabetically)*, cataloguer.
DIALOGUE *conversation to exchange ideas, seeking mutual understanding*, dialogize.
EPILOGUE *closing section of a novel or play (the actor directly addresses the audience)*, epilogic, epilogical, epilogistic, epilogize.
EULOGY (eu *good* + logos *discourse*) *a speech or writing in praise of a person*, eulogistical, eulogistically, eulogize.
LOGIC *the science of correct reasoning*, logical, logicality, logically, logicalness.
ILLOGICAL *ignorant of correct reasoning*, illogically, illogicalness.
MONOLOGUE (monos *alone* + legein *to speak*) *a long speech by one person*, monologuist, monologic, monology, monologic, monological.
ASTROLOGY *the pseudo science of foretelling the future by the relative position of the stars.*
CHRONOLOGY *the arrangement of events and dates in the order of occurrence.*
GENEALOGY *the naming of ancestors and descendants in the order of succession.*
METEOROLOGY *the study of weather and climate.*
MYTHOLOGY *the study of myths and legends.*
ORNITHOLOGY *the branch of zoology dealing with birds.*
PHILOLOGY *the study of written texts to determine authenticity and meaning.*
TECHNOLOGY *the science of the practical and industrial arts.*

LOQ
speak

LOQUOR, LOQUI *to speak*   32
COLLOGUE *to lay schemes in concert with another.*
COLLOQUY *the mutual discussion of two or more persons.*

LOQ — speak

COLLOQUIAL *informal conversation and writing*, colloquialism, colloquialize, colloquially, colloquiat.

ELOQUENCE *speech or writing in a fluent, forceful, and persuasive manner*, eloquent, eloquently.

ELOCUTION *the art of public speaking*, elocutionary, elocutionist.

LOCUTION *a particular style of speech*, locutory.

CIRCUMLOCUTION *an indirect and lengthy way of expressing something*, circumlocutional.

LOQUACIOUS *given to continual talking*, loquaciously, loquaciousness, loquacity.

OBLOQUY *verbal abuse of a person.*

SOLILOQUY (solus *alone* + loqui *to speak*) *in a drama, when a character reveals his thoughts to the audience alone*, soliloquist, soliloquize.

VENTRILOQUIST (venter *belly* + loqui *to speak*) *speaking from the stomach so the voice seems to come from a source other than the speaker*, ventrilocution, ventriloquial, ventriloquially, ventriloquism, ventriloquistic, ventriloquize.

LU — wash

LUERE *to wash*, LUTUM   30

ABLUENT *cleansing by water or liquids.*

ABLUTION *a washing, cleansing, purifying*, ablutionary.

AFFLUENCE *flowing toward; abundance in riches*, affluency, affluent, affluently, affluentness.

ALLUVIAL *thrown up by the action of waves*, alluvion, alluvium.

DILUVIAL *pertaining to a flood or deluge* (Noah), diluvialist, diluvian, diluvianism, diluvium.

ANTEDILUVIAN *before Noah's flood; person or thing of great age.*

DILUTE *to change or weaken by mixing with something else*, diluent, dilutedly, dilutedness, diluter, dilution.

POLLUTE *to taint; to corrupt*, pollutant, pollutedly, pollutedness, polluter, polluting, pollution.

LUC — light, clear

LUCEO, LUCERE *to shine;* LUMEN *light*   60

LUCENT *shining, bright*, lucency.

TRANSLUCENT *letting light pass, but diffusing it*, translucence, translucency, translucently.

LUCID *transparent; clear, bright*, lucidity, lucidly, lucidness.

ELUCIDATE (e *out* + lucidus *light*) *to explain*, elucidation, elucidative,

LUC / LUS / LUM
light
clear

elucidator, elucidatory.
LUCITE *a clear plastic.*
LUCIFER *Venus, the morning star; Satan,* Luciferian.
LUCIFEROUS *affording light or means of insight,* luciferin, luciferously, lucific.
LUCIFORM *having the form of light.*
LUSTER (lustre) *brilliancy; beauty or fame; renoun,* lusterless.
LUSTROUS *bright, shining,* lustrously.
LUSTRAL *used in ceremonial purification,* lustrate, lustration, lustrative.
ILLUSTRATE *pictures; to make clear,* illustration, illustrative, illustratively, illustrator, illustratory.
ILLUSTRIOUS *distinguished by greatness,* illustriously, illustriousness.
ILLUMINE *light up,* illuminer, illuminism, illuministic, illuminize.
ILLUMINATE *to light up; elucidate,* illumination, illuminatism, illuminative, illuminator.
LUMINATE *to illuminate,* lumination, luminesce, luminescence, luminescent.
LUMINOUS *readily understood,* luminosity, luminously, luminousness.
LUMINARY *one who sheds light on some subject; a famous intellectual.*

LUD
deceive
play

LUDO, LUDERE *to play, deceive,* LUSUM   **30**
ALLUDE *to refer to indirectly.*
COLLUDE *to conspire in a fraud; to have a secret share in a scheme,* colluder.
COLLUSION *a secret agreement among two or more, to defraud an outside person,* collusive, collusively, collusiveness, collusory.
DELUDE *to deceive; to beguile,* deludable, deluder.
ELUDE (e *out* + ludere *to play*) *to avoid by artifice; to escape,* eludible, elusive, elusively, elusiveness, elusory, elusoriness.
ILLUDE *to deride; to deceive.*
ILLUSION *misleading appearance; false perception,* illusional, illusionism, illusionist, illusive, illusively, illusiveness, illusory.
INTERLUDE *a short entertainment between acts; anything filling time between two events.*
LUDICROUS *ridiculous, causing laughter,* ludicrously, ludicrousness.
POSTLUDE *a phrase played at the end of a musical composition.*
PRELUDE *an introduction to the principal event,* preluder, preludious.

LUNA

LUNA *the moon*   **12**
LUNAR *pertaining to or resembling the moon,* lunarian, lunate *half-moon*

LUNA
moon

shaped.
LUNATION *lunar month of 29½ days.*
LUNETTE *a small moon; a word of many meanings.*
LUNACY *insanity (people's behavior was thought affected by the moon),* lunatic, lunatical.
LUNIFORM *shape of the moon, particularly the crescent.*
INTERLUNAR *between the old and new moon; when the moon is in line with the sun, and invisible.*
SUBLUNAR *earthly; beneath the moon,* sublunary.

MAGN
great

MAGNUS *great;* MAJOR *greater;* MAGISTER *master*   **39**
MAGNANIMOUS *noble in mind; elevated in sentiment,* magnanimity, magnanimously.
MAGNIFY *to increase the apparent size of a person or thing; to extoll,* magnifiable, magnific, magnifically, magnification, magnifier.
MAGNIFICENT *splendid, grand; beautiful,* magnificence, magnificently.
MAGNITUDE *greatness in size; importance, influence.*
MAGNILOQUENT *pompous and grandiose in speech,* magniloquently, magniloquence.
MAGNATE *an important or influential man, especially in big business.*
MAGISTRATE *civil officer; minor officer with limited powers,* magisterial, magisteriality, magisterially, magisterialness, magistracy.
MAJOR *greater in size or amount; legal age.*
MAJORITY *the greater part or larger number.*
MASTER *one who rules or has control of others,* masterful, masterfully, masterless, masterlessness, masterliness, masterly.
MAXIMUM *the greatest quantity or number.*
MAXIM *a concise rule of conduct or precept.*
MAYOR *chief officer of city,* mayoral, mayoralty, mayoress, mayorship.

MAL
bad
evil

MALUS **bad,** MALE **badly**   **45**
DISMAL (dies *day* + mali *evil*) "evil days," *cause of gloom or misery,* dismally, dismalness.
MALADROIT *clumsy, awkward,* maladroitly, maladroitness.
MALADY *any sickness or disease.*
MALARIA *"bad air"; disease formerly thought caused by swamp air,* malarial,

MAL
bad
evil

malarian, malarious.
MALAISE *a vague feeling of uneasiness or physical discomfort.*
MALCONTENT *a dissatisfied person*, malcontented, malcontentedly, malcontentedness.
MALEDICTION (male *badly* + dicere *to speak*) *invocation of evil*, maledictory.
MALEFACTOR *one who commits a crime*, malefaction, malefactress, malefic, maleficence, maleficent.
MALEVOLENCE *personal hatred*, malevolent, malevolently.
MALFEASANCE *misconduct in public affairs*, malfeasant.
MALFUNCTION *failing to function as it should.*
MALICE *desire to harm others*, malicious, maliciously, maliciousness.
MALIGN *very harmful*, malignant, malignantly, maligner, malignity, malignly.
MALINGER *one who feigns illness to avoid work*, malingerer, malingery.
MALNUTRITION *undernourishment from improper or insufficient food.*
MALPRACTICE *injurious or unprofessional care of patient by doctor.*

MAN
remain

MANERE *to remain*, MANSUM   **14**
MANSE *house of clergyman.*
MANSION *a stately residence.*
MANOR *in colonial times, a district granted as a manor and leased to tenants.*
IMMANENT (in *in* + manere *to remain*) *operating within; inherent*, immanence.
PERMANENCE *continuing, lasting indefinitely*, permanent, permanently.
IMPERMANENT *not enduring; temporary*, impermanency, impermanent.
REMAIN *to be left over when others have left; to stay*, remainder.
REMNANT *what is left over; residue.*

MAND
MEND
command

MANDARE *to command*, MANDATUM   **38**
MANDATE *a written authoritative order.*
MANDATORY *authoritatively commanded.*
MANDAMUS *in law, a writ requiring that a specified thing be done.*
COMMAND *to direct with authority*, commandable, commandant, commandeer, commander, commandery, commanding, commandingly, commandment, commando.
COUNTERMAND *to cancel or revoke an order*, countermandable.
DEMAND *to require as a right*, demandable, demandant.
REMAND *to order or send back*, remandment.

MAND
MEND
command

COMMEND *to represent as worthy of confidence*, commendable, commendableness, commendably, commendatary, commendation, commendator, commendatory, commender; uncommended.

RECOMMEND *to speak favorably as suited for some position*, recommendable, recommendableness, recommendably, recommendation, recommendative, recommendatory, recommender.

MANU
hand

MANUS ***the hand***   **60**

MANUAL *done by the hands*, manualist, manually.

MANACLE *an instrument for shackling the hands;* unmanacle.

MANAGE *to handle; to have charge of; to succeed in accomplishing*, manageability, manageable, manageableness, manageably.

MISMANAGE mismanagement, mismanager.

MANICURE *care of the hands, especially the nails*, manicurist.

MANIFEST *"struck by the hand"; easily understood; itemized list of cargo*, manifestable, manifestant, manifestation, manifestly, manifestness.

MANUDUCTION *to guide or lead by the hand*, manuductor, manuductory.

MANUFACTURE *making goods on a large scale by machinery (originally by hand)*, manufactory, manufactoral, manufacturer, manufacturing.

MANIPULATE *to control artfully or by shrewd use of influence*, manipulation, manipulative, manipulator, manipulatory.

MANNER *the way anything is done; personal behavior*, mannered, mannerism, mannerist, mannerless, mannerliness, mannerly.

MANEUVER (manus *the hand* + ouevre *work*) *to accomplish some stratagem or scheme*, maneuverability, maneuverable.

MANUSCRIPT *a document written by hand; author's copy of typewritten document*.

MANURE (*originally*) *to cultivate by hand labor*, manurer, manurial, manuring.

EMANCIPATE *to free from restraint of any kind*, emancipation, emancipationist, emancipator, emancipatory.

MAINTAIN (manu tenere *to hold in hand*) *to keep up*, maintainable, maintainer, maintainor.

MAINTENANCE *upkeep, support, assistance*.

MATR
mother

MATER ***a mother***   **21**

MATERNAL *like a mother*, maternalize, maternally, maternity.

MATRICIDE *killing of a mother by her child*.

MATR
mother

MATRICULATE *enrolling at a college*, matriculant, matriculation, matriculator.
MATRIMONY *the act and sacrament of marriage*, matrimonial, matrimonially.
MATRIX (*originally, the womb*) *that from which anything originates and develops.*
MATRON *an older married woman who has had children*, matronage, matronal, matronhood, matronize, matronlike, matronliness, matronly.

MATUR
mature

MATURUS *ripe, of full age* 18
MATURE *full grown; ripe; highly developed*, maturely, matureness, maturer, maturing, maturity.
MATURATE *to bring to maturity*, maturant, maturation, maturative.
IMMATURE *not completely grown; too early*, immaturely, immatureness, immaturity.
PREMATURE *coming to pass before the proper time*, prematurely, prematureness, prematurity.

MEDI
middle

MEDIUS *the middle* 32
MEDIEVAL *belonging to the Middle Ages*, medievalism, medievalist, medievally.
MEDIATE *to bring about by intervention*, mediately, mediateness, mediation, mediative, mediatization, mediatize, mediator, mediatorial, mediatorially, mediatorship, mediatory, mediatrix.
MEDIOCRE *of middle quality*, mediocrity.
MEDITERRANEAN *a sea in the middle of land.*
MEDIAN *a middle number, point, or line.*
MEDIUM *of middle degree; an intervening thing through which effects are produced.*
IMMEDIATE *nothing coming between; instantly*, immediacy, immediately, immediateness, immediatism.
INTERMEDIATE (inter *between* + medius *middle*) *in the middle; between two extremes*, intermediately, intermediation, intermediator.
INTERMEDIARY *acting between two persons, as a mediator.*

MEM
memory

MEMORIA *memory* 42
MEMORY *the process of remembering*, memorizable, memorization, memorize, memorizer.
MEMORIAL *commemorative; anything helping people to remember some person or event*, memorialist, memorialize.

MEM
memory

IMMEMORIAL *extending beyond memory; very old*, immemorially.
MEMORABLE *worthy to be remembered*, memorabilia, memorability, memorableness, memorably; immemorable.
MEMOIR *a report based on a writer's personal experiences; an autobiography*, memoirism, memoirist.
MEMORANDUM *a short note to remind*, memoranda (pl).
MEMENTO *anything serving as a remembrance or souvenir.*
MENTION *to speak about incidentally*, mentionable.
COMMEMORATE *to honor a person or event by some act*, commemorable, commemoration, commemorative, commemorator, commemoratory.
REMEMBER *to bring to mind*, rememberable, rememberably, rememberer, remembrance, remembrancer.
REMINISCE *to recall past experiences*, reminiscence, reminiscency, reminiscent, reminiscential, reminiscentially, reminiscitory.

MENT
mind

MENS, MENTIS *mind*   38

MENTAL *of the mind or intellect*, mentally, mentality, mentalization, mentalize.
DEMENTED (de *away from* + mentis *mind*) *devoid of reasoning*, dement, dementate, dementation, dementedness.
DEMENTI *in diplomacy, an official denial.*
DEMENTIA *loss of mental powers.*
COMMENT *to make remarks or criticism on anything*, commentarial, commentary, commentate, commentation, commentator, commentatorial, commentatorship, commenter.
COMMENTITIOUS *feigned, imaginary.*
MENTION *an incidental reference or statement*, mentionable.
MEMENTO *anything serving as a reminder or souvenir.*
VEHEMENT (vehere *to carry* + mentis *mind*) *moving with great force; violent, impetuous*, vehemence, vehemency, vehemently.
MIND (A-S gemynd *memory*) mindedness, mindful, mindfully, mindfulness, mindness.
REMIND *to cause a person to remember*, reminder, remindful.

MERC
trade

MERX, MERCIS *merchandise;* MERCES *hire*   29

MARKET (mercatus *market place*) *a gathering of people to buy and sell*, marketability, marketable, marketableness, marketer, marketing.
MERCHANT *one buying and selling goods for profit*, merchantable, mer-

MERC
trade

chantlike, merchantry.
MERCHANDISE *what is bought and sold in trade*, merchandizer.
MERCANTILE *relating to trade and commerce*, mercantilism, mercantilist, mercantilistic.
MERCENARY *motivated by a desire for money or other gain; a hired soldier;* unmercenary.
MERCURY *god of commerce, among other skills.*
MERCURIAL *like mercury, quick, volatile, changeable, fickle*, mercurialism, mercurialist, mercurially.
COMMERCE *the interchange of goods between individuals or nations*, commercial, commercialism, commercialization, commercialize, commercially.

MERG
dip

MERGO, MERGERE *to dip*, MERSUM   18
EMERGE *to come into view; to be known*, emergence, emergent, emergently.
EMERGENCY *an unexpected occurrence requiring prompt action.*
MERGE *to lose identity by being absorbed*, mergence, merger.
SUBMERGE *to put under; to suppress*, submergence, submergible, submerse, submersible, submersion.
EMERSION (e *out* + mergere *to dip*) *an emerging; the reappearance of a heavenly body after an eclipse.*
IMMERSE *to plunge completely under; to involve deeply*, immersible, immersion.

METR
measure

METRON [Gr] *a measure*   48
METE *to distribute, to apportion.*
METER (metre) *a device for measuring; rhythm in verse*, meterage.
METRIC *a measuring system of distances and weights*, metrical, metrically, metrication, metrician, metricize, metrify, metrist.
DIAMETER (dia *through* + metron *a measure*) *a straight line passing through the center of a circle*, diametral, diametrally.
DIAMETRICAL *as a diameter; directly opposed*, diametric, diametrically.
PERIMETER *the outer boundary of an area*, perimetric.
SYMMETRY *similarity of form; beauty of proportion*, symmetrical, symmetrically, symmetricalness, symmetrist, symmetrization, symmetrize.
BAROMETER *an instrument for measuring atmospheric pressure*, barometric, barometrically.
CHRONOMETER *an instrument that measures time precisely*, chronometric,

METR
measure

chronometrically, chronometry.
GEOMETRY *the mathematics and measurement of solids*, geometrize.
HYDROMETER *an instrument for measuring the specific gravity of liquids*, hydrometric, hydrometrical, hydrometry.
MICROMETER *an instrument for measuring very small distances and angles used in the microscope*, micrometry.
PEDOMETER *an instrument for measuring distances by the steps of the walker*, pedomatic, pedometrically.
THERMOMETER *an instrument for measuring temperature*, thermometric, thermometrical, thermometrically.

MIGR
depart

MIGRARE *to go from one place to another*, MIGRATUM   21
MIGRATE *to move from one country to another; birds seasonally changing regions*, migrant, migration, migrator, migratory.
EMIGRATE (e *out* + *migrare to move*) *to leave one's country for another*, emigrant, emigration, emigrational, emigrationist, emigrator, emigre.
IMMIGRATION *to come into a new country*, immigrant, immigration.
TRANSMIGRATE *passing through a country on way to another*, transmigrant, transmigrator, transmigratory.
TRANSMIGRATION *the supposed passing of the soul into another body after death*.
INTERMIGRATION *reciprocal migration; tribes exchanging lands*.

MIN
small

MINOR *less;* MINIMUS *least*   24
MIN′UTE *sixty seconds; a moment*, minutely.
MINUTE′ *very small; of little importance*, minutely, minuteness.
MINUTIAE *small details*, minutia(*sing*).
MINUS *less; reduced by subtraction*.
MINUSCULE *tiny; very small*.
MINIATURE *a model on a very small scale*, miniaturist.
MINIMUM *the smallest possible*, minimal.
DIMINISH *to lessen; to make smaller*, diminishable, diminisher, diminishing, diminishingly, diminishment.
UNDIMINISHED *not lessened*, undiminishable.
DIMINUTIVE *very small in size*, diminutively, diminutiveness.
DIMINUENDO *musically, gradually diminishing in volume*.

MIR
wonder

MIRARI *to wonder,* **MIRATUS**   **16**
ADMIRE *to regard with wonder and approval,* admiration, admirer, admiringly; unadmired.
MIRACLE *a wonderful example; caused by the supernatural,* miraculous, miraculously, miraculousness; unmiraculous.
MIRAGE *an optical illusion caused by layers of air at different tempeatures; something false appearing real.*
MIRROR *a polished substance that forms images by reflected light.*
MARVEL *an astonishing thing,* marvelous, marvelously, marvelousness.

MISS
MITT
send

MITTO, MITTERE *to send,* **MISSUM**   **138**
ADMIT *to permit to enter,* admittable, admittance, admittatur, admitter, admittedly; admission, admisive, admissory, admissibility, admissible, admissibleness, admissibly; inadmissable, inadmissibility; readmit, readmission.
COMMIT *to give in trust to or custody,* commitment, commitable, commital.
NONCOMMITAL *not revealing one's position,* noncommitally.
COMMITTEE *a group elected or appointed to attend the business referred to it,* committer, committor *legal application.*
COMMISSARY *an authorized person; where stores are kept.*
COMMISSION *an authorization to perform certain tasks,* commissioner; recommit, recommision; uncommitted, uncommissioned.
COMPROMISE *a settlement where both sides make concessions,* compromiser.
DEMISE (de *down* + mittere *to send*) *transfer of an estate; death,* demisable, demisability.
DEMISSION *resignation or abdication from office,* demissionary.
DEMIT *to resign voluntarily.*
DISMISS *to send away,* dismissal, dismissible, dismissive.
EMIT (e *out* + mittere *to send*) *to throw or give out,* emittent; emission, emissive, emissivity.
EMISSARY *an agent sent on a specific mission.*
IMMIT *to inject (the opposite of emit),* imission.
INTERMISSION *an interval of time between periods of activity,* intermissive.
INTERMIT *to cause to cease for a time,* intermittent, intermittence, intermittency, intermitter, intermittently.
INTROMIT (intro *within* + mittere *to send*) intromittent, intromitter.
MESSAGE (mittere) *any communication between persons.*
MESSENGER *one who carries messages or goes on errands.*

145

MISS / MITT
send

MISSILE *that can be hurled or fired or launched toward a target.*
MISSION *(n) being sent with authority to perform a certain duty, (v) one sent by his church to proselytize in a foreign country*, missionary, missioner.
MISSIVE *a letter.*
OMIT (ob *by* + mittere *to send*) *to pass by or neglect*, omitter; omission, omissive, omissively, omissible.
PERMIT *to allow by common consent*, permittance, permittee, permitter, permitting, permittivity, permission, permissively, permissibility, pemissibly, permissibleness, permissive, permissibly, permissory.
PREMISE *a previous statement that serves as the basis of the argument.*
PRETERMIT *to neglect or omit*, pretermission.
PROMISE (pro *forth* + mittere *to send*) *a vow to do or not to do something*, promisee, promiser, promisor *in law, a promiser*, promissorily, promissory.
REMISS *negligent in performance of duty*, remissibility, remissible, remission, remissive, remissly, remissory.
REMIT *to put back*, remitment, remittable, remittal, remittance, remittee, remitter, remittor *in law, the remitter;* unremitting.
SUBMIT (sub *under* + mittere *to send*) *to yield to the will of another*, submittal, submitter; submission, submissive, submissively, submissiveness; unsubmissible.
SURMISE *an opinion formed from evidence that is not conclusive*, surmiser, surmisable.
TRANSMISSION *auto part imparting motion; radio waves between stations*, transmissibility, transmissible, transmissive.
TRANSMIT *to go from one person or place to another*, transmittal, transmittable, transmittance, transmitter.

MOD
manner measure

MODERATUS **within bounds;** MODESTUS **modest;** MODUS **measure** 70
ACCOMMODATE (ac *to* + con *with* + modus *measure*) *to fit, adapt, make suitable*, accommodating, accommodation, accommodative, accommodativeness, accommodator.
COMMODE *an enclosed washstand.*
COMMODITY *convenience or advantage; an article sold or bought.*
COMMODIUS *roomy or spacious*, commodiously, commodiousness.
INCOMMODIOUS *to inconvenience*, incommode, incommodiously, incommodiousness, incommodity.
DISCOMMODE *to put to inconvenience*, discommodious, discommodiously,

MOD
manner
measure

discommodiousness, discommodity.
MODE *manner of acting; the common usage*, modal, modality, modally.
MODISH *in the latest style*, modishly.
MODISTE *woman who deals in women's clothing*.
MODEL *a particular form, a copy, a style or design;* remodel.
MODALITY *an attribute that marks individuals, things, or groups*.
MODERATE *avoiding excesses or extremes*, moderately, moderateness, moderation.
IMMODERATE immoderation.
MODERATOR *one who presides or moderates or restrains*.
MODERN *of the present or recent times*, modernism, modernist, modernistic, modernistically, modernity, modernization, modernize, modernizer.
MODICUM *a small quantity*.
MODEST *showing a humble opinion of one's achievements*, modestly.
IMMODEST *bold, indecent,* immodestly, immodesty.
MODIFY *to change the form of,* modifier, modifiable, modifiability, modification, modificative, modificatory.
MODULATE *to regulate; shift to another key,* modulant, modular, modulation, modulator.
MODULE *a unit of measurement*, modulus.
MODUS *manner; way*.
MODUS OPERANDI *manner of operating (MO)*.
MODUS VIVENDI *temporary agreement between parties until a final settlement is reached*.
A LA MODE *([Fr.] after the fashion) according to the fashion or mode, i.e., ice cream*.

MON
warn

MONERE to warn, MONITUM   **40**
ADMONISH *to caution against specific faults*, admonisher, admonishment, admonition, admonitively, admonitor, admonitorily, admonitory; unadmonished.
PREADMONISH *a previous warning*, preadmonition.
MONITOR *one on duty who informs*, monitorial, monitorially, monitory, monitoress.
MONUMENT *something to keep alive the memory of a person or event*, monumental, monumentality, monumentalization, monumentalize, monumentally.
SUMMON (sub *under* + monere *to warn*) *to call together; to issue a legal summons*, summoner, summons.

MON
warn

PREMONITION *a forewarning*, premonitor, premonitorily, premonitory.
MONEY (monere *to admonish*) *any measure or money used for exchange*, moneyed, moneyer, moneyless.
MONETARY *of the currency of the country*, monetarily, monetarian, monetarist, monetize, monetization.
DEMONETIZE *deprive currency of its standard value*.

MONO
one
alone

MONOS [Gr] *one, alone*   39

MONOCHROMATIC (monos *alone* + chroma *color*) *having a single color*, monochrome, monochromic, monochromical, monochromist.
MONOCLE *an eyeglass for one eye*.
MONOGAMY *marrying only once; marrying one at a time*, monogamist, monogamous.
MONOLOGUE *an extended speech by one peson*, monologist, monologic, monology.
MONOPOLIZE (monos *alone* + polein *to sell*) *exclusive control of a commodity or service*, monopolism, monopolist, monopolistic, monopolization, monopolize, monopolizer.
MONOSYLLABLE *a word consisting of only one syllable*, monosyllabic, monosyllabically, monosyllabism.
MONOTHEISM *belief in the existence of only one God*.
MONOTONE (monos *single* + tonos *tone*) monotonic, monotonical, monotonically.
MONOTONOUS *tiresome because unvarying*, monotonist, monotonously, monotonousness, monotony.
MONARCHY (monos *alone* + archeim *to rule*) *sole ruler of the state*.
MONASTERY *a place where monks retire from the world under religious vows*, monasterial, monasterially.
MONK *originally, a man who lived in solitary self-denial for religious reasons*.

MONS
show

MONSTRARE *to show*, MONSTRATUM   28

MONSTER *an imaginary creature, part human; anything of abnormal shape*.
MONSTROUS *abnormally large*, monstrously, monstrousness, monstrosity.
DEMONSTRATE *to make clear by examples or experiments*, demonstrability, demonstrable, demonstrableness, demonstrably, demonstrant, demonstrater, demonstration, demonstrative, demonstratively, demonstrativeness, demonstrator.
UNDEMONSTRABLE *cannot be clarified*, undemonstrably.

MONS
show

UNDEMONSTRATIVE *showing little outward expression of feelings.*
REMONSTRATE *to protect; to show strong reasons against an act,* remonstrance, remonstrant, remonstrantly, remonstration, remonstrative, remonstrator.
MUSTER (monstra *a review, show*) *an assembling of troops for inspection.*

MOR
manner
custom

MOS, MORIS *manner, custom*   20
MORAL *capable of making the distinction between right and wrong,* moralist, moralism, moralistic, morality, moralization, moralize, moralizer, morally.
AMORAL *neither moral or immoral; not concerned with moral standards.*
MORALE [*Fr*] *moral and mental conditions as regards courage, zeal, discipline, etc.*
DEMORALIZE *to lower the morale of; to weaken the spirit,* demoralization.
IMMORAL *contrary to the moral code of the community,* immorally, immorality.
MORES *folkways that are considered important to the functioning of a society, and, through many generations, develop the force of law.*
MOROSE *gloomy, surly, sullen,* morosely, moroseness.

MORT
death

MORTUUS *dead*   30
AMORTIZE *in accounting, paying of a note over a fixed period,* amortizement, amortizable, amortization.
MORTAL *that must eventually die,* mortality, mortalize, mortally, mortalness.
MORTGAGE (mort *dead* + gage *a pledge*) *pledging property as security of a debt.*
MORTGAGEE *the person to whom property is mortgaged.*
MORTGAGER *the one who mortgages property.*
MORTIFY *to punish one's body by self-denial; to humiliate,* mortifying, mortification, mortifier.
MORTUARY *where dead are held before burial or cremation.*
MORTICIAN *a funeral director.*
POST MORTEM *an examination of the body after death.*
MORBID *an unwholesome tendency to dwell on gloomy matters,* morbidly, morbidity, morbidness.
MORIBUND *dying or coming to an end.*
MORGUE *where dead are held awaiting identification.*
MURDERER (mors *death*) *the killing of a person by another,* murderer, murderess, murderous, murderously.

MOUNT
mount

MONS, MONTIS *mountain*   **24**

MOUND *a heap of earth; a small hill.*
MOUNT *a high hill; to ascend,* mountable, mounting, mountingly.
MOUNTAIN *a high, upward projection of rock,* mountaineer, mountainous, mountainousness.
MOUNTEBANK *one who "mounts a bench"—a boastful pretender.*
PROMONTORY *a headland; a high point of rock projecting over water.*
AMOUNT *to add up; to be equal in value.*
DISMOUNT *to get down; to descend.*
PARAMOUNT *higher than others; supreme,* paramountcy, paramountly.
REMOUNT *to get on again.*
SURMOUNT *to overcome,* surmountable, surmountableness, surmounter; insurmountable, unsurmountable.
TANTAMOUNT *equivalent in force, effect, significance.*

MOV MOT
move

MOVEO, MOVERE *to move;* **MOBILIS** *easily moved*   **81**

MOVE *to change place; to stir the emotions,* moveless, movement, mover, moving, movingly, movingness.
COUNTERMOVE *to move in retaliation,* countermovement.
MOVABLE *transportable,* movability; unmovable, unmoved.
IMMOVABLE *cannot be altered or shaken,* immovability, immovableness, immovably.
REMOVE *to take off; to go from one place to another,* removability, removable, removably, removal, removedness, remover; unremoved, unremovable.
IRREMOVABLE *cannot be removed,* irremovability, irremovably.
MOTION *movement of the body or any of its parts,* motionless.
COMMOTION (com *together* + movere *to move*) *disturbance.*
EMOTION *any specific feeling or reaction,* emote, emotional, emotionalism, emotionalist, emotionality, emotionalize, emotionally, emotive.
LOCOMOTION *moving from one place to another,* locomotive, locomotivity, locomotor.
PROMOTE *to advance; to contribute to the growth,* promotor, promotion, promotional, promotive.
REMOTE *distant in time or place,* remotely, remoteness.
MOTOR *anything that produces motion,* motorization, motorize.
MOTIVE *some inner drive that causes a person to behave as he does; a motif in music or literature,* motivate, motivation, motiveless, motivelessness, motivity.

MOV / MOT
move

MOMENT *a brief period of time*, momental, momentarily, momentariness, momentary, momently.

MOMENTOUS *very important*, momentously, momentousness.

MOMENTUM *the impetus of a moving object*.

MOB (mobile vulgus *the fickle crowd*) *a crowd of disorderly people*, mobbish, mobocracy, mobocrat, mobocratic.

MOBILE *easily moved*, mobility, mobilization, mobilize.

MULT
many

MULTUS *much* 21

MULTIPLE *consisting of many parts*, multiplex.

MULTIPLICATION *one amount times another amount*, multiplicative, multiply, multiplier.

MULTIPLICITY *a great many of the same kind*.

MULTILATERAL *having many sides*, multilaterally.

MULTILINEAL *having many lines*, multilinear.

MULTITUDE *large number of persons or things*, multitudinary, multitudinous, multitudinously, multitudinousness.

MULTIFARIOUS *of great diversity and variety*, multifariously, multifariousness.

MULTIFORM *having many shapes or appearances*, multiformity.

MUN
*gift
an office*

MUNUS, MUNERIS *a gift, an office* 55

COMMUNAL *belonging to the public*, communalism, communalist, communalistic, communalize.

COMMUNE *to talk together familiarly*.

COMMUNICATE *to have an exchange of thoughts*, communication, communicative, communicativeness, communicator, communicatory, communicability, communicable, communicableness, communicably.

COMMUNICANT *one who receives Holy Communion; one who communicates information*.

EXCOMMUNICATE (ex *out* + com *with* + mun *office*) *to expel from privileges of the church*, excommunicative, excommunication, excommunicator, excommunicatory.

INCOMMUNICABLE (in *not*) *cannot be told*, incommunicability, incommunicableness, incommunicably.

INCOMMUNICADO *cut off from the means of communicating*.

IMMUNE *exempt from anything harmful or disagreeable*, immunity, immunize, immunization.

MUN
gift
an office

REMUNERATE (re *again*) *to pay an equivalent for any service, expense, or loss*, remuneration, remunerative, remuneratively, remunerativeness, remunerable, remunerability.

MUNICIPAL *internal affairs of local government*, municipalism, municipalist, municipality, municipalize, municipalization, municipally.

MUNIFICENT (munos *a gift* + facere *to make*) *very generous in giving*, munificence, munificently.

COMMON (communis) *belonging to all the people*, commonable, commonality, commonly, commoner, commoness.

MUT
change

MUTO, MUTARE *to change*   40

COMMUTE *to exchange; to give a penalty less severe; daily travel to work*, commutability, commutable, commutate, commutation, commutative, commutatively, commutator, commuter, commutal.

IMMUTABLE *not capable of change*, immutability, immutableness, immutably.

MUTABLE *capable of alteration in its nature*, mutability, mutably, mutant, mutate.

MUTATION *the process of changing*, mutatis, mutative.

MUTINY *revolt against authority*, mutineer, mutinous, mutinously, mutinousness.

PERMUTATION *mutual change; rearrangement*, permutable, permutableness, permutably.

TRANSMUTE *to transform to another nature*, transmutability, transmutable, transmutableness, transmutably, transmutation, transmutationist, transmutative, transmutator.

NAT
born
natural

NASCI *to be born,* NATUS; NATURA *nature*   91

NATIVE *inforn*, natively, nativeness, nativism, nativist, natavistic, nativity.

NATIONAL *a person who belongs to a certain nation*, nationalistic, nationalist, nationalistically, nationality, nationalization, nationalize, nationally; denationalization, denationalize.

NAIVE (nativus *natural*) *unsophisticated*, naively, naivete.

INTERNATIONAL *between nations*, internationalism, internationalist, internationality, internationalization, internationalize, internationally.

NATAL *pertaining to one's birth*, natality.

NATALS *birthday celebration*.

NAT
born
natural

NASCENT *being born*, nascence, nascency.
PRENATAL *existing before birth*, prenatally.
RENAISSANCE *a new birth; European rebirth of learning in 1300s, 1400s, 1500s.*
NATURAL *what is expected in nature*, naturalism, naturalist, naturalistic, nuturality, naturalization, naturalize, naturally, naturalness; denaturalize.
CONNATURAL (com *together* + naturalis *natural*) connaturality, connaturalize, connaturally, connaturalness.
DENATURE *to take natural qualities from*, denaturant, denaturation.
SUPERNATURAL *caused by other than known forces in nature*, supernaturalism, supernaturalist, supernaturalistic, supernaturalize, supernaturally, supernaturalness.
UNNATURAL *artificial; abnormal*, unnaturalism, unnature.
AGNATE *relationship on the father's side*, agnatic, agnation.
COGNATE *having the same ancestor*, cognateness, cognation.
CONNATE *congenital*, connascent, connascence, connation, connatural, connaturality, connaturalize, connaturally, connaturalness.
ENATE *growing out; related through the mother*, enation.
INNATE *inborn, intuitive*, innately, innateness.
PREGNANT *carrying a child; prolific of ideas*, pregnantly, pregnance, pregnancy.
IMPREGNATE *to fertilize an ovum*, impregnation, inpregnator.

NAV
NAU
ship
sail

NAVIS *ship;* NAVIGARE *to sail,* NAVIGATUM   25
NAVAL *characteristic of the ships and personnel of a navy*, navalism.
NAVY *all of a nation's ships of war.*
NAVIGATE *to steer safely on water*, navigability, navigable, navigableness, navigably, navigation, navigator; unnavigable.
CIRCUMNAVIGATE *to sail around (the globe)*, circumnavigable, circumnavigation, circumnavigator.
NAUSEA *seasickness; stomach disorder; loathing*, nauseant, nauseate, nauseation, nauseous, nauseously, nauseousness.
NAUTICAL *in a shiply manner*, nautically.
NAUTILUS *a tropical mollusk with spiral shells; a diving bell.*

NEC
bind

NECTO, NECTERE *to bind,* NEXUM   19
CONNECT *to join one thing to another; to show as related*, connectedly, connection, connective, connectively, connectivity, connector.

NEC / NEX — *bind*

DISCONNECT *to separate; to turn off current,* disconnected, disconnectedly, disconnection.

UNCONNECTED *not united; not coherent.*

ANNEX (ad *to* + nectere *to bind*) *to add at the end; to unite a smaller thing to a greater,* annexation, annexational, annexationist.

REANNEX *to add once again,* reannexation.

NEXUS *a connection between individuals or characteristics within a population.*

NEG — *deny*

NEGARE *to deny,* **NEGATUM** 32

ABNEGATE (ab *from* + negare *to deny*) *to renounce; to oppose,* abnegation, abnegator.

NEGATE *to deny the existence or truth of,* negation.

NEGATIVE *saying "no"; implying denial,* negatively, negativeness, negativism, negativist, negativistic, negativity, negatory.

NEGLECT *to ignore or disregard,* neglectedness, neglecter, neglectful, neglectfully, neglectfulness, neglective.

NEGLIGENT *habitually failing to do the needed act,* negligence, negligently.

NEGLIGIBLE *disregard because unimportant,* negligibility, negligibly.

NEGLIGEE *a woman's loose fitting dressing gown.*

RENEGADE *one who abandons his principles, religion or party for another; a deserter.*

RENEGE *in cardgames, a failure to follow suit.*

DENY (de *intens.* + negare *to deny*) *to contradict; to refuse to grant,* denyingly.

UNDENIABLE *indisputable,* undenied, undeniably.

NERV / NEUR — *nerve*

NERVUS *a sinew;* **NEURON** [*Gr*] *a nerve* 18

ENERVATE (e *out* + nervus *a nerve*) *to deprive of strength,* enervative, enervator.

NERVE *bundle of fibers connecting body organs with the nervous system,* nerveless, nervelessness; unnerved.

NERVOUS *showing emotional tension,* nervously, nervousness, nervosity.

NEURON *the functional unit of the nervous system.*

NEURAL *belonging to the nervous system,* neuralgia, neuralgic.

NEURITIS *inflammmation of the nerves, causing pain.*

NEUROSIS *any baseless disorder characterized by anxieties and phobias.*

NEUROLOGY *medical practice of the nervous system, structure, and diseases.*

NOC
hurt

NOCERE *to harm;* **NOXIUS** *hurtful*   **23**

INNOCENT *free from sin or guilt*, innocence, innocency, innocently.
INNOCUOUS *harmless*, innocuity, innocuousness, innocuously.
NOCUOUS *hurtful, harmful*, nocuously, noxious, noxiously, noxiousness.
OBNOXIOUS *very unpleasant; offensive*, obnoxiously, obnoxiousness.
ANNOY *to irritate or vex*, annoyance, annoyer, annoying, annoyingly, annoyingness.
NUISANCE (nocere *to hurt*) *an incident or person causing trouble or annoyance.*

NOM
name

NOMEN, NOMINIS *a name*   **42**

NOMINAL *in name only, not in fact; hardly worth mention*, nominalism, nominalist, nominalistic, nominalize, nominally.
BINOMINAL *a mathematical equation of two terms with a plus or minus.*
MULTINOMINAL *having many names*, multinominous.
NOMINEE *one who has been nominated as a candidate for office.*
NOMINATE *to propose for office*, nomination, nominative, nominatively, nominator; renominate.
DENOMINATE *to designate; to give a name to*, denominant, denomination, denominational, denominationalism, denominationalist, denominationally, denominative, denominatively, denominator.
NAME *a word or phrase by which a thing is known.*
MISNOMER *to misname; to designate wrongly.*
NOMENCLATURE *the system of names used in a branch of learning or activity*, nomenclatural.
NOUN *a word used to describe a person or thing or action*, nounal.
PRONOUN *a word used as a substitute for a noun.*
RENOWN (re *again* + nomen *a name*) *fame and celebrity from great achievements*, renownedly, renowner, renownless.
IGNOMINY *shame; dishonor; loss of one's reputation*, ignominious, ignominiously.
AGNOMEN (ad *to* + nomen *name*) *a nickname; an epithet honoring some exploit.*
COGNOMEN *family name; surname; last name.*

NORM
rule

NORMA *square, rule, pattern*   **17**

NORM *a standard, rule, or pattern for a group.*
NORMAL *conforming to the standard or average*, normalcy, normality, nor-

NORM
rule

malization, normalize, normally.
ABNORMAL *not typical; irregular*, abnormality, abnormally, abnormity.
SUBNORMAL *less than normal*, subnormality.
ENORMOUS (e *out* + norma *rule*) *immense in size*, enormity, enormously, enormousness.

NOT
know

NOTARE *to mark*   **52**
NOTE *a token by which a thing may be known*, noted, notedly, notedness, noteless, noteworthy, noteworthily, noteworthiness.
NOTABLE *remarkable, memorable*, notably, notability, notableness.
NOTABILIA *things worthy of notice*.
NOTARY *an official authorized to certify or take depositions*, notarize, notarial, notarially.
NOTICE *announcement*, noticeable, noticeably, noticer.
NOTIFY (notus *know* + facere *to make*) *to give notice to*, notifier, notification, notifiable.
NOTION *conception; mental image*, notional, notionality, notionally, notionist.
NOTORIOUS *widely but unfavorably known about*, notoriety, notoriously, notoriousness.
NOTATE *a system of symbols to represent words or numbers*, notation, notative, notational.
ANNOTATE *to make notes by way of explanation*, annotation, annotative, annotator, annotatory.
CONNOTE *an idea suggested beyond its explicit meaning*, connotation, connotative, connotatively.
DENOTE (de *down* + notare *to mark*) *to signify by a visual sign*, denotable, denotation, denotative, denotatement, denotatively.

NOUN NUNC
announce

NUNTIO, NUNTIARE *to announce*, NUNTIATUM   **40**
ANNOUNCE *to give formal notice*, announcement, announcer.
RENOUNCE *to inform against; to condemn*, denouncement, denouncer.
PRONOUNCE *to articulate a sound; to declare*, pronounceable, pronouncement, pronouncer, pronouncing; unpronounceable.
MISPRONOUNCE *to pronounce different from accepted standard*.
RENOUNCE *to give up a right or opinion; to disown*, renouncement, renouncer.
NUNCIO *a papal ambassador*.
ANNUNCIATE *a proclamation or promulgation*, annunciation, annunciative,

NOUN
NUNC
announce

annunciator, annunciatory.
DENUNCIATE *an accusation against,* denunciation, denunciative, denunciator, denunciatory.
ENUNCIATE *pronounce clearly; state definitely,* enunciable, enunciative, enunciatively, enunciator, enunciatory.
PRONUNCIATION *pronouncing words with reference to stress, intonation, etc.,* pronunciative, pronunciator, pronunciatory; mispronunciation.
RENUNCIATION *a repudiation,* renunciatory.

NOV
NEW
new

NOVUS *new*   27
NOVEL (*adj*) *new, unusual,* novelty.
NOVEL (*n*) *a long fictional prose narrative,* novelette, novelist, novelistic, novelization, novelize, novella.
NOVICE *one new to any endeavor; one who has not completed religious vows.*
NOVITIATE *the period of being a novice in the religious order.*
NOVOCAIN *a local anesthetic resembling cocaine but less toxic.*
RENOVATE *to make like new,* renovation, renovator.
NEW (novus *new*) *never existing before; just discovered,* newly, newness.
RENEW *to begin again; to become restored,* renewability, renewable, renewal, renewedly, renewedness, renewer.
NEWS *newspaper.*
NEWSPEAK *use of deceptive talk to mold public opinion.*

NUMER
number

NUMERUS *a number;* NUMERO, NUMERARE *to count*   29
NUMBER *a symbol or word for 1,6,34, etc.; the sum of persons or things,* numberer, numberless; outnumber; unnumbered.
NUMERAL *a figure or letter expressing a number,* numerable, numeracy, numerary, numerate, numeration, numerative, numerator.
NUMERICAL *expressing by letters, not numbers,* numeric, numerically.
NUMEROUS *consisting of a great many persons or things,* numerously, numerousness.
ENUMERATE (e *out* + numerare *to count*) *to count one by one,* enumeration, enumerative, enumerator.
INNUMERABLE *too many to be enumerated,* innumerability, innumerableness; innumerate, innumerous.
SUPERNUMERARY *on the stage, one above the necessary number.*

NUR / NUT — *nourish*

NUTRIRE *to nourish,* **NUTRITUM**   **27**

NURSE *one trained to attend the sick or injured,* nurser, nursery, nursing.
NURTURE *that which nourishes; the process of upbringing;* unnurtured.
NUTRIENT *promoting growth,* nutrify.
NUTRITION *the science of proper diet to promote health,* nutritional, nutritionally, nutritionist, nutritious, nutritiously, nutritiousness, nutritive, nutritively, nutritiveness, nutritory.
NUTRIMENT *that which promotes growth and development,* nutrimental.
NOURISH *to feed; to support,* nourishable, nourisher, nourishing, nourishingly, nourishment.

ORA — *speak, plead*

ORARE *to speak, plead,* **ORATUM**   **29**

ADORE (ad *to* + orare *to speak*) *to regard with utmost esteem,* adorer, adoringly, adorable, adorability, adorableness, adorably, adoration; unadored.
EXORABLE *susceptible of persuasion by pleas.*
INEXORABLE *that cannot be moved by persuasion,* inexorability, inexorableness, inexorably.
ORACLE *a divine revelation by a medium or priest,* oracular, oracularly.
ORISON *a prayer or supplication.*
ORAL *words spoken not written,* oralism, orally.
ORATION *an elaborate speech delivered in public,* orator, oratoric, oratorical, oratorically, oratory, oratress.
ORATORIO *a long, dramatic musical composition, usually on a religious theme.*

ORD — *order*

ORDO, ORDINIS *order, rank*   **54**

ORDER *a fixed plan; rank; succession; a command,* orderer, ordering, orderless, orderliness, orderly.
DISORDER *confusion; irregularity,* disorderly, disorderedness, disorderliness, disorderly.
PREORDER *to arrange beforehand.*
UNORDERED unorderly.
ORDAIN *to decree; to order,* ordainable, ordainer; unordained.
PREORDAIN *to decree beforehand,* preordination.
REORDAIN *to ordain again after a defective ordination,* reordination,.
ORDNANCE *all weapons and ammunition used in warfare.*
ORDINANCE *an authoritative command; a practice established by usage or authority.*

ORD
order

ORDINATION *arranging in regular code*, ordinator.

CO-ORDINATE *being of equal order*, co-ordinately, co-ordinateness, co-ordination, co-ordinative, co-ordinator.

INORDINATE *not regulated; immoderate*, inordinacy, inordinately, inordinateness.

SUBORDINATE *placed inferior to another in rank or importance*, subordinacy, subordinal, subordinately, subordinateness, subordination, subordinationism, subordinative.

INSUBORDINATE *disobedient*, insubordination.

ORDINARY *usual, normal, regular*, ordinarily, ordinariness, ordinaryship; unordinary.

EXTRAORDINARY *out of the common order, remarkable, rare*, extraordinarily, extraordinariness.

ORG
instrument

ORGANUM *an instrument* 26

ORGAN *a large wind instrument; part of the body having a specific function*, organism, organist, organistic.

ORGANIC *inherent; systematically arranged*, organically, organicalness, organicism.

INORGANIC *composed of substance not animal or matter*, inorganical, inorganically.

ORGANIZE *to provide with an organic structure*, organizability, organizable, organization, organizer; unorganizable.

DISORGANIZE *to break up the order*, disorganization, disorganizer.

INORGANIZED *not having organic structure*, inorganizable, inorganization.

REORGANIZE *to organize anew*, reorganization.

PAN
all

PAN [Gr] *all, whole* 30

PANACEA *a supposed remedy for all ills*, panacean.

PANCREAS (pan *all* + kreas *flesh*) *a gland in stomach secreting a digestive juice*, pancreatic, pancreation, pancreatize.

PANDEMIC *prevalent over a whole area*.

PANDEMONIUM *a scene of wild disorder*, pandemoniac.

PANEGYRIC *eulogy bestowed on some person*, panegyrical, panegyrically, panegyrist, panegyrize.

PANOPLY *magnificent covering or array*, panoplied.

PANORAMA *a comprehensive survey; continuous series of scenes*, panoramic,

PAN
all

panoramical, panoramically.
PANTHEISM *belief that God is in everything*, pantheist, pantheistic, pantheistically, pantheologist.
PANTOMIME *a drama where only action and gestures are used*, pantomimic, pantomimical, pantomimically, pantomimist.

PAR
appear

PARERE *to come forth, appear*, PARITUM   17
APPARITION *a strange or extraordinary vision*, apparitional.
APPARENT *readily understood; seemingly true*, apparently, apparentness.
TRANSPARENT *see through; easily understood*, transparence, transparency, transparently, transparentness.
SEMITRANSPARENT *partial opaqueness*, semitransparency.
APPEAR (ad *to* + parere *to appear*) *to be in view; to be known*, appearance, appearer.
DISAPPEAR *to vanish from sight*, disappearance.

PAR
prepare

PARARE *to prepare*, PARATUM *making ready;* SEPARATUM *separate*   63
APPAREL *clothing; garments.*
APPARATUS *instruments, etc. enabling something to be accomplished.*
PARE *to cut or trim away.*
PARRY *to ward off; to deflect; to avoid.*
PARADE *any organized procession; military display.*
COMPARE *to examine things relative to each other*, comparability, comparable, comparableness, comparably, comparative, comparator, comparer.
INCOMPARABLE *having no basis of comparison*, incomparability, incomparableness, incomparably.
PREPARE *to make ready*, preparation, preparative, preparatively, preparator, preparatory, preparatorily, preparedly, preparedness, preparer.
REPAIR *to restore or mend after injury*, repairable, repairer.
REPARATION *restoration to good condition; amends or compensation done for a harm*, reparability, reparable, reparably, reparative.
IRREPARABLE *cannot be mended*, irreparability, irreparably, irreparate, irreparately.
SEPARATE (se *apart* + parare *to arrange*) *to set apart; to distinguish*, separability, separable, separableness, separably, separately, separateness.
INSEPARABLE *cannot be separated*, inseparability, inseparableness, inseparably, inseparate, inseparately.

PAR
prepare

SEVER *to separate; to divide by violence*, severable, severance.
DISSEVER (dis *apart* + separare *to sever*) *to disunite; to divide into parts*, disseverance, disseverment.
SEVERAL *separate; distinct; a small number more than two*, severally, severalty.

PAR
PEER
equal

PAR *equal*   **25**

PAR *the average or normal state; common status.*
PAIR *two similar things*, pairer, pairing.
PARITY *state of the same power, value, rank, etc.*
COMPARE *to examine the relationship things bear to each other*, comparer, comparison.
INCOMPARABLE *that admits of no comparison; beyond comparison*, incomparableness, incomparably.
DISPARITY *difference in degree, amount, excellence, etc.*
DISPARATE *essentially not alike.*
DISPARAGE *to speak slightingly of*, disparagement, disparager, disparaging, disparagingly.
PEER *one of the same rank; a British nobleman*, peeress.
PEERAGE *the body and ranking of noblemen of a country*, peerdom.
PEERLESS *unequaled*, peerlessly, peerlessness.
COMPEER *a person of the same rank or status.*

PART
share

PARS, PARTIS *a part;* **PORTIO** *a share*   **87**

PART *a proportion or division of the whole*, partage, partake, partaker.
PARTIAL *favoring one person or thing over another*, partialism, partialist, partiality, partialize, partiability, partible.
IMPARTIAL *not biased in favor of one party*, impartiality, impartially, impartialness.
PARTIBLE *that can be divided*, partibility.
IMPARTIBLE *that cannot be divided*, impartibly, impartibility, impartment.
PARTICLE *a minute part of matter; a very small proportion.*
PARTICULAR *special as to one and not others*, particularity, particularly, particularize, particularization.
PARTICULARISM *a theological doctrine; adherence to one party or system*, particularist, particularization.
PARCEL *a small package; a portion or collection.*

PART
share

PARSE *to break a sentence into parts, explaining each part.*
PARTISAN *one who strongly supports one side; a guerilla,* partisanship.
PARTITION *the act of separating,* partitionment, partitive; partite; tripartite *divided threefold;* repartition.
PARTNER *one who shares with another,* partnership.
PARTICIPATE (partis *a part* + capere *to take*) *share an activity with others,* participant, participantly, participation, participative, participator.
PARTY *a group of people working together for a common goal.*
PARTAKE *to take part in an activity,* partaker.
APART *separately from others,* apartment *a room or suite of rooms to live in.*
COMPART (com *with* + partire *to divide*) *to divide into parts,* compartition, compartment.
COUNTERPART *a person or thing resembling another.*
DEPART *to go away from,* departer, departure.
DISPART (dis *apart* + partire *to divide*) *to divide, to burst.*
IMPART *to communicate or bestow on another,* impartation.
PORTION *a part divided from the whole,* portioner, portionless.
APPORTION *to divide according to some plan,* apportioner, apportionment.
PROPORTION (pro *before* + portio *part*) *a share in relation to the whole,* proportionable, proportional, proportionate, proportionately, proportionality, proportionally, proportionateness, proportionment, proportionless.
DISPROPORTION *lack of symmetry between parts of a thing,* disproportionable, disproportionableness, disproportionably, disproportional, disproportionally, disproportionate, disproportionateness.
REPARTEE′ *a quick, witty reply.*

PASS PAN
spread step

PANDO, PANDERE *to spread;* PASSUS *a step*   41

COMPASS (com *with* + passus *a pace*) *stretch; limits; an instrument for showing direction,* compassable.
ENCOMPASS *to contain; to include,* encompassment.
PASS (*a word of many meanings*) *to proceed from one place to another,* passable, passableness, passably; unpassable.
PASSAGE *movement from one place to another.*
PASSENGER *one who travels by a public conveyance.*
IMPASSABLE *cannot be passed,* impassability, impassableness, impassably.
OVERPASS *a passageway over a road, railroad track, etc.*
SURPASS *to be superior to,* surpassable, surpassing, surpassingly, surpass-

PASS / PAN
spread, step

ingness.
TRESPASS *to go beyond what is considered right*, trespasser.
PACE *a measure of a stride; rate of walking or moving.*
PASSOVER *a Jewish holiday.*
PASSPORT *a government document for travel, proving citizenship.*
SPAN *the full extent between two limits.*
EXPAND *to cause to fill more space*, expander, expanding.
EXPANSE *a large, open area*, expansibility, expansible, expansibleness, expansibly, expansion, expansionism, expansionist, expansive, expansively, expansiveness.

PAT / PASS
bear

PATIOR, PATI *to bear, suffer*, PASSUS   39
PATIENT (*adj*) *bearing without complaint*, patiently (*adv*)
PATIENT (*n*) *one receiving treatment*, patience.
IMPATIENT *uneasy or fretful*, impatiently.
COMPATIBLE *capable of living together harmoniously*, compatibility, compatibleness.
INCOMPATIBLE *irreconcilably different*, incompatibleness, incompatibly.
PASSION *compelling emotion; being affected by an external influence*, passional, passionary, passionate, passionately, passionateness.
COMPASSION *a suffering with another*, compassionate, compassionately, compassionateness.
DISPASSION *free from bias*, dispassionate, dispassionately, dispassionateness.
IMPASSION *to arouse emotionally*, impassionable, impassionate, impassioned.
PASSIVE *unresisting; inactive*, passively, passiveness, passivism, passivity.
IMPASSIVE *not feeling or showing emotion*, impassively, impassiveness, impassivity.

PATH
feeling

PATHOS [*Gr*] *suffering, feeling*   22
ANTIPATHY (anti *against* + patheia *to suffer*) *inherent revulsion of feeling*, antipathetic.
APATHY *lack of interest*, apathetic, apathetical, apathetically, apathist.
EMPATHY (em *in* + pathos *feeling*) *the subjection of one's own personality to the personality of another in order to understand him better.*
PATHOS *the pity or compassion caused by something experienced or seen.*
PATHETIC *a feeling of pity or sorrow*, pathetically, patheticalness.
PATHOLOGY *medical training of the causes and symptoms of disease, especially*

PATH
feeling

their functional changes, pathologic, pathological, pathologically, pathologist.

SYMPATHY *affinity between persons; compassion for another's troubles*, sympathetic, sympathetically, sympathize, sympathizer.

PATR
father

PATER *father;* PATRIA *one's native country*   35

PATERNAL *like a father; from a father*, paternalism, paternalistic, paternalistically, paternally.

PATERNITY *male parentage; authorship or origin in general.*

PATRICIAN *noble, aristocratic*, patricianism, patriciate.

PATRIMONY *anything inherited from one's father or ancestors*, patrimonial, patrimonially.

PATRONYMIC (pater *father* + onoma *name*) *derived from the name of a father or ancestor.*

PATRON *a wealthy person who supports some person or cause*, patronage, patronal, patronate, patroness, patronize, patronizer, patronizing, patronizingly, patronless; unpatronized.

PATRIOT *one who loyally supports his own country*, patriotic, patriotical, patriotically, patriotism; unpatriotic, unpatriotical.

COMPATRIOT *a fellow countryman*, compatriotism.

EXPATRIATE *one who renounces rights of citizenship where born*, expatriation.

PED
foot

PES, PEDIS *the foot*   37

EXPEDITE *to facilitate; to quicken*, expeditely, expediteness, expediter.

EXPEDITION *haste; going on a trip for a special purpose*, expeditionary, expeditionist.

EXPEDITIOUS *efficient and speedy*, expeditiously, expeditiousness.

EXPEDIENT *suitable for a purpose; politic*, expediency, expediential, expedientially, expediently.

INEXPEDIENT *not suitable for a given situation*, inexpedience, inexpediency, inexpediently.

IMPEDE *to hinder or obstruct.*

IMPEDIMENT *anything that impeded (a speech defect, or the making of a legal contract)*, impedimenta, impedimental, impeditive.

PEDIMENT *triangular ornament in architecture over openings*, pedimental.

PEDESTRIAN *going on foot; prosaic, lacking in imagination*, pedestrianism, pedestrianize.

PEDESTAL *a base support for a column, statue or vase.*

PED — foot

PEDAL *a lever operated by the foot.*
PEDIGREE (*OFr.* pie de grue *"crane's foot"*) *a list of descent (like a crane's foot) of ancestors.*
PEDICURE *care of the toenails.*
PEDICAB *a three-wheeled vehicle in Asia pedalled like a bicycle.*
BIPED *an animal having two feet.*
QUADRUPED *an animal with four feet.*
CENTIPEDE *a worm-like animal with very many feet.*

PED — child

PAIS, PAIDOS [*Gr*] *a child*   **18**
PEDAGOGUE *Greek or Roman slave who took children to school and also taught them; a pedantic teacher.*
PEDAGOGY *the science of teaching and methods.*
PEDANT *a narrow-minded teacher who adheres to trivialities and rules,* pedantic, pedantically, pedantism, pedantize, pedantocracy.
PEDIATRICS *branch of medicine dealing with care of children and treatment of their diseases,* pediatrician.
ENCYCLOPEDIA (enkiklios *in a circle, general,* + paideia *education*) *books with information of all branches of knowledge,* encyclopedic, encyclopedical, encyclopedism, encyclopedist.
PEDERASTY *a form of sodomy between men, especially by a man with a boy,* pederast, perderastic.

PEL PULS — drive

PELLO, PELLERE *to drive,* PULSUM   **58**
COMPEL *to urge with physical or moral force,* compellable, compellably, compeller.
DISPEL *to scatter and drive away.*
EXPEL (ex *out* + pellere *to drive*) *to force to leave,* expellable, expeller, expellant.
IMPEL *to drive forward,* impellant, impeller.
PROPEL *to drive forward,* propellant, propeller, propelment.
REPEL *to drive back; to ward off,* repellence, repellency, repellent, repeller.
INTERPELLATE *to formally request of a government minister an explanation of his policy,* interpellant, interpellation.
PULSE (pulsus *a beating*) *any regular beat, as in arteries; the underlying feelings of the people,* pulsate, pulsation, pulsative, pulsator, pulseless, pulselessness, pulsive.

PEL
PULS
drive

COMPULSION *coercion*, compulsive, compulsively, compulsiveness, compulsorily, compulsoriness, compulsory.

EXPULSION *the act of driving out*, expulsive.

IMPULSE *an impelling force*, impulsion, impulsive, impulsively, impulsiveness, impulsor.

PROPULSION *being propelled*, propulsive, propulsory.

REPULSE *to beat or drive back*, repulseless, repulser.

REPULSION *aversion, repugnance*, repulsive, repulsively, repulsiveness, repulsory.

PEN
punish-ment

POENA *punishment*   40

PAIN *the suffering one feels for mental or physical hurt*, painful, painfully, painfulness, painless, painlessly, painlessness; unpainful.

PENALTY *a punishment fixed by law or contract for an offense*, penal, penalization, penalize, penally.

PENANCE *a voluntary suffering for repentance of wrongdoing*, penanceless.

PENITENCE *regret for offense committed*, penitency, penitencer, penitent, penitential, penitentially, penitently.

IMPENITENT *not repenting of sin*, impenitence, impenitency, impenitently.

PENITENTIARY *a prison for those convicted of various crimes.*

REPENT (re *again* + poena *punishment*) *to feel regret for something done or not done*, repentable, repentance, repentant, repentantly, repenter, repentingly, repentless.

UNREPENTED unrepenting, unrepentance.

SUBPOENA *a writ directing appearance in court of the person served*, subpoenal.

PEND
PENS
POND
hang
weigh

PENDO, PENDERE *to weigh, hang,* PENSUM; PONDUS, PONDERIS *weight*   207

APPEND *to add as a supplement*, appendage, appendant.

APPENDIX *supplementary material at the end of a book; in anatomy, the outgrowth of an organ*, appendical.

APPENDICITIS *inflammation of the vermiform appendix.*

APPENDECTOMY *in surgery, removal of the vermiform appendix.*

COMPENDIUM *an abridged form of a subject containing its general principles*, compendious, compendiously, compendiousness.

DEPEND (de *down* + pendere *to hang*) *to have full confidence*, dependable, dependability, dependableness, dependably, dependent, dependence, dependency,

PEND / PENS / POND
hang
weigh

dependently, depender, depending.

INDEPENDENT *not subject to the influence of others*, independence, independency, independently.

EXPEND *to dispurse*, expendable, expenditor, expenditure,

IMPEND *to hang over, or about to happen*, impendent, impendence, impendency, impending.

PEND *to await decision*, pendency, pending.

PENDANT *a hanging object, as an earring.*

PENDULOUS *hanging freely, fastened at one end with the other end free*, pendulously, pendulousness.

PENDULUM *a body suspended from a fixed point so that it moves freely to and fro.*

PENTHOUSE *a house built on the roof of a building.*

PERPEND or PERPENDER *a large stone extending through both sides of a wall, serving as a binder.*

PERPENDICULAR *exactly vertical*, perpendicularity, perpendicularly.

SPEND *to use up*, spender, spendable, spending, spent, spendthrift.

SUSPEND *to bar from privileges for a specified time*, suspender.

STIPEND *any periodical payment for services or an allowance.*

COMPENSATE (com *with* + pendere *to weigh*) *to make up for*, compensation, compensational, compensative, compensator, compensatory.

DISPENSE *to give out; to administer*, dispenser.

DISPENSABLE *not important*, dispensableness.

INDISPENSABLE *absolutely necessary*, indispensability, indispensableness, indispensably.

DISPENSARY *a place where medicines and treatment are administered.*

DISPENSATION *giving out; any release from an obligation*, dispensative, dispensatively, dispensator, dispensatory.

EXPENSE *money paid for services.*

EXPENSIVE *costly*, expensively, expensiveness.

RECOMPENSE *to compensate; to make payment*, recompenser, recompensive.

PENCHANT *a strong liking.*

PENSILE *a hanging bell or nest.*

PENSIVE *thinking deeply, often sadly*, pensively, pensiveness.

PENSION *a payment made regularly to a person who has reached a certain age and fulfilled conditions*, pensionable, pensionary, pensioner.

PROPENSITY *a natural inclination; a bent.*

PEND / PENS / POND
hang / weigh

SUSPENSE *a state of being uncertain,* suspensibility, suspensible, suspension, suspensive, suspensively.

PONDER *to weigh in the mind,* ponderer, ponderable, ponderableness, ponderability.

IMPONDERABLE *what cannot be weighed or solved,* imponderability, imponderableness.

PREPONDERANT *greater in weight and influence,* preponderance, preponderancy, preponderantly, preponderate, preponderation, preponderatingly.

PONDEROUS *very heavy; bulky,* ponderosity, ponderously, ponderousness.

POUND *a weight of 16 ounces.*

POISE *balance; keep steady; ease of manner.*

AVOIRDUPOISE *a system of weights based on the pound (16 oz).*

COUNTERPOISE *a weight or influence that balances another.*

EQUIPOISE *equal distribution of weight; equilibrium of moral or political interest.*

PERSON
person

PERSONA *a mask* 27

PERSONA *a character represented by an actor,* personae (*pl*), personate.

PERSON *an individual human being,* personal, personalism, personally, personalize.

PERSONABLE *an attractive personal appearance.*

PERSONAGE *a person of importance (sometimes ironical).*

IMPERSONAL *without reference to any particular person,* impersonality, impersonally.

PERSONATE *to assume a character,* personation, personative, personator.

IMPERSONATE *to mimic the appearance and manner of a person,* impersonation, impersonator.

PERSONNEL *employees of an establishment.*

PERSONIFICATION (persona *a person* + facere *to make*) *a figure of speech in which a thing or idea is represented by a person,* personifier, personify.

PERSONALITY *the individuality of a particular person; the qualities that make each person unique.*

PARSON *person of the church.*

PARSONAGE *dwelling for parson or minister.*

PET

PETO, PETERE *to ask, seek,* PETITUM 39

APPETENCE *a strong desire for that which gratifies the senses,* appetency.

PET
seek
ask

APPETITE *a desire for food or drink; a natural desire for gratification of the body or mind*, appetition, appetize, appetizer, appetizing, appetizingly.

COMPETE (com *together* + petere *to seek*) *to strive for the same thing as another.*

COMPETENCE *adequate ability*, competency, competent, competently.

COMPETITION *seeking for the same thing as another*, competitive, competitor.

INCOMPETENCE *without adequate ability*, incompetency, imcompetent, incompetently.

IMPETUS *the force with which a body moves against resistance.*

IMPETUOUS *acting suddenly with little thought*, impetuosity, impetuously, impetuousness.

PETITION *a formal writing of a request; a solemn application*, petitionarily, petitionary, petitionee, petitioner, petitioning.

REPETITION *doing the same thing for a second time*, repetitionary, repetitious, repetitive.

REPEAT (re *again* + petere *to seek*) *to say or do again*, repeatedly, repeater, repeating.

PHAN
show

PHAINEIN [Gr] *to show*   37

DIAPHANOUS *some fabric, or the like, that can be seen through.*

EMPHASIS *force of expression; special stress*, emphasize, emphatic, emphatically, emphatical.

EPIPHANY *appearance or apparition of a supernatural being.*

PHANTOM *an apparition, an illusion.*

PHASE *any of the ways in which something may be observed or represented; an aspect.*

SYCOPHANT *a toady; one who seeks influence by flattering people of influence*, sycophantic, sycophantical sycophantish, sycophantishly, sycophantism, sycophantize.

PHENOMENON *extremely unusual*, phenomenal, phenomenalism, phenomenalist, phenomenalistic, phenomenally, phenomenalist, phenomenology.

FANCY (phantasia *the look of a thing*), *capricious imagination*, fancier, fanciful, fancifully, fancifulness, fanciless.

FANTASTIC (phantasticus *imaginary*) *incredible; having a strange appearance; unrestrained fancy*, fantastical, fantastically, fantasticality, fantasticalness, fantasticism.

FANTASY *an unreal mental image.*

PLA / PLEA
please

PLACERE *to please,* **PLACITUM** 44

COMPLAISANT *desirous to please,* complaisance, complaisantly.

PLACATE *to appease,* placation, placative, placatory.

IMPLACABLE *that cannot be appeased,* implacability, implacableness, implacably.

PLACID *serene,* placidity, placidness.

PLACEBO ("*I will please*") *a medicine given for psychological effect; a test used when testing other medicines.*

PLEASE *to give pleasure to and satisfy,* pleasing, pleaser, pleasingly, pleasingness.

PLEASANT pleasantly, pleasantness, pleasantry.

PLEASURE pleasureful, pleasureless, pleasurer, pleasuring.

DISPLEASE *to offend,* displeaser, displeasing, displeasingly, displeasingness, displeasure.

UNPLEASANT *disagreeable,* unpleasantness, unpleasantry.

PLEA *a statement by or for a defendant, answering the charges or claiming no answer is needed.*

PLEAD *to argue the case for either party,* pleader, pleadable, pleading, pleadingly.

PLAU
applause

PLAUDO, PLAUDERE *to applaud,* **PLAUSUM** 20

PLAUSIBLE *seemingly true,* plausibility, plausibleness, plausibly.

IMPLAUSIBLE *not likely to be believed,* implausibility, implausibleness, implausibly; unplausible.

PLAUDIT *an expression of approval,* plauditory.

APPLAUD *clapping the hands, etc.,* applauder, applause, applausive, applausively.

EXPLODE (ex *off* + plaudere *to clap*) *to burst with violence,* explosion, explosive, explosively.

PLE
full
plenty

PLENUS *full;* **PLENITAS** *plenty* 61

PLENTY *an abundance,* plentiful, plentifully, plentifulness.

PLENITUDE *fullness, completeness,* plenteous, plenteously, plenteousness.

PLENARY *attended by all members.*

PLETHORA *state of overabundance,* plethoric, plethorically; deplethoric *not overabundant.*

PLENIPOTENTIARY (plen *full* + potus *powerful*) *having full authority.*

PLE
full
plenty

ACCOMPLISH (ac *to* + complere *to complete*) *to succeed in doing*, accomplishable, accomplisher, accomplishment; unaccomplished, unaccomplishment.

COMPLIMENT *something said in praise, or an act of civility*, complimentary, complimentative, complimenter.

COMPLEMENT *the full amount*, complemental, complementary.

COMPLETE *full or finished*, completely, completeness, completion.

INCOMPLETE *not whole or finished*, incompletely, incompleteness, incompletion.

DEPLETE (de *from* + plere *to fill*) *to reduce or exhaust*, depletion, depletive, depletory.

EXPLETIVE *something not needed but added for ornament*.

IMPLEMENT (in *in* + plere *to fill*) *something needed in a given activity; to fulfill*, implemental, implementation, impletion.

MANIPULATE (manu *hand*) *artful control by shrewd use of influence, often unfairly*, manipulation, manipulative, manipulator, manipulatory.

REPLETE (re *again* + plere *to fill*) *plentifully supplied*, repleteness, repletion, repletive, repletively.

SUPPLEMENT (sub *under*) *something added to fill a need*, supplemental, supplementary, supplementation.

SUPPLY *to furnish what is needed*, supplier.

PLI
PLE
fold

PLICARE *to fold;* PLEXUM *twisted*   142

APPLICABLE *appropriate, relevant*, applicability, applicableness, applicably.

INAPPLICABLE *inappropriate*, inapplicability, inapplicableness, inapplicably, inapplication.

APPLY *to put one thing to another; to employ for a particular purpose*, applicable, applied, appliedly, applier, applicable, applicably.

MISAPPLY *use incorrectly or dishonestly*, misapplication.

APPLIANCE *something applied to a particular use*.

APPLICANT *one who applies for an opening*.

APPLICATE *to put to practical use*.

APPLICATION *the act of laying out; making the request*, applicative, applicatively, applicator, applicatory.

ACCOMPLICE *an associate in crime*.

COMPLEX *"fold together"; involved, complicated*, complexed, complexedness, complexly, complexity.

PLI / PLE
fold

COMPLEXION *originally the four humors: cold, heat, dryness, and moisture; now, the general appearance of anything, as the face.*

COMPLY *to act in accordance with a request*, compliable, compliably, compliance, compliancy, compliant, compliantly.

COMPLICATE *to entangle, to become intricate*, complicant, complicacy, complicated, complication.

COMPLICITY *the state of being an accomplice.*

DUPLICITY *double dealing; exhibiting contrary conduct and sentiments in relation to the same thing.*

DISPLAY (dis *apart* + plicare *to fold*) *to show, to unfold for the mind*, displayed, displayer.

DEPLOY *to unfold, to spread out.*

EMPLOY *to keep busy.*

EXPLOIT *to make use of; to turn to one's advantage.*

EXPLICIT *"unfolded"; in plain language*, explicitly, explicitness.

EXPLICATE *to unfold the meaning; to make clear*, explication, explicative, explicator, explicable, explicableness.

IMPLY *to entangle, to indicate without saying openly*, implied, impliedly.

IMPLICATION *to entangle*, implication, implicative, implicatively, implicatory.

IMPLICIT *to indicate without openly saying so*, implicitly, implicitness.

MULTIPLY *"many folds"; to increase*, multiple, multiplying, multiplication, multiplicity.

PERPLEX *"to twist thoroughly"; to confuse a person*, perplexedly, perplexedness, perplexingly, perplexity.

PLY *having a specified number of layers or strands; to keep busy at something*, plyer.

PLIABLE *easily bent or influenced*, pliableness, pliably.

PLIANT *capable of being easily bent*, pliantly, pliantness, pliancy.

PLICA *in anatomy, the folding of the skin; in medicine, the matting of the hair.*

PLICATE *folded or in pleats, like a fan*, plicately, plicatile, plication, plicative, plicator, plicature, pliciferous, pliciform, plier.

REPLICA *a copy of a work.*

REPLICATE (re *back* + plicare *to fold*) *to fold as a leaf; to repeat.*

REPLICATION *in law, the reply of a plaintiff to the defendant's plea.*

REPLY *an answer.*

SIMPLE *"without fold"; easy to understand*, simpleness, simplicity, simplification, simplifier, simplistic.

PLI
PLE
fold

SIMPLEX *having only one part.*
SUPPLE (sub *under* + plicare *to fold*) *"to fold under"; easily bent,* supplely.
SUPPLIANT *entreating, beseeching,* suppliantly, suppliantness.
SUPPLICATE *to seek by earnest prayer,* supplicatingly, supplication, supplicator, supplicant, supplicantly.
DUPLEX *twofold,* duplicate, duplication, duplicative, duplicator.
TRIPLICATE *threefold,* triplication, triplicity.
QUADRUPLE *fourfold,* quadruplicate, quadruplication, quadruplicity.
QUINTUPLE *to multiply by five,* quintuplicate,
SEXTUPLE *sixfold.*

POL
city

POLIS [Gr] ***a city***   23
POLICE *department for keeping order and preventing crime,* policemen, policewomen.
POLICY *a governing principle or course of action.*
POLITIC *wise, prudent, sagacious measures;* unpolitic.
IMPOLITIC *imprudent; not expedient,* impoliticly, impoliticness.
POLITICAL *behavior of government or political parties,* politicalism, politically; unpolitical.
COSMOPOLITAN (*Gr* kosmos *world* + polites *a citizen*) *"citizen of the world,"* cosmopolitanism, cosmopolite, cosmopolitism.
METROPOLIS (*Gr* meter *mother* + polis *city*) *any large city,* metropolitan, metropolitic, metropolitical.
ACROPOLIS *highest part of the city.*
NEAPOLITAN (neos *new* + polis *city*) *a native of Naples.*

POP
PUB
people

POPULUS ***the people;*** PUBLICUS ***public***   30
PEOPLE (plebs *the common people*) *all the persons of a community or nation having common traditions,* peopleless; repeople; unpeople.
POPULATE *to furnish with people,* population, populator.
DEPOPULATE depopulation, depopulator.
POPULAR *very well liked by one's acquaintances; liked by most people,* popularity, popularization, popularize, popularizer, popularly, popularness; depopularize.
POPULOUS *thickly populated,* populously, populousness.
PUBLIC *belong to the people of a community or nation,* publicly.
PUBLICATION *public notification by printing;* republication.

PUB
people

PUBLICITY *any information that brings a person or thing to the attention of the public*, publicist, publicize.

PUBLISH (publicare *to make public*) *to cause to be printed and offered for sale*, publishable, publisher, publishment.

PORT
carry

PORTO, PORTARE *to carry*, PORTATUM   **65**

ASPORTATION *carrying away; in law, the felonious removal of goods.*

PORCH or PORTICO *originally a covered walk.*

PORT *to carry a rifle or sword diagonally in front of one, as for inspection; a harbor.*

PORTABLE *that can be easily carried*, portability, portableness, portative.

PORTAGE *the act of carrying.*

PORTAMENTO *in music, a glide from one note to another.*

PORTCULLIS *the falling gate to a fortified town.*

PORTER *one who carries things.*

PORTFOLIO (port *carry* + folium *a leaf*) *a brief case; a selection of representative items.*

PORTLY *a stocky person.*

PORTMANTEAU *a stiff leather suitcase that opens like a book.*

COMPORT *to agree with; to behave in a specified manner*, comportable, comportment.

DEPORT *expulsion of an undesirable alien*, deportation, deportee.

DEPORTMENT (de *from* + portare *to bring*) *conduct and demeanor.*

DISPORT *to frolic, to indulge in amusement.*

EXPORT *to sell and send goods to another country*, exportable, exportability, exportation, exporter.

IMPORT *to buy and bring in goods from a foreign country*, importable, importableness, importer, importation.

IMPORTANT *having significance and value*, importance, importancy, importantly; unimportant, unimportance.

OPPORTUNE *right for the purpose; well-timed*, opportunely, opportuneness, opportunism, opportunist, opportunistic, opportunity.

PURPORT *to profess or claim; to give the appearance, even falsely*, purportless.

RAPPORT *a close or sympathetic relationship.*

REPORT *to give or write an account of*, reportable, reporter, reporting, reportorial; unreported.

PORT
carry

SPORT *any activity that gives enjoyment or recreation*, sportability, sportful, sportfully, sportily, sportiness, sporting, sportive, sportiveness, sportsman.

SUPPORT (sub *under* + portare *to carry*) *to bear, sustain, endure*, supportable, supportableness, supportably, supporter.

INSUPPORTABLE *cannot be sustained*, insupportableness, insupportably; unsupported, unsupportable.

TRANSPORT (trans *across* + portare *to carry*) *to carry from one place to another*, transportability, transportable, transportation, transporting.

POS
*put
set*

PONERE *to put or set,* POSITUM   173

POSE *to put forward or advance*, poser *an affected person; a questioner.*

POSIT *to place in proper relation to other objects.*

POSITION *the manner or place or attitude*, positional.

POSITIVE *explicitly laid down*, positively, positiveness, positivism, positivist, positivistic, positivity.

POST *a piece of wood; a system of mail; a situation*, postage, postal, postman.

POSTURE *the position of the body; the way things stand*, posturer, posturize.

APROPOS *opportunely; at the right time.*

APPOSE (ad *to* + ponere *to put*) *to put something to another*, apposite, appositely, appositeness, apposition, appositional, appositive, appositively; inapposite, inappositely.

CIRCUMPOSITION *the act of placing in a circle.*

COMPOSE *to form by uniting two or more things; to create*, composedly, composedness, composer.

COMPOSITE *made up of distinct elements*, composition, compositive, compositor, compositorial.

DECOMPOSE *to break up into basic components*, decomposer, decomposite, decomposition.

DISCOMPOSE *to unsettle; to disarrange*, discomposedly, discomposalness, discomposure.

COMPOST *a mixture of decomposing refuse.*

COMPOSURE *the act of composing; a settled state of mind.*

CONTRAPOSE *to set in opposition*, contraposition.

DEPONE (de *from* + ponere *to put*) *in law, to testify*, deponent.

DEPOSE *to divest of office; to testify*, deposer; deposition.

DEPOSIT *anything entrusted in care of another*, depositary, depositor, depository.

POS
put
set

DEPOT *a place for storage; a transportation center.*
DISPONE *in Scots law, to make over to another,* disponee, disponer, disponent.
DISPOSE (dis *apart* + ponere *to place*) *to arrange to place or distribute,* disposal, disposable, disposer, disposingly.
PREDISPOSE *to make susceptible,* predisposition, predispositional.
DISPOSITION *the manner in which things are arranged; one's customary frame of mind,* dispositional.
EXPONENT (ex *out* + ponere *to place*) *a person who sets forth or interprets or is a symbol,* exponible.
EXPOSE *to set to view; to uncover,* exposer, exposedness, exposure.
EXPOSÉ *a disclosure.*
EXPOSITION *setting forth facts and ideas,* expositive, expositor, expository.
EXPOUND (ex *out* + ponere *to put*) *to set forth point by point,* expounder.
IMPOSE (im *into* + ponere *to put*) *to inflict; to force oneself; to pass off,* imposer, imposingly, imposingness, imposition.
SUPERIMPOSE *to lay on top of something else,* superimposition.
IMPOST *an tax imposed by authority.*
IMPOSTURE *assuming a character for deception,* impostor, impostrous.
INTERPOSE *to put between; to put in as an interruption,* interposal, interposer, interposition.
JUXTAPOSE *to place side by side,* juxtaposition.
OPPONENT *an adversary.*
OPPOSE *to set against; to resist by physical force or logic,* opposer, opposite, oppositeness, opposition, oppositionist, oppositive.
POSTPONE (post *after* + ponere *to put*) *to put off; to defer,* postponement, postponer, postponable.
POSTPOSITION *a placing after,* postpositional, postpositive, postpositively.
PREPOSITION *the relation word that connects the noun form with another element,* prepositional, prepositionally, prepose.
PREPOSITIVE *prefixed; put before,* prepositor, prepositive.
PROPONE *to propose* [Scot].
PROPONENT *one who makes a proposition or supports a cause.*
PROPOSE (pro *forth* + ponere *to put*) *to put forth for consideration,* proposer, proposition, propositional.
PURPOSE *to intend; the end in view,* purposer, purposely, purposeful, purposefully, purposeless, purposelessness.
RECOMPOSE *to restore to composure,* recomposition *act of recomposing.*

POS
put set

REPOSE *to put to rest*, reposedly, reposedness, reposeful, reposer.
SUPERIMPOSE *imposing on top of something else*, superimposition.
SUPERPOSE *to place a figure on another so they match*, superposable, superposition.
SUPPOSE *to assume to be true, to imagine*, supposable, supposableness, supposably, supposal, supposer, supposedly.
SUPPOSITION *laying down a hypothesis*, suppositional, suppositious, suppositiously, suppositiousness, suppositive, suppositively.
SUPPOSITORY *a capsule introduced into the vagina or rectum*.
PRESUPPOSE *to take for granted*, presupposal, presupposition.
TRANSPOSE (trans *across* + ponere *to place*) *to change the normal order*, transposible, transposing, transposition, transpositional.

POS POT
able

POSSE *to be able;* POTENS *powerful*   **34**
POTENT *powerful, convincing; sexually capable*, potency.
IMPOTENT *powerless; lacking strength*, impotence, impotency, impotently.
PREPOTENT (pre *before* + potentia *power*) *superior in power or influence*, prepotency.
OMNIPOTENT *possessing unlimited power*, omnipotence, omnipotency, omnipotently.
POTENTIAL *a latent ability not yet realized*, potentiality, potentially, potentiate.
POTENTATE *one who possesses great power; a ruler*.
PLENIPOTENTIARY *having full power or authority*.
POWER *capacity to act; great ability to do*, powerful, powerfully, powerfulness, powerless, powerlessness.
POSSE *a body of men armed with legal authority*.
POSSIBLE *that can be done*, possibility, possibly.
IMPOSSIBLE *not capable of being done*, impossibility, impossibly.
PUISSANT (poetical) *powerful, forcible*, puissantly, puissantness.

PRACT
to do

PRASSEIN [Gr] *to do*   **19**
PRACTICE *to do or perform frequently or habitually*, practicer, practitioner.
IMPRACTICAL *not capable of being dealt with*, impracticability, impracticable, impracticableness, impractically, impracticality.
MALPRACTICE *misconduct in any professional or official position*.
UNPRACTICED *not skilled or experienced*, unpractical, unpracticable.
PRAGMATISM *a philosophy that tests the validity of concepts by their practical*

results, pragmatic, pragmatical, pragmatically, pragmaticalness, pragmatist.

PREC *pray*

PRECOR, PRECARI *to pray,* **PRECATUS** 22

PRAY *to beg for imploringly*, prayer, prayerful, prayerfully, prayerfulness, prayerless, prayerlessly, prayerlessness.

PRITHEE *"I pray thee"; please.*

DEPRECATE (de *from* + precari *to pray*) *to pray against; to express strong disapproval*, deprecatingly, deprecation, deprecative, deprecatively, deprecator, deprecatory.

IMPRECATE *to pray for misfortune; to invoke a curse*, imprecation, imprecatory.

PRECARIOUS *uncertain; dependent upon circumstances*, precariously, precariousness.

PREC *value esteem*

PRETIUM *a price* 37

APPRAISE *to judge the quality or worth of*, appraisable, appraisal, appraisement, appraiser.

PRAISE *commendation, approbation*, praiseless, praiser, praiseworthy, praiseworthiness, praiseworthily.

APPRECIATE *to be fully aware of; to esteem*, appreciable, appreciably, appreciatingly, appreciation, appreciative, appreciatively, appreciativeness, appreciator, appreciatorily, appreciatory.

DEPRECIATE (de *from* + pretium *price*) *to lessen in value*, depreciable, depreciation, depreciative, depreciatively, depreciator, depreciatory.

PRECIOUS *of great value; held in high esteem*, preciously, preciousness.

PRECIOSITY *great fastidiousness; over refinement.*

PRICE *the cost of something*, priceless *invaluable.*

PRIZE *to value highly*, prizable.

PREH *seize*

PREHENDO, PREHENDERE *to seize,* **PREHENSUM** 80

APPREHEND *to take hold of physically; to perceive with the mind*, apprehender, apprehendingly, apprehensibility, apprehensible, apprehension, apprehensive, apprehensively, apprehensiveness.

MISAPPREHEND *to understand wrongly*, misapprehension, misapprehensively.

UNAPPREHENDED unapprehensible.

PREH
seize

COMPREHEND *to grasp by the understanding*, comprehendibility, comprehensible, comprehensibleness, comprehensibly, comprehension, comprehensive, comprehensively, comprehensiveness, comprehensor.

INCOMPREHENSIVE *cannot be understood*, incomprehensibility, incomprehensible, incomprehensibleness, incomprehensibly, incomprehension, incomprehensively incomprehensiveness.

UNCOMPREHENDING uncomprehensible, uncomprehensibility, uncomprehensible, uncomprehensibleness, uncomprehensibly, uncomprehension, uncomprehensive, uncomprehensively, uncomprehensiveness.

REPREHEND (re *back* + prehendere *to seize*) *to censure; to blame*, reprehender, reprehensibility, reprehensible, reprehensibleness, reprehensibly, reprehension.

IRREPREHENSIBLE *free from fault*, irreprehensibly, irreprehensibility.

APPRISE *to notify*, apprisal; unapprised.

COMPRISE *to consist of*, comprisable, comprisal.

ENTERPRISE *an undertaking; readiness to take risks*, enterpriser, enterprising, enterprisingly.

REPRISAL *doing an injury in return for an injury received.*

SURPRISE *to come on unawares; to astound*, surprisal, surprisedly, surpriser, surprising, surprisingly, surprisingness.

APPRENTICE *a beginner of a trade or profession*, apprenticeship.

REPRIEVE *to delay the punishment; to defer.*

PREGNABLE *capable of being won by force.*

IMPREGNABLE *unyielding*, impregnability, impregnableness, impregnably.

PRISON *place where convicted persons are confined*, prisoner.

PRIZE *something taken by force; a lever for prying.*

PRESS
press

PREMERE *to press*, PRESSUM   68

PRESS *to act on with steady force*, pressable, presser, pressingly, pressingness.

PRESSURE *a condition of distress; a compelling influence*, pressure point, pressurize.

APPRESSED *in botany or zoology, lying flat against a surface.*

COMPRESS (com *together* + premere *to press*) *to press together; to condense*, compressibility, compressible, compressibleness, compression, compressive, compressor, compressure.

DEPRESS (de *down* + premere *to press*) *to press down; to discourage*,

PRESS
press

depressant, depressible, depressingly, depression, depressive, depressiveness, depressor.

EXPRESS (ex *out* + premere *to press*) *to squeeze out; to put into words; to make known*, expressible, expressibly.

EXPRESSION *a meaningful manner of speaking*, expressional, expressionless, expressive, expressively, expressiveness.

EXPRESSIONISM *early 20th century movement in art (especially drama) to use symbols, etc. to give objective expression to inner experience*, expressionist, expressionistic, expressionistically.

INEXPRESSIVE *that cannot be expressed*, inexpressible, inexpressibility, inexpressibly.

IMPRESS *to mark by using pressure*, impressibility, impressible, impressibleness; unimpressive, unimpressionable.

IMPRESSION *the act of impressing*, impressionability, impressionable, impressionableness, impressional; unimpressionable.

IMPRESSIONISM *a theory of painting which produces the immediate impression*, impressionist, impressionistic.

OPPRESS *to lie heavily on; to keep down by cruel use of power*, oppression, oppressive, oppressively, oppressiveness, oppressor.

REPRESS (re *back* + premere *to press*) *to put down; to subdue; to prevent natural development*, represser or repressor, repressible, repression, repressive, repressively.

SUPPRESS (sub *under* + premere *to press*) *to put down by force; to prevent the publication*, suppressible, suppression, suppressive, suppressor.

REPRIMAND *to reprove severely*, reprimander.

PRINT *originally a mark made on paper by pressing with a die*, printable, printer, printing, printless; imprint.

IMPRIMATUR *"let it be pressed upon"; sanction approval.*

PRIM PRIN
first

PRIMUS *first;* **PRINCEPS, PRINCIPIS** *chief* 34

PRIME *first in time, rank, or quality*, primeness.

PRIMACY *state of being first in rank and importance.*

PRIMARY *original in order of development.*

PRIMATE *the highest-ranking bishop.*

PRIMEVAL *belonging to the earliest period*, primevally.

PRIMITIVE *pertaining to the earliest times*, primitively, primitiveness, primitivism.

PRIM
PRIN
first

PRIMOGENITOR *a forefather*, primogeniture *in English law, the right of the eldest son to inherit the father's estate.*

PRIMORDIAL *existing from the beginning*, primordialism, primordiate, primordiality, primordially.

PRIMROSE *an early flowering plant.*

PRINCE *one who holds first rank; son of a sovereign*, princess, princedom, princehood, princely, princeliness.

PRINCIPAL *that of highest rank*, principally, principalness, principality.

PRINCIPLE *the ultimate source or cause of something; a fundamental doctrine or force*, principled; unprincipled.

PRIOR *previously*, priority.

PRIOR/PRIORESS *heads of religious orders.*

PRISTINE *an original; still pure and untouched.*

PRIV
one's own

PRIVO, PRIVATUM **apart from others;** PRIVUS **one's own**   12

PRIVATE (*adj*) *belonging to a person; not known to the public*, privately.

PRIVATE (*n*) *lowest rank of enlisted man in the U.S. army.*

PRIVACY *a place of seclusion.*

PRIVATION *the lack of usual necessities or comforts.*

PRIVATEER *an authorized private ship of war.*

PRIVILEGE (privus *separate* + legis *a law*) *a right granted to some person or class not granted to others.*

PRIVY *privately known; knowledge of a secret transaction.*

DEPRIVE *to keep away from having; dispossess*, deprivable, deprivation, depriver.

PROV
PROB
prove
like

PROBO, PROBARE **to prove,** PROBATUM   62

APPROVE *to like, to commend*, approvable, approvableness, approval, approvedly; self-approving; unapproved.

DISAPPROVE *to reject, to consider wrong*, disapproval, disapprover, disapprovingly.

PROVE *to establish as truth or fact, by testimony or evidence*, provable, provableness, provably.

IMPROVE *to make better*, improvability, improvable, improvableness, improvement, improver.

REPROVE (re *again* + probare *to prove*) *to blame, censure, condemn*, reprovable, reprovableness, reprovably, reproval, reprover, reprovingly.

PROV / PROB
prove like

PROBABLE *likely; what reasonably can be expected*, probability, probably.
IMPROBABLE *not likely to be true*, improbability, improbableness, improbably.
APPROBATION *approval*, approbative, approbativeness, approbatory; self-approbation.
PROBATION *conditional suspension of a sentence dependant upon behavior*, probational, probationary, probationer.
PROBATE *in law, official proof or validity of a document.*
IMPROBATION *the act of disapproving*, improbative, improbatory.
REPROBATE *depraved, vicious, unprincipled*, reprobateness, reprobater, reprobation, reprobative, reprobatory.
PROBE *a surgical instrument; a searching investigation of illegal practices.*
PROBITY *complete honesty and integrity*; improbity.
PROOF *something serving as evidence*, proofing, proofless, prooflessly.

PROPR
one's own

PROPRIUS *one's own*   24
PROPER *specially suitable for a specific purpose; seemly*, properly, properness.
IMPROPER *not suitable for the purpose or circumstances; not in accordance with the truth or fact*, improperly.
PROPERTY *the right to possess something; a thing owned.*
PROPRIETOR *one who has exclusive right to some property*, proprietorial.
PROPRIETARY *one who has the exclusive legal right to something.*
PROPRIETY *conformity with what is proper and fitting*; impropriety *improper behavior.*
APPROPRIATE (ad *to* + proprius *one's own*) *to assign for a particular use; fit or proper*, appropriately, appropriateness, appropriator, appropriative, appropriateness.
APPROPRIATION *money, etc. set apart for a given purpose.*
DISAPPROPRIATE *to withdraw from an appropriate use*, disappropriation.
EXPROPRIATE *to take private land for public use, by eminent domain.*
IMPROPRIATE *to appropriate for private use*, impropriation, impropriator.

PROP / PROX
near

PROPE *near;* PROPIUS *nearer;* PROXIMUS *nearest*   47
PROPINQUITY *nearness of relationship; affinity of nature.*
PROPITIOUS (*origin uncertain*) *favorably inclined; advantageous*, propitiously, propitiousness; unpropitious.
PROPITIATE *to appease; to win or regain the good will of*, propitiable, propitiation, propitiative, propitiator, propitiatorily, propitiatory.

PROP
PROX
near

UNPROPITIATED unpropitiable.

APPROACH *to draw near; resemblance*, approachability, approachable, approachableness, approacher, approaching, approachless.

UNAPPROACHABLE unapproachably, unapproached.

REPROACH (re *back* + prope *near*) *rebuke, reprove; to blame for a fault*, reproachable, reproacher, reproachful, reproachfully, reproachfulness, reproachless.

IRREPROACHABLE *above reproach*, irreproachableness, irreproachably.

APPROXIMATE *closely resembling*, approximately, approximating, approximation, approximative, approximatively, approximativeness, approximator.

PROXIMATE *nearest in space or time*, proximad, proximal, proximally, proximately.

PROXIMITY *nearness in place, time, or alliance*.

PUG
fight

PUGNUS *a fist;* PUGNARE *fight;* PUGIL *a boxer*   **22**

PUGILISM *the art of fighting with fists*, pugilist, pugilistic, pugilistically.

PUGNACIOUS *quarrelsome; disposed to fight*, pugnaciously, pugnaciousness, pugnacity.

IMPUGN *to challenge one's motives; to contradict*, impugnable, impugnation, impugner, impugnment.

OPPUGN (ob *against* + pugna *a fight*) *to reason against; to conflict with*, oppugnancy, oppugnant, oppugner.

REPUGNANT *highly distasteful; inclined to oppose*, repugnance, repugnancy, repugnantly, repugnatorial.

PUNC
PUNG
point

PUNGO, PUNGERE *to prick, point,* PUNCTUM   **44**

PUNCH *a tool for impressing or piercing*, puncher.

PUNCTATE *pointed: dotted*, punctation, punctator.

PUNCULATE *marked with small dots*, punctulation.

PUNCTUAL *on time; prompt*, punctualist, punctuality, punctually, punctualness; unpunctual.

PUNCTILIO *careful observance of behavior*, punctilious, punctiliously, punctiliousness.

PUNCTUATE *insert punctuation marks for clarity; to interrupt from time to time*, punctuation, punctuative, punctuator.

PUNCTURE *a small wound or hole*, punctureless.

COMPUNCTION *twinge of conscience; regret for wrong done*, compunctionless,

PUNC / PUNG — *point*

compunctious, compunctiously.
PUNGENT *acrid; sharp sensation of taste and smell*, pungency, pungently.
EXPUNGE *to rub out; to delete*, expunction.
POIGNANT *a pointed and piercing feeling*, poignancy, poignantly.
POINT (punctus *prick*) *a dot; a definite position in space; a condition*, pointable, pointal, pointedly, pointedness, pointing, pointless, pointly.
POUNCE *a swoop by a bird of prey*.

PUR — *cleanse*

PURGO, PURGATUM *cleanse;* PURUS *clean*   37
PURGE *to cleanse by separating and carrying off the impurities*, purgation, purgative, purgatively; unpurged.
PURGATORY *a state of temporary punishment*, purgatorial, purgatorian.
EXPURGATE (ex *out* + pugere *to cleanse*) *to remove objectionable matter*, expurgation, expurgator, expurgatorial, expurgatory.
PURE *clear; absolute, faultless*, purely, pureness.
IMPURE *adulterated, obscene*, impurely, impureness, impurity.
PURITY *freedom from improper materials or views*.
PURIFY (purus *pure* + facere *to make*) *rid of impurities; free from corrupting influences*, purification, purificative, purificator, purificatory, purifier.
PURITAN *one strict in morals and religion*, puritanic, puritanical, puritanically, puritanism, puritanize.
PURISM *strict usage and purity of language*, purist, puristic, puristical.

PUT — *think*

PUTO, PUTARE *to trim, to think,* PUTATUM   68
AMPUTATE (amb *about* + putare *to trim*) *to cut off (as a human limb)*, amputation, amputator, amputee.
COMPUTE *to reckon; to ascertain*, computation, computer, computerize.
DEPUTE *to appoint an agent*, deputable, deputation, deputator, deputize, deputy.
DISPUTE *to argue; to quarrel*, disputable, disputeness, disputably, disputant, disputation, disputatious, disputatiously, disputatiousness, disputative, disputer.
INDISPUTABLE *incontravertible*, indisputability, indisputableness, indisputably.
IMPUTE *to attribute a fault to another*, imputability, imputable, imputableness, imputably, imputation, imputative, imputatively, imputer.

PUT
think

PUTATIVE *supposed; reputed*, putation.

REPUTE *to hold in general opinion*, reputability, reputable, reputableness, reputably, reputation, reputedly; unreputable.

DISREPUTE *dishonor; disfavor*, disreputability, disreputable, disreputably.

ACCOUNT *a sum; a computation; a narrative*, accountable, accountableness, accountably, accountancy, accountant, accounting.

UNACCOUNTABLE *not responsible*, unaccountability, unaccountableness, unaccountably.

DISCOUNT *a deduction*, discountable, discounter.

RECOUNT *to relate, to narrate*, recountal.

QUAD
four

QUATTUOR *four*   **25**

QUADRABLE *in mathematics, capable of being square.*

QUADRANGLE *in geometry, a plane having four angles (and sides)*, quadrangular, quadrilateral.

QUADRANT *"the fourth part" or 90°; an instrument for measuring elevations and altitudes.*

QUADRATE *a square or rectangle.*

QUADRENNIAL *lasting for four years.*

QUADRILINGUAL *using or speaking four languages.*

QUADRILLE *a French square dance with four couples.*

QUADRILLION *a fifth power of a thousand; a 1 followed by 15 zeros.*

QUADRIPARTITE *divided in four parts or shared by four people.*

QUADROON *offspring of a mulatto and white; has one quarter Negro blood.*

QUADRUPLE *to make four times as many*, quadruplicate, quadruplication.

QUADRUPLET *one of four born together.*

QUARANTINE *a 40-day period of isolation for anyone suspected of an infectious disease.*

QUARRY *small square tiles.*

QUART *a fourth of a gallon.*

QUARTERLY *four times a year.*

QUARTET *music in four parts, or four players or singers.*

QUATRAIN *a poem of four lines, which lines rhyme among themselves.*

SQUARE *having four equal sides and angles.*

SQUAD *the smallest military tactical unit; a group of players.*

SQUADRON a square body of troops.

QUES / QUIR — seek, gain

QUAERO, QUAERERE *to seek, gain,* **QUAESITUM**   65

QUERY *an inquiry or question.*

QUEST *an act of seeking.*

QUESTION *an asking; inquiry; doubt,* questionability, questionable, questionableness, questionably, questionary, questioner, questionist, questionless.

UNQUESTIONABLE *certain; not disputed,* unquestionably, unquestionability, unquestioning.

CONQUEST *the process of conquering.*

CONQUER *to subdue; to gain by force,* conquerable, conquerableness, conqueress, conqueringly, conqueror.

UNCONQUERED unconquerable.

INQUEST *a judicial inquiry.*

REQUEST (re *again* + quaerere *to seek*) *that which is asked or begged for,* requester.

ACQUIRE *to get by one's own actions,* acquirement.

ACQUISITION *the act of acquiring; the thing acquired,* acquisitive, acquisitively, acquisitiveness, acquisitor.

DISQUISITION *a formal written discussion on a subject,* disquisitional, disquisitionary, disquisitive, disquisitorial.

INQUIRE *to ask questions; to seek for the truth,* inquirer, inquiring, inquiringly, inquiry.

INQUISITION *a religious or legal inquest,* inquisitional, inquisitionist.

INQUISITIVE *asking more questions than necessary,* inquisitively, inquisitiveness, inquisitor, inquisitorially, inquisitorious.

PERQUISITE *something to which a person is entitled to by status or position.*

PERQUISITION *a thorough search.*

REQUIRE *to demand; to have a need for,* requirable, requirement, requirer.

REQUISITE *required by the nature of the circumstances,* requisitely, requisiteness.

REQUISITION *a formal written order requesting,* requisitionist.

PREREQUISITE *a necessary condition for something to follow.*

QUIE — quiet

QUIES, QUIETIS *rest, peace*   30

QUIET *calm; hushed, still,* quietly, quietness, quietude.

DISQUIET *to make anxious,* disquieter, disquieting, disquietful, disquietment, disquietness, disquietude.

QUIESCE *to be silent or quiet,* quiescence, quiescent, quiescently.

QUIE
quiet

ACQUIESCE *apparently satisfied to accept without opposition,* acquiescence, acquiescent, acquiescently.
ACQUIT *to exonerate; to release from duty,* acquitment, acquittal, acquittance, acquitter.
REQUIEM *a musical service for the dead.*
REQUIESCAT *prayer for the repose of the dead.*
COY *pretending shyness to attract,* coyish, coyly, coyness.

RAD
ray
spoke

RADIUS *spoke of a wheel*   18
RAY *beams of light from a bright source; several lines radiating from a center,* rayless.
RADIUS *any straight line from the center to the edge of a circle.*
RADIAL *spreading in all directions from a common center,* radially.
RADIANT *filled with light; showing pleasure and joy,* radiantly.
RADIATE *to send out rays of heat or light; to spread happiness and love,* radiately.
RADIATOR *anything that radiates heat or cools the engine.*
ERADIATE *to shoot out, as rays of light,* eradiation.
IRRADIATE *to illuminate; to enlighten intellectually,* irradiance, irradiancy, irradiant, irradiation, irradiative.

RADI
root

RADIX, RADICIS *a root*   15
RADICAL *going to the source of something; one favoring extreme change,* radicalism, radicality, radically, radicalness.
RADICAND *the quantity under a radical sign.*
RADICANT *in botany, rooting.*
RADICLE *in anatomy, the rootlike beginning of a nerve or vein.*
RADISH *a pungent root, eaten raw or in salad.*
RADIX *in linguistics, a root or base.*
ERADICATE (e *from* + radix *root*) *"to pull out by the roots,"* eradicable, eradication, eradicative, eradicator.

RAP
seize

RAPIO, RAPERE *to seize,* RAPTUM   28
RAPE *carrying off by force; a flagrant violation; unconsented sexual relations with a female,* rapacious, rapaciously, rapaciousness, rapacity, rapist.
RAPINE *the act of plundering.*

RAP
RAV
seize

RAPID *swift; quick*, rapidity, rapidly.
RAPIDS *where a stream moves swiftly because of land drop.*
RAPTURE *an expression of great pleasure*, rapturize, rapturously, rapturely.
ENRAPTURE *to delight greatly*, enrapt.
RAVAGE *to devastate by any means*, ravager.
RAVISH *to seize by force; to carry away with emotion.*
RAVINE *a gorge; a long narrow gully worn down by a stream.*
SURREPTITIOUS (sub *under* + rapere *to seize*) *done by stealth; clandestine*, surreptitiously.
USURP (usus *use* + rapere *to seize*) *assume possession by force or without right*, usurpation, usurpatory, usurper, usurpingly.

RAT
think

REOR, RATUS *think, reckon*   41
RATE (*vb*) *to value,* (*n*) *a fixed charge*, rateable, rateably, rater; underrate, overrate.
RATIFY (ratus *firm* + facere *to make*) *to give formal approval to*, ratification, ratifier.
RATIO *a relation in number between two similar things.*
RATIOCINATE *to reason using formal logic*, ratiocination, ratiocinative.
RATION *a fixed share or allowance.*
RATIONAL *showing reason, not foolishness*, rationalism, rationalist, rationalistic, rationalistically, rationality.
RATIONALE *the fundamental reasons of something.*
RATIONALIZE *to explain; a sympathetic explanation of behavior blacking out the true motivation.*
IRRATIONAL *contrary to reason*, irrationalism, irrationality, irrationally, irrationalness.
REASON *ability to make judgments*, reasonability, reasoner, reasoning, reasonless; unreason, unreasoning.
REASONABLE *moderate; not excessive or unjust*, reasonableness, reasonably; unreasonable, unreasonableness, unreasonably.

RECT
rule

REGO, REGERE *to rule*, RECTUM; RECTUS *straight*; REX *king*   101
ARRECT *erect, upright*, arrected.
CORRECT *to make right*, correctable, correction, correctional, correctitude, corrective, correctly, correctness, corrector, correctress; uncorrected.

RECT
REG
rule
straight

INCORRECT *wrong, untrue, improper,* incorrectly, incorrectness.

DIRECT (a) *straight, not deviating.*

DIRECT (v) *manage the affairs of,* direction, directional, directive, directly, directness.

DIRECTOR *a person who directs or controls,* directorate, directorial, directorship, directory, directress, directrix.

INDIRECT *deviating from a direct line,* indirectness.

ERECT (e *out, up* + regere *to make straight*) *to raise or set up in an upright position,* erectable, erecter, erector, erectile, erectility, erection, erective, erectly, erectness.

RECTIFY (rectus *right* + facere *to make*) *"to make right,"* rectifiable, rectification, rectificator, rectifier.

RECTITUDE *conduct according to moral principles.*

RIGHTEOUS *acting in a just and virtuous manner,* righteously, righteousness; uprighteous.

RECTOR *a particular minister; headmaster of certain schools.*

RECTUM *lowest segment of the large intestine.*

REALM *a royal jurisdiction.*

REGAL (regere *to rule*) *in a splendid or stately manner,* regalism, regality, regally.

INTERREGUM *period between two successive reigns.*

REGALIA *the privileges and trappings of a king.*

REGALE *to entertain,* regalement.

REGENCY *the authority of a regent or group of regents.*

REGICIDE *the killing of a sovereign,* regicidal.

ROYAL *of a king or kingdom,* royalism, royalist, royally, royalty.

REGIME *a political or social system,* regimen.

REGIMENT *a military unit of three battalions.*

REGION *a particular part of the world,* regional, regionalism.

REGULAR *conforming in arrangement and form to rule and standard,* regularity, regularize, regularly, regularness.

IRREGULAR *not according to the common form,* irregularity, irregularly.

REGULATE *to govern or control according to rule or system,* regulation, regulative, regulator, regulatable.

REIGN *royal authority; dominance.*

RULE (regula *a straight piece of wood*) *an established guide for action or conduct,* rulable, ruler, ruling, rulingly, ruleness, rulelessness; unruly; misrule.

RHE
flow
speak

[Gr] **RHEO** *I speak;* **RHETOR** *an orator;* **RHEUMA** *that which flows*   27

RHETOR *an instructor in rhetoric.*
RHETORIC *art of using words effectively in speaking and writing*, rhetorical, rhetorically, rhetoricalness, rhetorician.
RHEUM *a watery discharge from the eyes, nose, or mouth*, rheumic, rheumy.
RHEUMATIC *a person suffering from rheumatism.*
RHEUMATISM *painful conditions of the muscles or joints*, rheumatismal, rheumatismoid, rheumatoid.
HEMORRHAGE (*Gr.* haima *blood* + rheginai *burst*) *heavy bleeding*, hemorrhagic.
HEMORROID *painful swelling in the region of the anus*, hemorrhoidal.
DIARRHEA (*Gr.* dis *through* + rheein *to flow*) *a frequent discharge from the bowels.*
GONORRHEA (gonos *semen*) *a discharge in venereal complaints.*
RESIN *a material exuded from trees, or made artificaly*, resinify, resiniferous.
CATARRH *a mucous secretion of the nose*, catarrhal.
CHOLER *anger; irritation of the passions.*
CHOLERA *a formerly widespread fatal disease of the intestines.*

RID RIS
laugh

RIDEO, RIDERE *to laugh,* **RISUM**   19

RIDICULE *derision; contempt; mockery*, ridiculer.
RIDICULOUS *ludicrous; absurd*, ridiculosity, ridiculously, ridiculousness; unridiculous.
DERIDE *make fun of; laugh in comtempt*, deridingly, derisible.
DERISION *scorn; ridicule*, derisive, derisively, derisiveness, derisory.
RISIBLE *inclined to laugh; causing laughter*, risibility, risibleness, risibly.

RIV
river

RIVUS *a river;* **RIPA** *a bank*   21

ARRIVE (ad *to* + ripa *bank*) *"to come to the shore"; to reach one's destination*, arrival, arriver.
DERIVE *to draw from; to deduce or infer*, derivability, derivable, derivably, derivation, derivational, derivationalist, derivative, derivatively, derivativeness, deriver.
RIVER *a large stream emptying into more water.*
RIVULET *a small stream.*
RIPARIAN *legal rights of one owning land bordering a waterway.*

RIV
river

RIVAL *thought to be early competitors on a stream; one in pursuit of the same object as another*, rivalry.
OUTRIVAL *to surpass.*
UNRIVALED *not equal to.*

ROG
ask

ROGO, ROGARE *to ask,* ROGATUM   42

ABROGATE *to repeal; to abolish*, abrogable, abrogation; unabrogated.
ARROGATE *to lay claim in an overbearing manner*, arrogation, arrogative.
ARROGANCE *full of unwarranted pride and self-importance*, arrogancy, arrogant, arrogantly.
DEROGATE (de *from* + rogare *to ask*) *degenerate; to worsen one's position*, derogation.
DEROGATORY *disparagingly; belittling*, derogative, derogatively, derogator, derogatorily, derogatoriness.
INTERROGATE *to formally examine by questioning*, interrogatee, interrogation, interrogative, interrogatively, interrogator, interrogatorily.
INTERROGATORY *a formal set of questions; in law, a question asked in writing.*
PREROGATIVE *a superior advantage; an exclusive right of rank*, prerogatively.
SUPEREROGATE *to do more than duty requires*, supererogation, supererogative, supererogatory.
SURROGATE *one appointed to act for another*, surrogateship, surrogation.
SUBROGATE *to substitute one person or thing for another*, subrogation.
PROROGUE *to discontinue a legislative session*, prorogate, prorogation.
ROGATION *prayer chanted in three days before Ascension Day.*

RUPT
break

RUMPO, RUMPERE *to break,* RUPTUM   44

ABRUPT *broken off suddenly*, abruption, abruptly, abruptness.
BANKRUPT *one who fails in business*, bankruptcy.
CORRUPT (com *together* + rumpere *to break*) *morally unsound; debased*, corrupter, corruptibility, corruptible, corruptibleness, corruptibly, corruption, corruptionist, corruptive, corruptless, corruptly, corruptness, corruptress.
INCORRUPT *upright; honest*, incorruptibility, incorruptible, incorruptibleness, incorruptibly, incorruption, incorruptly, incorruptness.
UNCORRUPT *integrity*, uncorrupted, uncorruptness.
DISRUPT *to break apart*, disruption, disruptive, disruptor.
ERUPT *to burst forth or out*, eruption, eruptional, eruptive.

RUPT
break

INTERRUPT *to break into or upon*, interruptedly, interruption, interruptive, interruptively.

IRRUPT *burst in*, irruption, irruptive.

RUPTURE *breaking apart; breaking off friendly relations*, ruption, rupturable.

SACR
SECR
holy

SACER *holy* 41

SACRED *made holy, dedicated to person or purpose*, sacredly, sacredness.

SACERDOTAL *belief in divine authority of the priesthood*, sacerdotalism, sacerdotally.

SACRAMENT *a solemn oath or pledge, as ratified by a rite*, sacramental, sacramentalism, sacramentalist, sacramentally.

SACRIFICE *foregoing of some valued thing for the sake of something considered better*, sacrificable, sacrificator, sacrificatory, sacrificer, sacrificial.

SACRILEGE *disrespectful of treatment of persons, things, or ideas held sacred*, sacrilegious, sacrilegiously, sacrilegiousness.

SACRISTAN *a sexton; an officer in charge of sacristy.*

SACRISTY *room of the church where sacred utensils are kept.*

SACROSANCT *very holy; inviolable*, sacrosanctity.

CONSECRATE *declare to be sacred*, consecratedness, consecration, consecrator, consecratory; unconsecrated.

DESECRATE *to profane*, desecrater, desecration, desecrator.

EXECRATE *to curse; to detest utterly*, execration, execrative, execratively, execrator, execratory.

SAL
SULT
SIL
leap

SALIO, SALIRE *to leap*, SALTUM 51

SALACIOUS *lustful, lecherous*, salaciously, salaciousness, salacity.

SALIENT *standing out from the rest*, salience, saliency.

SALLY *a sudden start of activity; a quick witticism.*

SALMON *"a leaper"; a game fish*, salmonet.

ASSAIL (ad *to* + salire *to leap*) *to leap upon with violence; to attack with arguments*, assailable, assailant, assailer, assailment.

UNASSAIL *impregnable*, unassailable, unassailably.

ASSAULT (ad *to* + salire *to leap*) *to attack with weapons; to attack with hostile words; in law, a threat or attempt to attack physically*, assaultable, assaulter; unassaulted.

DESULTORY *random; passing from one subject to another disconnectedly*, desultorily, desultoriness, desultorious.

SAL / SULT / SIL — *leap*

EXULT *to rejoice greatly,* exultance, exultant, exultation, exultingly.
INSULT *any act or speech intended to hurt the feelings of another,* insultant, insulter, insulting, insultless.
RESULT *to happen as a consequence of some cause,* resultance, resultant, resulting, resultless.
SUBSULTORY *moving by sudden leaps,* subsultive, subsultorily, subsultus.
DISSILIENT *bursting apart.*
RESILIENT *recovering quickly,* resile, resilience.
TRANSILIENT *leaping from one thing to another,* transilience.

SAL — *healthy, safe*

SALUS, *health;* SALVUS *safe;* SALUBRIS *healthgiving*   35
SALUBRIOUS *promoting health,* salubriously, salubriousness, salubrity.
INSALUBRIOUS insalubrity.
SALUTARY *promoting a beneficial purpose;* insalutary, unsalutary.
SALUTATION *an act of greeting or paying respect,* salutatorian, salutatorily, salutatory.
SALUTE *to welcome in a customary manner;* unsaluted.
SALVAGE *saving of a crew or cargo, and compensation,* salvor.
SALVATION *rescue from danger; redemption of man from sin,* salvationism, salvationist.
SALVE *to sooth, assuage; to flatter.*
SALVO *burst of shouts or gunfire; in law, a reservation.*
SAFE *free from danger; cautious,* safely, safeness, safety; unsafe.
SAVE *remove from harm; to preserve for further use,* saveable, saver, saving, savingly, savingness; unsaved.
SAVIOR *one who saves; Jesus Christ.*

SANCT — *holy*

SANCTUS *holy*   20
SAINT *a holy person,* sainthood, saintlike, saintness, saintly.
SANCTION *authorization; approval; something that makes a rule of conduct binding;* unsanctioned.
SANCTITY *anything held sacred,* sanctitude.
SANCTUARY *church or temple; a place of refuge or protection.*
SANCTIFY (sanc *holy* + facere *to make*) "to make holy," sanctification, sanctifier, sanctifyingly; unsanctified.
SANCTIMONIOUS *saintly; pretending to be holy or pious,* sanctimoniously, sanctimoniousness, sanctimony.
SANCTUM SANCTORUM *"holy of holies."*

SAP / SIP — *taste*

SAPIO, SAPERE *to taste;* **SAPOR** *flavor*   27
SAPID *a pleasing taste; having interest,* sapidity, sapidness.
SAPIENT *discerning; sagacious (sometimes used ironically),* sapience, sapiential, sapientially, sapiently.
HOMO SAPIENS *man, the only living species of the genus Homo.*
SAPOR *that quality producing taste or flavor,* saporific, saporosity, saporous.
RESIPISCENCE *wisdom derived from severe experience.*
INSIPID *tasteless; lacking ability to excite,* insipidity, insipidly, insipidness.
INSIPIENCE *foolishness; lack of understanding,* insipient.
SAVOR *power to excite interest; something that affects taste and smell,* savorily, savoriness, savorless, savorly, savory.
UNSAVORY *unpleasant taste or smell; morally offensive.*

SCEND — *climb*

SCANDO, SCANDERE *to climb,* **SCANSUM**   44
ASCEND *to move upward,* ascendable, ascendance, ascendancy, ascendant, ascender, ascending, ascendingly, ascensive, ascent.
ASCENSION *the bodily rising of Jesus to heaven,* ascensional.
REASCEND *to climb again,* reascension, reascent.
UNASCENDABLE unascended.
CONDESCEND *to be affable with inferiors,* condescendence, condescending, condescendingly, condescension.
DESCEND *to come downward,* descendable, descendent, descender, descendibility, descendible, descending, descendingly, descension, descensional, descensive, descent; undescendible.
DESCENDANT *an individual offspring of certain ancestors.*
TRANSCEND (trans *over* + scandere *to climb*) *to surpass; to exceed,* transcendence, transcendent.
TRANSCENDENTAL *Kant transcending experience but not knowledge,* transcendence, transcendent.
SCAN *to glance at quickly; to analyze; to scrutinize;* unscanned.

SCI — *know*

SCIO, SCIRE *to know,* **SCITUM; SCIENTIA** *wisdom*   34
CONSCIENCE *feeling of right or wrong; moral judgment,* conscienceless.
CONSCIENTIOUS *faithfully; scrupulously,* conscientiously, conscientiousness.
CONSCIONABLE *according to conscience.*
UNCONSCIONABLE *unscrupulous,* unconscionableness, unconscionably.
CONSCIOUS *awake; having a feeling of one's own sensations,* consciously,

SCI
know

consciousness.
SELF-CONSCIOUS *ill-at-ease; embarrassed*, self-consciousness.
UNCONSCIOUS *not known or realized*, unconsciously, unconsciousness.
SCIENCE *systematized knowledge to determine principles being studied*, sciential, scientific, scientifically, scientism, scientist.
UNSCIENTIFIC unscientifically.
PRESCIENCE *foreknowing*, prescient, presciently.
OMNISCIENCE *universal knowledge (God)*, omniscient, omnisciently.
SCIOLIST *a pretender of learning*, sciolism, sciolistic.

SCOP
see

[Gr] SKOPEO *I see;* SKEPTOMAI *I consider*   **35**
SCOPE *range of view; area the mind can cover; extent of action.*
SKEPTIC *one who habitually doubts*, skeptical, skeptically, skepticalism, skepticism, skepticize.
MICROSCOPE (mikro *small* + skopein *to view*) *an instrument for examining very small objects*, microscopic, microscopical, microscopically, microscopist, microscopy.
STETHOSCOPE *a hearing instrument for examining the heart, lungs, etc.*, stethoscopic, stethoscopically, stethoscopist, stethoscopy.
TELESCOPE *an instrument for making distant objects appear near*, telescopic, telescopical, telescopically, telescopist, telescopy.
EPISCOPACY *government of the church by bishops*, episcopal, episcopalian, episcopalianism, episcopally, episcopate, episcoture, episcopize.
BISHOP (epi *upon* + skopos *look*) *a high-ranking clergyman with authority over a church district*, bishopdom, bishopric.

SCRIB
SCRIPT
write

SCRIBO, SCRIBERE *to write,* SCRIPTUM   **80**
ASCRIBE *to attribute to a source; to consider to belong to*, ascription, ascriptious.
CIRCUMSCRIBE *to enclose within a certain limit*, circumscribable, circumscriber, circumscriptible, circumscription, circumscriptive, circumscriptively, circumscriptly; uncircumscribed.
CONSCRIPT *to draft for the military*, conscription.
DESCRIBE (de *from* + scribere *to write*) *to give a detailed account; to picture*, describable, describer; undescribed, undescribable.
DESCRIPTION *the act of delineating*, descriptive, descriptively, descriptiveness.
INDESCRIBABLE indescribability, indescribably.

SCRIB / SCRIPT — *write*

NONDESCRIPT *hard to classify or describe.*
INSCRIBE *to mark or engrave the name on; briefly dedicate something,* inscribable, inscriber.
INSCRIPTION inscriptional, inscriptive.
PRESCRIBE *to set down as a rule,* prescriber, prescript, prescriptibility, prescriptible.
PRESCRIPTION *a written direction or order for one to follow,* prescriptive, prescriptively.
PROSCRIBE *to forbid; exile, banish,* proscriber, proscript, proscription, proscriptional, proscriptionist, proscriptive.
RESCRIPTION *a writing back; a new copy,* rescript, rescriptive.
SCRIBE *a pointed metallic instrument; a professional writer.*
SCRIBAL *arising from the process of writing,* scribable.
SCRIBBLE *writing that is careless or illegible,* scribbler.
SCRIPT *handwriting.*
POST SCRIPT *a note added to a letter after it is concluded and signed.*
SCRIPTURE *the Biblical Scripture,* Scriptural, Scripturalism, Scripturalist, Scripturally.
SUBSCRIBE (sub *under* + scribere *to write*) "to write one's name beneath," *to support,* subscribable, subscriber.
SUBSCRIPTION *a written signature or consent,* subscript, subscriptive, subscriptively.
SUPERSCRIBE *to write or engrave on the top or outer surface,* superscript, superscription.
TRANSCRIBE *to make a copy of a speech; to arrange music for another instrument or voice; to pre-record for radio,* transcriber.
TRANSCRIPT *a copy or reproduction of any kind,* transcription, transcriptive, transcriptively.

SECT — *cut*

SECO, SECARE *to cut,* SECTUM   43

SECANT *any straight line intersecting a curve at two or more points,* secancy.
SECT *a part of a section; any group holding certain veiws with common leadership.*
SECTARIAN *devoted to some sect; narrow-minded,* sectarianism, sectarianize.
SECTION *the process of cutting; a distinct part,* sectional, sectionalism, sectionalization, sectionalize, sectionally; subsection.
SECTOR *a part of a circle divided by two radii,* sectoral.

SECT
cut

SEGMENT *any of the parts in which a body is divided*, segmental, segmentally, segmentary, segmentation, segmented; intersegmented.
BISECT *to divide into two (equal) parts*, bisection, bisector.
TRISECT *to divide into three (equal) parts*, trisection, trisector.
DISSECT *to examine closely; to cut a body into parts for study*, dissectible, dissecting, dissection, dissector.
VIVISECTION *an operation of a living animal to determine research results.*
INTERSECT *to meet and cross each other*, intersection, intersectional.
INSECT (in *into* + secare *to cut*) *so called because some insects appear to be cut into segments.*
INSECTIFUGE *any preparation that will drive away insects.*
INSECTICIDE *any substance used to kill insects*, insecticidal.
INSECTIVORA *any mammal that feeds primarily on insects*, insectivorous.

SENS SENT
feel

SENTIO, SENTIRE *to feel*, SENSUM   98
ASSENT *to agree*, assenter, assentor, assentient, assenting, assentingly, assentive, assentment.
CONSENT *to be of the same opinion*, consensus, consentable.
DISSENT *to disagree in opinion*, dissenter, dissenterism, dissentient, dissension.
INSENSATE *lacking sensation or feeling*, insensately, insensateness.
INSENSIBLE *unaware, void of feeling*, insensibility, insensibleness, insensibly, insensible.
NONSENSE *words or actions of absurd meaning or no meaning*, nonsensical, nonsensicality, nonsensically, nonsensicalness.
PRES'ENT (*n*) (*adj*) *existing or happening now.*
PRESENT' (*v*) (*n*) *introduce, exhibit, perform; make a gift*, presentability, presentable, presentably, presentative, presentee, presenter, presently.
PRESENTATION *something that is presented, such as a plea for something or a gift*, presentational.
PRESENTIMENT *a previous conception or foreboding.*
RESENT (re *again* + sentire *to feel*) *to feel or show displeasure*, resenter, resentful, resentfully, resentingly, resentment.
SCENT *to smell; to have a suspicion of*, scentful, scentless.
SENTENCE *a judgment; a complete group of words with a subject and predicate.*
SENTIENT *capable of peception*, sentience, sentiency, sentiently.

SENS / SENT — *feel*

INSENTIENT *not having consciousness or perception.*

SENTENTIOUS *expressing much in words; pithy, using maxims; trite and moralizing,* sententiously, sententiousness.

SENTIMENT *generalized emotional attitude,* sentimental, sentimentalism, sentimentalist, sentimentality, sentimentalize, sentimentally.

SENSE *an impression through the sense or intellect,* senseful, senseless, senselessly, senselessness.

CONSENSUS *unanimity; general opinion.*

SENSATION *the power of impressions through bodily organisms,* sensate, sensational, sensationalism, sensationalist, sensationalistic, sensationalize.

SENSIBLE *possessing sense and reason; easily perceived,* sensibility, sensibleness, sensibly; supersensible, supersensibly.

SENSITIVE *keen sensibilities; easily offended by others,* sensitively, sensitiveness, sensitivity, sensitization, sensitize, sensitizer; supersensitive, supersensitiveness.

DESENSITIZE *to make less sensitive.*

SENSUAL *preoccupation with bodily or sexual pleasure,* sensualism, sensualist, sensualistic, sensuality, sensualization, sensualize, sensually, sensualness; supersensual.

CONSENSUAL *in law, formed by mere mutual consent.*

SENSUOUS *easily affected through the senses,* sensory, sensitory, sensorium; supersensory, supersensuous.

SENTINEL *a person or animal that guards against surprise.*

SENTRY *a military guard posted to give warning.*

SENTENTIAL *of a grammatical sentence; nature of a decision or judicial sentence.*

SEQ / SEC — *follow*

SEQUOR, SEQUI *to follow,* SECUTUS   78

CONSEQUENCE *an event cause by preceeding act,* consequent, consequently, consequential, consequentially, consequentialness.

INCONSEQUENCE *lack of relevance or logical sequence,* inconsequent, inconsequential, inconsequentiality, inconsequentially, inconsequentness.

OBSEQUIOUS *excessively willing to obey,* obsequiously, obsequiousness; unobsequiousness.

SEQUACIOUS *pliant; tending to follow any leader,* sequaciously, sequaciousness, sequacity.

SEQ
SEC
follow

SEQUEL *something that comes as a result of something else.*
SEQUENCE *a particular order of succession*, sequent, sequential, sequentially.
SUBSEQUENCE *following in time or order*, subsequency, subsequent, subsequently.
CONSECUTIVE *folowing in order*, *successive*, consecution, consecutively, consecutiveness.
EXECUTIVE (ex *out* + sequi *to follow*) *to carry into effect*, executable, executant, executer, execution, executioner; unexecuted.
INEXECUTION *failure to do something*, inexecutable.
EXECUTOR *a doer, one who executes a will*, executorial, executorship, executory, executrix.
PERSECUTE (per *through* + sequi *to follow*) *to harrass constantly so as to distress*, persecution, persecutive, persecutor, persecutrix.
PROSECUTE *to institute legal proceedings against*, prosecutable, prosecution, prosecutor, prosecutrix.
SUE *in law, to institute legal action*, suer, suable, suability.
ENSUE *to follow as a consequence; to come afterward.*
PURSUE (pro *forth* + sequi *to follow*) *to follow after, to chase*, pursuance, pursuant, pursuantly, pursuer, pursuit.
SUIT *in law and also in clothes*, suited.
SUITABLE *fitting, appropriate*, suitability, suitableness, suitably.
SUITE *retainers; a series of related things; a musical form.*
SUITOR *one who sues; a petitioner; a wooer.*

SERT
join

SERO, SERERE *to bind*, SERTUM   37
ASSERT (ad *to* + serere *to bind*) *to affirm positively*, asserter, assertion, assertional, assertive, assertively, assertiveness, assertor, assertorial, assertory.
REASSERT *to say again after stopping*, reassertion.
DES'ERT (*n*) (*a*) *a dry barren region.*
DESERT' (*n*) *deserving reward or punishment*, desertlessly.
DESERT' (*vb*) *to forsake; to leave without permission*, deserter, desertion.
DISSERTATION *an elaborate formal discourse on a subject*, dissertational, dissertationist, dissertator.
EXERT (ex *out* + serere *to join*) *to bring into active operation*, exertion, exertive.
INSERT *to put something into something else*, inserting, insertion.
REINSERT *to insert a second time*, reinsertion.

SERT
join

SERIAL *appearing in a succession of continuous parts*, seriality, serialize, serially.
SERIATIM *point by point; in regular order.*
SERIES *a continual series of similar things*, seriation.

SERV
save

SERVO, SERVARE *to save, keep,* SERVATUM   53
CONSERVE *to keep in a safe and sound state*, conservant, conservable, conservancy, conserver.
CONSERVATION *the official protection of natural resources*, conservational, conservationalist.
CONSERVATIVE *one who wishes to preserve traditions or resist innovations*, conservativeness, conservatism.
CONSERVATORY *a greenhouse; a school for teaching arts or music*, conservatoire.
CONSERVATOR *a guardian appointed by the court*, conservatrix.
OBSERVE (ob *before* + servare *to keep*) *to adhere to rules, laws, customs; to perceive something; to mention casually*, observer, observing, observingly; unobserved.
OBSERVANCE *keeping the laws, customs, rules*, observancy, observant, observantly; unobservant.
OBSERVABLE *that can be perceived*, observableness; inobservable; unobservable.
INOBSERVANCE *lack of attention*, inobservancy, inobservant, inobservantly.
OBSERVATORY *any place with an extensive view; for astronomical and meteorological research.*
OBSERVATION *the practice of noting and recording facts; comments on such facts*, observational.
PRESERVE *to protect, to keep from harm or damage*, preservable, preserver, preservation, preservative, preservatory; self-preservation.
RESERVE (re *back* + servare *to keep*) *to hold for a later time*, reservedly, reservedness, reserver, reservist.
UNRESERVE *frankness, candor*, unreserved, unreservedly.
RESERVATION *a withholding; public lands for Indians or the military.*
RESERVOIR [*Fr*] *storeplace for community water.*

SERV

SERVIO, SERVIRE *to serve, obey;* SERVITIUM *servitude*   38
DESERVE *to merit, to be worthy of*, deservedly, deservedness, deserver,

SERV
serve

deserving, deservingly; undeserved, undeserving.
DISSERVE (dis *away* + servire *to serve*) *to injure, to harm*, disservice, disserviceable, disserviceableness, disserviceably.
SERVE *to work for; carry out the duties of*, server.
SUBSERVE (sub *under* + servire *to serve*) *to be helpful in an inferior capacity*, subservience, subserviency, subservient, subserviently.
SERVICE *work done for a superior*, serviceability, serviceable, serviceableness, serviceably; unserviceable.
SERVANT *one employed to perform services*, servantry.
SERVITOR *a servant, a follower, an adherent*.
SERVILE *like a slave; humbling, yielding or submissive*, servilely, servileness, servility.
SERVITUDE *slavery; involuntary subjection to a master*.
SERF *a slave; anyone oppressed*, serfage, serfdom, serfhood.
SERGEANT *a policeman or armyman below a lieutenant*.

SES SED SID
sit

SEDEO, SEDERE *to sit*, SESSUM   80

ASSESS *to set the amount of damages; to critically view*, assessable, assessably, assession, assessment, assessorial, assessor.
OBSESS *to preoccupy, to haunt the mind*, obsession, obsessive.
POSSESS *to occupy in person; to cause to have*, possessed, possession, possessionary, possessioner, possessive, possessively, possessor, possessory.
DISPOSSESS *to deprive of a possession*, dispossession, dispossessor.
PREPOSSESS *to preoccupy beforehand; to impress favorably beforehand*, prepossessing, prepossessingly, prepossession, prepossessor.
SESSION *one meeting or a group of meetings*, sessional.
SEDAN *a chair or special enclosed automobile*.
SEDATE *serene, dignified*, sedately, sedateness.
SEDIMENT *anything that settles to the bottom in liquid*, sedimental, sedimentarily, sedimentary, sedimentation.
SEDENTARY *liking to sit; remaining in one spot*, sedentarily, sedentariness.
SEDULOUS *diligent in application*, sedulity, sedulousness, sedulously.
SUPERCEDE (super *above* + sedere *to sit*) *to move to make way for another*, supercedure.
ASSIZE *certain courts of England; a former weight regulation*, assizer.
ASSIDUOUS *performed with constant diligence*, assiduity, assiduousness.
INSIDIOUS *treacherous, wily, crafty*, insidiously, insidiousness.

SES SED SID
sit

PRESIDE (pre *before* + sidere *to sit*) *to have control or authority.*
PRESIDIO *a garrison*, presidiary.
PRESIDENT *the highest officer of an organization*, presidency, presidential, presidentship.
RESIDE *to dwell for a length of time*, residence, residency, resident, residential, residentiary, residentship, resider.
RESIDUAL *what is left at the end of the process*, residuary, residue, residuum.
SIEGE *a continual endeavor to gain possession.*
BESIEGE *to beset*, besiegement, besieger, besieging, besiegingly.

SIGN
mark
sign

SIGNO, SIGNARE *to mark*   68

ASSIGN (ad *to* + signare *to mark*) *to designate or appoint for a particular purpose*, assignability, assignable, assignee, assigner, assignment, assignor.
ASSIGNATION *a secret meeting of lovers; in law, a transference of a claim.*
CONSIGN *to transfer over.*
CONSIGNMENT *goods sent to an agent for sale or safekeeping*, consignation, consignee, cosigner or cosignor.
COUNTERSIGN *a signature added to signed writing to authenticate it*, countersignal, countersignature.
DESIGN (de *out, from* + signare *to mark*) *to plan the outline, to contrive*, designable, designedly, designee, designer, designful, designfulness, designing, designless, designlessly.
DESIGNATE designation, designative, designator; undesignated.
INSIGNIA *marks or signs by which anything is distinguished.*
RESIGN *to give up an office*, resignation, resignedly, resignee, resigner, resignment.
SIGN (vb) *to attach a signature;* (n) *a mark; a remarkable event*, signable; unsigned; undersigned.
CO-SIGNER *one who signs a note, being equally responsible*, co-sign, co-signatory.
ENSIGN *a flag or banner; lowest officer of the navy.*
SIGNAL (n) *a token or indication;* (adj) *remarkable, memorable*, signally, signalize; unsignalized.
SIGNATURE *a person's name written by himself*, signatory.
SIGNIFY *to make a sign or indication.*
SIGNIFICANCE *full of meaning*, significancy, significant, significantly, signification, significative, significatively, significativeness, significator, significatory.
INSIGNIFICANCE *meaningless*, insignificancy, insignificant, insignificantly.

SIMI
SEMB
like

SIMILIS *like* **53**

ASSIMILATE *to make alike; to absorb and incorporate*, assimilability, assimilable, assimilation, assimilative, asssimilatory.

FACSIMILE *an exact copy or likeness.*

SIMILE *a figure of speech in which one thing is likened to another.*

SIMILAR *resembling but not exactly the same*, similarity, similarly.

DISSIMILAR *unlike in nature or form*, dissimilarity, dissimilarly, dissimilate, dissimilation, dissimilative, dissimilitude.

SIMILITUDE *a person or thing resembling another.*

SIMULATE *to pretend; to give a false indication*, simulant, simular, simulation, simulative, simulator, simulatory.

DISSIMULATE *to pretend, to simulate the opposite of*, dissimulation, dissimulative, dissimulator.

VERISIMILAR *having the appearance of truth*, verisimilitude.

SIMULTANEOUS *happening at the same time*, simultaneity, simultaneousness.

ASSEMBLE (ad *to* + simul *together*) *to bring together*, assemblage, assembler, assembling, assembly.

DISSEMBLE *to hide under false appearance*, dissemblance, dissembler, dissembling, dissemblingly.

RESEMBLE *to be alike in appearance or nature*, resemblance, resembler, resembling, resemblingly.

SEMBLANCE *the look of something else*, semblable, semblative.

SIST
stand

SISTO, SISTERE *to stand* **96**

ASSIST *to help; to lend aid*, assistance, assistant, assistantly, assister, assistful, assistive, assistor, assistless; unassisted.

CON'SIST (*n*) *bill of lading.*

CONSIST' (*v*) *to be composed of*, consistency, consistence, consistent, consistently.

INCONSISTENT *incompatible*, inconsistence, inconsistency, inconsistently.

CONSISTORY *an assembly of bishops or prelates*, consistorial, consistorian.

DESIST (de *from* + sistere *to stand*) *to cease to act*, desisting, desistance, desition *end*; undesisting.

EXIST *to live; to be; be present*, existence, existent, existible.

EXISTENTIALISM *Sartre philosophy that free will must combat hostile environment*, existential, existentially.

CO-EXIST *to exist together at the same time or place*, co-existent, co-existing, co-existence.

SIST
stand

PRE-EXIST *to exist before*, pre-existent, pre-existence, pre-existency, pre-existentism *philosophical doctrine that the soul has an existence prior to that of the human body.*

INSIST *to make a firm demand*, insistence, insistency, insistent, insistently.

PERSIST *to refuse to give up*, persistence, persistency, persistent, persistently, persisting, persistingly, persisive.

RESIST *to oppose actively*, resistance, resistant, resister, resistful, resistibility, resistible, resistibleness, resistibly, resisting, resistingly, resistive, resistivity, resistless, resistlessly, resistlessness; unresisted, unresistant, unresisting.

RESISTOR *an electrical device to provide resistance.*

IRRESISTANCE *non-resistance; submission*, irresistibility, irresistible, irresistibleness, irresistibly.

UNRESISTANT unresisted, unresisting; nonresistance, nonresisted.

SUBSIST (sub *under* + sistere *to stand*) *to remain alive by specific means*, subsistence, subsistency, subsistent.

SOCI
companion

SOCIO, SOCIARE *to join together,* SOCIATUM   **34**

ASSOCIATE (ad *to* + sociare *to join*) *to bring one into relationship to oneself and others; to connect in the mind*, association, associational, associationism, associationist, associative, associator; unassociated.

CONSOCIATE *to join together*, consociation, consociational.

DISSOCIATE *to sever the association of*, dissociation, dissociative, disassociate, disassociation.

SOCIABLE *enjoying the company of others*, sociability, sociableness, sociably.

DISSOCIABLE *ill-matched; incongruous*, dissociability.

UNSOCIABLE *avoiding association with others*, unsociability, unsociably.

SOCIAL *living as a member of a group that has dealings with one another*, sociality, socialization, socialize, socialness, socially; unsocial.

DISSOCIAL *tending to avoid society*, dissocialize.

SOCIETY *all people regarded as constituting a community; an organized group joined together with some interest in common.*

SOLI
alone

SOLUS *alone*   **21**

SOLE *one; without others*, solely.

SOLO *any performance by one person alone*, soloist.

SOLILOQUY *a character onstage who reveals his thoughts to the audience, but not to the other characters*, soliloquist, soliloquize.

SOLI
alone

SOLITARY *done in solitude,* solitarily, solitariness.
SOLITUDE *the state of being alone.*
DESOLATE (de *away* + solus *alone*) *deserted; laid waste,* desolately, desolateness, desolater, desolation, desolator, desolatory.
SULLEN *gloomy, dismal, depressing,* sullenly, sullenness.

SOLV
loosen
solve

SOLVO, SOLVERE *to loosen,* SOLUTUM   64

ABSOLVE (ab *from* + solvere *to loosen*) *to release from some obligation,* absolvable, absolvatory; unabsolved.
ABSOLUTE *complete within itself,* absolutely, absoluteness.
ABSOLUTION *in civil law, an acquital; in some churches, a remission of sins.*
DISSOLVE *to convert from solid to liquid,* dissolvability, dissolvable, dissolvableness, dissolvent, dissolver, dissolving, dissolvingly, dissolubility, dissoluble, dissolubleness; undissolved.
DISSOLUTE *loose in behavior and morals,* dissolutely, dissoluteness, dissolution.
RESOLVE (re *again* + solvere *to loosen*) *to cause a person to make up his mind,* resolvability, resolvable, resolvableness, resolvedly, resolvedness, resolvent, resolver.
IRRESOLVABLE *cannot be solved,* irresolvability, irresolvableness, irresolvedly.
RESOLUTE *unwavering, showing a fixed purpose,* resolutely, resoluteness.
RESOLUTION *a thing resolved; a statement adopted by the assembly,* resolutioner, resolutionist.
IRRESOLUTE *given to doubt,* irresolutely, irresoluteness, irresolution.
SOLVE *to find a satisfactory solution,* solver.
SOLVENT *a substance that dissolves or makes a new substance,* solvency.
INSOLVENT *bankrupt; unable to pay debts,* insolvency.
NONSOLVENT *not able to pay debts;* insolvent, nonsolvency.
SOLUBLE *capable of being solved,* solubility, solubleness, solubly.
INSOLUBLE *cannot be explained, or dissolved,* insolubility, insolubleness.

SON

SONUS *a noise, sound*   35
ASSONANCE *likeness; where the stressed vowel sounds are alike but the*

SON
sound

consonants are unlike, assonant, assonantal, assonate.
CONSONANCE *agreement; a pleasing arrangement of simultaneous musical sounds,* consonancy, consonant, consonantal, consonantize, consonantly.
DISSONANCE (dis *from* + sonus *sound*) *an inharmonious sound(s),* dissonancy, dissonant.
RESONANCE *prolongation of sound by vibration of other bodies,* resonant, resonantly; resonate, resonator.
SOUND *the sensation of hearing,* soundable, sounder, sounding, soundless, soundlessly, soundlessness, soundly, soundness.
RESOUND (re *again* + sonare *to sound*) *to reverberate.*
SONOROUS *a full, deep, rich sound,* sonority, sonorously, sonorousness.
SONATA *a composition of a special form for a solo instrument.*
SONNET *a poem of fourteen lines, of several rhyme schemes, with a theme.*
SONIC *a speed equal to sound: 1,088 feet per second, or 738 miles per hour.*

SPECT
SPIC
see
a kind

SPECIO, SPECERE *to look;* SPECIES *a kind*   152
ASPECT *the countenance; appearance as seen by the mind or eye,* aspectant.
ESPECIAL *outstanding,* especially.
EXPECT *to look for as likely to occur,* expectancy, expectant, expectation, expectative, expectedly, expecter, expectingly, expective.
UNEXPECTED *not looking for,* unexpectedly, unexpectedness.
CIRCUMSPECT (circum *around* + specere *to look*) *cautious, watchful, prudent,* circumspection, circumspective, circumspectively, circumspectly, circumspectness.
INSPECT *to examine,* inspection, inspective, inspector, inspectorial, inspectorship.
INTROSPECTION *to look into one's own mind,* introspectionist, introspective.
PERSPECTIVE *showing the relative distance; the relationship of parts to the whole.*
PROSPECT *a probable outcome; a view from a particular point,* prospection, prospective, prospectively, prospectiveness, prospector.
PROSPECTUS *a brief plan of a proposed commercial undertaking.*
RESPECT (re *back* + specere *to look*) *to consider with some deference,* respectability, respectable, respectableness, respectably, respecter, respectful, respectfully, respectfulness, respectably, respecter, respectful, respectfully, respectfulness, respecting.
DISRESPECT *rudeness; lack of respect,* disrespectability, disrespectable,

SPECT
SPIC
see
a kind

disrespectly, disrespectful, disrespectfully, disrespectfulness.
RESPECTIVE *relating personally to two or more things or persons.*
IRRESPECTIVE *without regard to persons or circumstances,* irrespectively.
UNRESPECTED unrespectable, unrespectful.
RETROSPECT (retro *backward* + specere *to look*) *contemplation of something past,* retrospection, retrospective, retrospectively.
SUSPECT *to believe someone guilty with little evidence, to distrust,* suspectedly, suspectedness, suspecter.
UNSUSPECTED *not under suspicion,* unsuspecting.
SPECIAL *unusual, exceptional; designed for a particular purpose,* specialism, specialist, specialistic, speciality, specialization, specialize, specialty.
SPECTATOR *one who looks on,* spectatorial, spectatorship, spectatress.
SPECTACULAR *unusual to a striking degree.*
SPECTER *an apparition; any kind of fear.*
SPECTRAL *ghostly, like a specter.*
SPECTRUM *diffracted white light showing colored bands.*
SPECIFY (species *kind* + facere *to make*) *to define in detail,* specifiable, specific, specifical, specifically, specificalness, specification, specificity, specificness.
SPECIMEN *a part of the whole.*
SPECULATE *to think or theorize on any subject,* speculation, speculatist, speculator, speculative, speculatively, speculativeness, speculativism, speculatory.
SPECIES *a distinct plant or animal with distinguishing characteristics.*
SPECIOUS *plausible but not genuine,* speciosity, speciously, speciousness.
AUSPICE *an omen or sign.*
AUSPICATE *to begin formally or auspiciously.*
AUSPICIOUS *having omens of success or favorable appearances,* auspiciously, auspiciousness.
CONSPICUOUS *easy to see or perceive,* conspicuously, conspicuousness.
DESPICABLE *that which deserves to be despised,* despicability, despicableness, despicably.
DESPISE (de *down* + specere *to look*) *to hold in scorn or disdain,* despisedness, despiser, despisingly.
DESPITE *extreme malice,* despiteful, despitefully, despiteous, despiteously.
PERSPICACIOUS *having clear judgment and understanding,* perspicaciously, perspicaciousness, perspicacity.
PERSPICUOUS *clear in statement and easily understood,* perspicuity, perspicuously, perspicuousness.

see SUSPICION *the act of believing something harmful with little supporting evidence,* suspicious, suspiciously, suspiciousness.

SPIR
breathe

SPIRO, SPIRARE *to breathe,* SPIRATUM   **79**

ASPIRE *to long for advancement, etc.,* aspirer, aspirant.

ASPIRATE *to pronounce with an emission of breath,* aspiration, aspiratory; unaspirated.

ASPIRATOR *a suction to remove fluid or gas from a body cavity; an instrument for creating a vacuum.*

CONSPIRE *planning or acting together for an unlawful or harmful purpose,* conspirator, conspiratorial.

DISPIRIT *to lower the spirits of,* dispiritly, dispiritness, dispiritment.

EXPIRE *"to breathe out"; to die,* expirable, expirant, expiration, expiratory, expiring; unexpired.

INSPIRE *to have an animating effect upon,* inspired, inspirer, inspirable, inspiring.

INSPIRATION *any stimulus to creative action or thought,* inspirational, inspirationist, inspiratory.

PERSPIRE *"to breathe through"; to sweat,* perspirability, perspirable, perspiration, perspiratory.

RESPIRE (re *back* + spirare *to breathe*) *to breathe freely after exhaustion or anxiety,* respirability, respirable, respirableness, respiration, respirational, respirator, respiratory.

TRANSPIRE *to pass through the tissues; to leak out, to be known,* transpirable, transpiration, transpiratory.

SPIRACLE *an air hole,* spiraculum, spiracula, spiracular, spiraculate; spiraculiferous, spiraculiform.

SPIRIT *the life principle; the thinking, feeling part of man,* spiritedly, spiritedness, spiriting, spiritism, spiritless, spiritlessly, spiritlessness; inspirit; reinspirit; unspirited.

SPIRITUAL *the religious and moral aspect of the soul,* spiritualism, spiritualist, spiritualistic, spirituality, spiritualization, spiritualize, spiritualizer, spiritually, spiritualty.

UNSPIRITUAL unspiritually.

SPRITE *an apparition or ghost.*

. . .

SPON
promise

SPONDEO, SPONDERE *to promise*, **SPONSUM** 49

CORRESPOND *to be similar; to communicate*, correspondence, correspondency, correspondent, correspondently, corresponding, correspondingly, corresponsively.

DESPOND *to be depressed*, despondence, despondency, despondent, despondently, desponder, desponding, despondingly.

ESPOUSE *to advocate; to betroth*, espousal, espousement, espouser.

RESPOND *to act in return, to answer*, respondence, respondency, respondent; responsion, responsive, responsively, responsiveness.

RESPONSIBLE *involving accountability and obligation*, responsibility, responsibleness, responsibly.

IRRESPONSIBLE *not answerable*, irresponsibility, irresponsibly, irresponsive.

UNRESPONSIBLE unresponsive.

SPONSOR *one who binds himself to answer for another*, sponsorial, sponsorship.

SPONSION *a formal promise made on behalf of another*.

SPONTANEOUS *acting on its own impulse without influence*, spontaneity, spontaneously, spontaneousness; unspontaneous.

SPOUSE *husband or wife*, spousal.

STA STIT
stand

STO, STARE *to stand*, **STATUM** 182

ARREST *to check the motion of; to seize by authority*, arrestee, arrester or arrestor, arresting, arrestive, arrestment.

CIRCUMSTANCE (circum *around* + stare *to stand*) *something relative to a fact or event*, circumstantial, circumstantiality, circumstantially, cimcumstantiate, circumstantiation; uncircumstantial.

CONSTANT *remaining the same*, constancy, constantly.

INCONSTANT *changeable*, inconstantly, inconstancy.

CONTRAST (contra *against* + stare *to stand*) *to show the comparative excellence or difference*.

DISTANCE *an interval between points in time or space; a remoteness in relationship*, distantly.

EQUIDISTANCE *an equal distance*, equidistant, equidistantly.

ESTATE *rank; fortune; landed property*.

ESTABLISH *to settle on a firm basis*, establisher, establishment.

RE-ESTABLISH *to establish anew*, re-establisher, re-establishment.

INSTANCE *a request, an example; urgency*, instancy.

INSTANT *urgent, imminent*, instantaneity, instantaneous, instantaneously,

STA
STIT
stand

instantaneousness, instanter, instantly.

INSTEAD *as an alternative or substitute.*

OBSTACLE (ob *against* + stare *to stand*) *anything that hinders or obstructs.*

OBSTETRICS *medical care of women during pregnancy and childbirth*, obstetrician.

REINSTATE *to replace to a former state*, reinstatement, reinstation.

REST (re *back* + stare *to stand*) *that which is left* [*restrictive meaning*] restive, restore.

STANCE *manner of posture.*

STAND *remain upright; to maintain one's ground; to remain firm*, stand-by, standing, standoff; outstanding *prominent, conspicuous.*

UNDERSTAND *to perceive, comprehend, interpret*, understandable, understandably, understanding, understandingly.

STANDARD *something established as a basis of comparision; a banner used as a symbol*, standardize, standardization.

STABLE *not easily moved off balance; a standing place for animals*; instable, instability.

CONSTABLE *"count of the stable"; now, a policeman.*

STEADY *firm in position.*

STAMEN *male reproduction organ of flowers*, staminate.

STAMINA *resistance to fatigue*, staminal.

STANCHION *an upright prop or support.*

STANZA *a group of lines of verse.*

STAID *sober, sedate*, staidly, staidness.

STAGE *platform for plays; part of route; level of growth.*

STATE *circumstances characterizing a person at a given time; conditions of a physical structure; governmental authority*, stately, stateless.

STATEMENT *act of stating verbally or in writing.*

STATESMAN *a person who shows wisdom in handling public issues*, statesmanlike, statesmanly, statesmanship.

STATION *a place where a person or thing is located; regular stopping place; rank, status*, stationary *fixed.*

STATIC *bodies at rest; interference on radio.*

STATISTICS *facts and data assembled and classified to give significant information on a subject*, statistical, statistically, statistician.

STATUE *form of person or animal carved or cast*, statuesque, statuesquely, statuesqueness.

STA
STIT
stand

STATUTE *an established rule or law,* statutory.

STATUS *position or standing in social, scholarly or legal affairs.*

STAY *remain,* stayer, staying.

STEAD *a place for a person or thing filling as a substitute,* steady, steadily, steadiness, steadfast, steadfastly, steadfastness.

SUBSTANTIAL *having substance, of considerable worth,* substantialism, substantialist, substantiality, substantialize, substantially, substantialness, substantiate, substantiation; unsubstantial; supersubstantial.

SUBSTANTIVE *a matter of substance rather than form; independent, actual, essential,* substantively, substantiveness, substantivize.

COSUBSTANTIAL *having the same essential nature (relative to the Trinity),* cosubstantiation, cosubstantiationist, cosubstantially, cosubstantiate, cosubstantiation.

TRANSUBSTANTIATE *change of one substance for another in church ritual,* transubstantiation, transubtantiator.

ARMISTICE (arms *arms* + stare *to stand still*) *a temporary stopping of warfare by mutual consent.*

CONSTITUTE *to set up or establish,* constituter; preconstitute; unconstituted.

CONSTITUENT *necessary component in forming of the whole,* constituency.

CONSTITUTION *the way by which a person or organization or government is organized,* constitutional, constitutionalism, constitutionalist, constitutionality, constitutionally, constitutive, constitutively; unconstitutional, unconstitutionality, unconstitutionally.

DESTITUTE *not possessing the necessities of life,* destitutely, destituteness, destitution.

INSTITUTE *to establish or found,* institution, institutional, institutionalism, institutionalize, institutionary, institutive, institutively, institutor; superinstitution.

INTERSTICE *a small space that intervenes between one thing and another,* interstitial.

OBSTINATE *unreasonably determined to have one's own way,* obstinately, obstinateness.

PROSTITUTE *one who sells one's own body or integrity for an unworthy purpose,* prostitution, prostitutor.

RESTITUTION *the act of making good for any loss, damage or injury,* restitutive.

SOLSTICE (sol *sun* + stare *to stand*) *a point where the sun appears to recede*

STA / STIT
stand

from the equator, solstitial.

SUBSTITUTE *a person or thing used in place of another*, substitution, substitutional, substitutionally, substitutionary, substitutive.

SUPERSTITION *any belief inconsistent with the known laws of science*, superstitionist, superstitious, superstitiously, superstitiousness.

STING / STINCT
mark extinguish

STINGUO, STINGUERE *to mark, extinguish*, STINCTUM   51

DISTINGUISH *to ascertain differences by perception*, distinguishable, distinguishableness, distinguishably, distinguisher, distinguishing, distinguishingly, distinguishment; contradistinguish.

DISTINGUISHED *separated from others by extraordinary qualities*, distinguishedly.

INDISTINGUISHABLE *cannot be separated*, indistinguishably.

UNDISTINGUISHED undistinguishable, undistinguishing.

EXTINGUISH *to put to an end; to quench*, extinguishable, extinguisher, extinguishment.

INEXTINGUISHABLE *unquenchable*, inextinguishably.

UNEXTINGUISHED unextinguishable.

PRESTIGE (pre *before* + stinguere *to mark*) *to obscure; distinction based on achievement*, prestigious.

DISTINCT *individual; not the same*, distinction, distinctive, distinctively, distinctiveness, distinctly, distinctness; undistinctive.

INDISTINCT *not plainly defined*, indistinctible, indistinction, indistinctive, indistinctiveness, indistinctly, indistinctness.

CONTRADISTINCT *distinguished by opposite qualities*, contradistinction, contradistinctive.

EXTINCT *no longer in existence*, extinction, extinctive.

INSTINCT *an inborn way of behaving; a natural or acquired tendency*, instinctive, instinctively, instinctual.

STRI
bind

STRINGO, STRINGERE *to bind*, STRICTUM   51

ASTRINGENT *causing to shrink or contract*, astringency, astringently.

CONSTRINGENT *causing constriction*, constringe, constringency.

STRINGENT *making strict requirements*, stringently, stringentness.

CONSTRICT *to make smaller by squeezing*, constricted, constriction, constrictive, constrictor.

STRICT *enforcing a rule with great care*, strictly, strictness.

STRI
bind

STRICTURE *adverse criticism; in medicine, abnormal narrowing of a passage.*
RESTRICT *to restrain within bounds,* restricted, restriction, restrictionist, restrictive, restrictively, restrictiveness.
CONSTRAIN *to confine by force,* constrainable, constrainedly, constrainer, constraint.
DISTRAIN *in law, to hold as security for a debt,* distrainable, distrainer or distrainor, distraint.
STRAIN *to force beyond the normal limits,* strainable, strainably, strainer.
RESTRAIN (re *back* + stringere *to draw tightly*) *to hold back by physical or moral force,* restrainable, restrainedly, restrainer, restraint.
STRAIGHT (*A-S* streht) *not crooked or bent,* straightaway, straighten, straightly, straightness.
STRAIT *a narrow waterway connecting two large bodies of water.*
STRAITEN *to bring to financial hardship.*

STRU
build

STRUO, STRUERE *to build, place in order,* **STRUCTUM** 70
CONSTRUE *to deduce the meaning of,* construable.
MISCONSTRUE *to interpret erroneously,* misconstruer.
CONSTRUCT *to put into an orderly arrangement,* constructor, construction, constructional, constructionist, constructive, constructively, constructiveness, constructivism, constructor.
MISCONSTRUCT *wrongly arrange a building or a statement,* misconstruction.
DESTROY *to tear down,* destroyable.
DESTROYER *one who destroys; a small, fast armed warship.*
DESTRUCTION *a pulling down,* destruct, destructibility, destructible, destructibleness, destruction, destructionist, destructive, destructively, destructiveness, destructivity.
INDESTRUCTIBLE *cannot be destroyed,* indestructibility, indestructibleness.
INSTRUMENT *a thing by means of which something is done,* instrumental, instrumentalism, instrumentalist, instrumentality, instrumentally, instrumentalness, instrumentivity.
INSTRUCT *"to build into"; to teach,* instruction, instructional, instructive, instructively, instructiveness, instructor, instructress; preinstruct.
OBSTRUCT (ob *against* + struere *to pile up*) *to hinder,* obstructer, obstructor, obstruction, obstructionism, obstructionist, obstructive, obstructively, obstructiveness; unobstructed.
STRUCTURE *something constructed; interrelation of the parts to the whole,*

STRU
build

structural, structuralism, structuralist, structuralization, structuralize, structurally, structureless.

SUPERSTRUCTURE *a structure build on top of another; the part above deck of a warship.*

SUAD
advise

SUADEO, SUADERE *to advise, exhort,* SUASUM   38

ASSUAGE *to pacify; to lessen distress,* assuagement, assuager, assuasive.

DISSUADE (dis *away* + suadere *to persuade*) *to turn one aside by giving reasons,* dissuader, dissuasion, dissuasive, dissuasively.

PERSUADE *to convince one to believe something,* persuadable, persuadably, persuader, persuasibility, persuasible, persuasibleness, persuasion, persuasive, persuasively, persuasiveness.

IMPERSUADABLE *unyielding,* impersuadableness, impersuasibility, impersuasible.

MISPERSUADE *to lead to a wrong notion,* mispersuasion.

UNPERSUADED unpersuadable, unpersuasive.

SUAVITY *graciousness of manner,* suave.

SWEET *pleasing, fragrant; having an agreeable taste,* sweetened, sweetener, sweetening, sweetish, sweetly, sweetness.

SUM
take
cost

SUMO, SUMERE *to take,* SUMPTUM; SUMPTUS *cost*   37

ASSUME *to take for granted,* assumedly, assumer, assuming; assumption, assumptive, assumptively.

UNASSUMED unassuming.

ASSUMPSIT *in law, a verbal or written promise.*

CONSUME *to use up,* consumable, consumedly, consumingly; unconsumed.

CONSUMPTION *the using up of goods; tuberculosis,* consumptive, consumptively, consumptiveness.

INCONSUMABLE inconsumably.

CONSUMMATE *to finish by fulfilling,* consummately, consummation, consummative, consummator.

PRESUME *"to take before"; to suppose to be true without examination.*

UNPRESUMING unpresumptious.

RESUME (re *from* + sumere *to take*) *to begin again,* resumable, resumption, resumptive.

SUMPTUOUS *involving great expense,* sumptuously, sumptuosity, sumptuousness.

TAC
TEG
touch

TANGO, TANGERE *to touch,* **TACTUM**   **60**

ATTAIN (attingere *to touch upon*) *to reach a goal,* attainability, attainable, attainableness, attainment.
ATTAINT *to find guilty of a crime; to disagree,* attainder, attainment, attainture.
CONTACT (com *together* + tangere *to touch*) *the state of being in touch.*
TACT *a fine perception of the thing to say or do,* tactful, tactless, tactlessness.
TACTILE *having the sense of touch,* tactility.
INTEGER *"not touched"; a whole number.*
INTEGRANT *making parts of a whole; integral.*
INTEGRATE *to make whole by bringing together parts,* integration, integrative, integrator.
REDINTEGRATE *to make whole or perfect again,* redintegration.
INTEGRITY *the quality of being of sound moral principle.*
TANGENT *touching; in geometry, meeting a curved line but not intersecting it,* tangential, tangentially.
TANGIBLE *that can be felt, touched or understood,* tangibility, tangibleness, tangibles, tangibly.
INTANGIBLE *that cannot be easily defined,* intangibility, intangibleness.
CONTAGION *"a touching"; the communicability of a disease or idea,* contagioned, contagionist, contagious, contagiously, contagiousness.
CONTAMINATE *corrupt by contact,* contamination, contaminative, contaminator.
CONTIGUOUS *meeting or joining; close together,* contiguity, contiguously, contiguousness.
CONTINGENT *depending upon something uncertain,* contingence, contingency, contingently, contingentness.
ENTIRE (integer *untouched*) *complete in all its parts,* entirely, entireness, entirety.

TEC
TEG
cover

TEGO, TEGERE *to come,* **TECTUM**   **30**

DETECT *to find out,* detectable, detecter, detection, detective, detector; undetected.
PROTECT *"to cover before"; to shield from danger,* protectingly, protection, protectional, protectionism, protectionist, protective, protectively, protector, protectoral; unprotected.
PROTECTORATE *a weaker state under control of a stronger state.*
PROTEGE *one under the care and protection of another,* protegee.

TEC
TEG
cover

TEGUMENT *the natural covering of a body or plant*, tegumental, tegumentary.
INTEGUMENT *an outer covering; skin, hide, husk*, integumentary, integumation.
TEGULAR *arranged like tiles*, tegularly.

TEMP
time
temper

TEMPUS, TEMPORIS *time;* TEMPERARE *to regulate, temper*   43
COMTEMPORARY *living or happening at the same period*, contemporaneity, contemporaneous, contemporaneously, contemporaneousness, comtemporize.
EXTEMPORARY (ex *out of* + tempore *time*) *improvised; spoken without preparation*, extemporaneous, extemporaneousness, extemporarily, extempore, extemporize, extemporizer, extemporization.
TEMPORARY *lasting for a time only*, temporality, temporally, temporalness, temporarily, temporariness.
TEMPORIZE *to suit one's actions to the time or occasion*, temporization, temporizer, temporizingly.
TEMPER *to make suitable; tendency to become angry.*
DISTEMPER *a mental or physical disorder; a disease of young dogs.*
TEMPERANCE *moderation in eating and drinking.*
INTEMPERANCE *excess in any kind*, intemperate, intemperately, intemperateness.
TEMPEST *a violent storm; tumult of words*, tempestuous, tempestuously, tempestuousness.
TENSE *forms of verbs that show time of action or state of being.*
TIME (A-S tima) *the period between two events*, timeful, timeless, timeliness, timely.
UNTIMELY *coming at the wrong time, prematurely*, untimeliness.

TEN
TIN
TAIN
hold

TENEO, TENERE *to hold,* TENTUM   132
ABSTEMIOUS *sparing in enjoyment of appetites or pleasures*, abstemiously, abstemiousness, abstention, abstentious.
CONTENT' (v) *to satisfy the mind of*, contentedly, contentedness, contently, contentment.
CON'TENT (n) *anything inside; main substance.*
CONTENTION *controversy*, contentious, contentiously, contentiousness.
DISCONTENT *dissatisfaction, uneasiness*, discontentedly, discontentedness, discontentful.

TEN
TIN
TAIN
hold

MALCONTENT *rebellious*, malcontented, malcontentedness.
COUNTENANCE *the expression of the face; approval*, countenancer.
DISCOUNTENANCE *to shame; to discourage*, discountenancer.
DETENTION *keeping in custody*, detentive.
DETENTE [Fr] *a lessening of tension between nations*.
LIEUTENANT *lowest army officer*, lieutenancy, lieutenantship.
RETENTION *act of keeping*, retentive, retentively, retentiveness, retentivity.
SUSTENANCE *that which supports life*.
TENABLE *capable of being held or defended*, tenability, tenableness.
TENACIOUS *holding fast or firmly*, tenaciously, tenaciousness, tenacity.
TENANT *one who pays rent to occupy a building*, tenancy.
TENEMENT *a set of rooms tenanted as a separate dwelling*, tenemental, tenementary.
TENET *any opinion or principle a person or sect believes*.
TENNIS *a net, a ball, and two or four with racquets*.
TENON *a projecting piece of wood to be inserted into a mortise*.
TENOR *general direction; course of thought; highest adult male voice*.
TENURE *the right to hold or possess something*.
ABSTINENCE *the act of voluntarily refraining from some action*, abstinent, abstinently.
APPERTINENCE *belonging*, appertinent.
CONTINENT *one of six largest land masses on earth*, continental.
CONTINENCE *moderation; restraint a person places on his desires*, continent, continently.
INCONTINENCE *without restraint of passions or appetites*, incontenent, incontinently.
CONTINUE (com *together* + tenere *to hold*) *endure*, continual, continually, continualness.
DISCONTINUE *to cease*, discontinuance, discontinuation, discontinuee, discontinuer, discontinuor, discontinuity, discontinuous, discontinuously.
PERTINACIOUS *exhibiting unyielding purpose*, pertinaciously, pertinaciousness, pertinacity.
PERTINENCE *relevant, to the point*, pertinency, pertinent, pertinently, pertinentless.
IMPERTINENCE *insolent, rude; imappropriate*, impertinency, impertinent, impertinently.
RETINUE *an escort; a body of retainers*.

TEN / TIN / TAIN — *hold*

ABSTAIN *to refrain from*, abstainer.
APPERTAIN *as part of a function; to relate.*
CONTAIN (com *together* + tenere *to hold*) *hold, enclose*, containable, container, containerize, containment.
DETAIN *keep from, withhold*, detainer, detainment.
ENTERTAIN *to receive and treat with hospitality*, entertainer, entertaining, entertainingly, entertainingness, entertainment.
MAINTAIN (manu *hand* + tenere *to hold*) *to carry on, keep up*, maintainable, maintainer, maintainor, maintenance.
OBTAIN *to achieve, to get possession of*, obtainable, obtainer; preobtain.
PERTAIN *to belong; suitable, relevant.*
RETAIN *to keep in possession*, retainable, retainal, retainer, retaining, retainment.
SUSTAIN *keep in existence; support, endure*, sustainable, sustainer, sustaining, sustainment.

TEND / TENS / TENT — *stretch*

TENDO, TENDERE *to stretch*, TENSUM   125

ATTEND *to accompany, to be present, to serve*, attendance, attendancy, attendant, attender; unattended.
ATTENTION *careful observation*, attentive, attentively, attentiveness.
INATTENTION *heedless, careless, negligent*, inattentive, inattentively, inattentiveness.
CONTEND (com *together* + tendere *to stretch*) *to strive in opposition, controversy or competition*, contendent, contender.
CONTENTION *verbal strife*, contentious, contentiously, contentiousness.
DISTEND *to spread, enlarge, expand in all directions*, distensibility, distensible, distension, distensive, distention.
EXTEND *to carry forward in length, distance or time*, extendedly, extender, extendible, extensibility, extensible, extensibleness, extensile.
EXTENT *the degree to which a thing is extended*, extenuate, extenuating, extenuation, extenuative, extenuator, extenuatory.
EXTENSION *the act of extending*, extensional, extensionist, extensity, extensive, extensiveness.
EXTENSOR *in anatomy, a muscle that serves to extend or straighten any part of the body.*
INTEND *to have in mind to accomplish*, intended, intender.
INTENSE *to a high degree*, intensely, intenseness, intensification, intensifier,

TEND
TENS
TENT
stretch

intensify, intension, intensity, intensive, intensely, intensiveness.

INTENT *firmly directly or fixed*, intention, intentional, intentionally, intentioned, intently, intentness.

OSTENSIBLE *apparent, evident*, ostensibility, ostensibly, ostention, ostensive, ostensively.

OSTENTATION *boastful, showy, pretentious*, ostentatious, ostentatiously, ostentatiousness; unostentatious.

PORTEND (pro *forth* + tendere *to stretch*) *an omen or warning*, portent, portention, portentious, portentiousness, portentiously.

PRETEND *to claim falsely, to feign, to simulate*, pretendant, pretendedly, pretender; unpretending.

PRETENSE *a claim as to some distinction*, pretension, pretentious, pretentiously, pretentiousness.

SUPERINTEND *to exercise oversight of*, superintendence, superintendency, superintendent, superintender.

TEND *to move in a certain direction*, tendency.

TENDER *to offer for acceptance; very sensitive, easily impressed*, tenderly, tenderness.

TENDON *in anatomy, an inelastic bundle of tissue attached to a bone.*

TENSOR *any muscle that stretches a part of the body.*

TENSE *rigid; showing mental or nervous strain*, tensely, tenseness, tension, tensity, tensive.

TENSILE *capable of being stretched*, tensibility, tensible, tensibly, tensility.

TENT *a portable cloth shelter*, tenter, tentful.

TERM
limit

TERMINUS **limit, boundary**　　55

CONTERMINOUS *contiguous; having a common boundary at some point*, conterminable, conterminate.

DETERMINE *to reach a decision after thought; set limits to*, determinability, determinable, determinant, determinantal, determinate, determinately, determinateness, determinedly, determiner, determinism, deterministic, determination, determinative, determinator.

INDETERMINABLE *that cannot be ascertained*, indeterminableness, indeterminability, indeterminacy.

INDETERMINISM *the doctrine that one's actions are not altogether determined outside his will.*

PREDETERMINE *to determine beforehand; to prejudice*, predetermination,

TERM
limit

predeterminer, predeterminism.

SELF-DETERMINATION *right of the people to decide on their form of government without outside influence*, self-determined.

TERM *a period of time having definite limits*.

TERMINABLE *that terminates after a specified time*, terminability, terminableness, terminably.

INTERMINABLE *apparently endless*, interminableness, interminably, interminate.

TERMINATE *to put an end to*, terminally, termination, terminative, terminatively, terminator, terminatory.

EXTERMINATE *to destroy completely*, exterminable, extermination, exterminative, exterminator, exterminatory.

TERMINOLOGY *the terms collectively used in any art or science*, terminologist, terminologically.

TERR
earth

TERRA *earth*   **20**

INTER *to place in the earth; to bury*.

DISINTER *to take from the grave; to bring something hidden to light*.

TERRACE *flat earth with sloping sides*.

TERRESTRIAL *existing on earth*, terrestrially, terrestrialness; superterrestrial.

TERRAQUEOUS (terra *earth* + aqua *water*) *consisting of both land and water*.

TERRITORY *land and water under a State*, territorial, territorialism, territoriality, territorialization, territorialize, territorially.

TERRIER *several breeds of dogs who burrow after game*.

MEDITERRANEAN *a sea in the middle of two lands*.

SUBTERRANEAN *an underground cave*.

SUPERTERRANEAN *lying on or above the ground*, superterrene.

TEST
witness

TESTIS *a witness*; TESTAMENTUM *a will*   **58**

ATTEST (ad *to* + testis *a witness*) *to make a solemn declaration*, attestant, attestation, attestative, attester or attestor, attestive; unattested.

CON'TEST (n) *strife, struggle*.

CONTEST' (v) *to strive earnestly; to hold or maintain*, contestable, contestableness, contestant, contestation, contestingly; uncontested, uncontestable.

INCONTESTABLE *too clear to be controverted*, incontestability, incontestableness, incontestably.

TEST
witness

DETEST *to abhor,* detestive, detestively, detestiveness, detestability, detestable, detestableness, detestably, detester; undetesting.
OBTEST *to beseech; to call to witness.*
PRO'TEST *(n) an objection.*
PROTEST' *(v) "to witness against"; to make a solemn declaration or objection,* protestation, protester or protestor, protestingly.
PROTESTANTISM *the religion of Protestants,* Protestantly.
TEST *an examination; questions, etc. to determine a person's ability and knowledge,* testable; untested.
TESTATE *a deceased having left a legally valid will,* testator, testrix.
INTESTATE *dying without a valid will.*
TESTAMENT *a covenant; a will,* testamental, testamentary.
TESTIFY *to make a solemn declaration; (in law) under oath,* testification, testificator, testifier.
TESTIMONY *a written or oral statement establishing some fact.*
TESTIMONIAL *the honoring of a person for good deeds.*
TESTICLE *the sex gland of the male.*
TESTICULATE *in botany, shaped like a testicle.*

TEXT
woven

TEXO, TEXERE *to weave,* TEXTUS   16
TEXT *the substance of a book,* textual, textualism, textualist, textually, textuary.
TEXTILE *woven fabrics.*
TEXTURE *the character of a woven fabric; the structural quality or composition of any material or act,* textual.
CONTEXT *"a weaving together"; the whole situation relevant to some incident,* contextual, contextually, contextural, contexture.
PRETEXT *"to weave before," an ostensible motive covering the real motive,* pretexted.

THEO
God

THEOS [Gr] *god*   52
ATHEISM *the belief there is no God,* atheist, atheistical, atheistically, atheisticalness.
ATHEOLOGY *opposition to theology,* atheological.
APOTHEOSIS (apo *from* + theos *god) an honoring or glorification of any kind,* apotheosize.
ENTHUSIASM *excitement of the mind in pursuit of a goal,* enthusiast, enthusiastic, enthusiastical, enthusiastically.

THEO — God

PANTHEISM *belief that God is everything and everything is God,* pantheist, pantheistic, pantheistical, pantheistically, pantheologist, pantheology.

POLYTHEISM *the worship of many gods,* polytheist, polytheistic, polytheistical, polytheistically, polytheize.

THEISM *belief in one God who is ruler of the universe,* theist, theistic, theistical, theistically.

THEOCRACY *government by priests who claim to rule by divine authority,* theocrat, theocratic, theocratical, theocratist.

THEOCRASY *mixture of several dieties into one; mystical union of the soul with God.*

THEOLOGY *study of God; studies of religious doctrines,* theologize, theologer.

THEOSOPHY *establishment of divine principles through contemplation and revelation,* theosopher, theosophic, theosophical, theosophism, theosophist, theosophistical, theosophize.

THEOTECHNIC *matters operated and carried on by the gods.*

THEOTHERAPY (theos *god* + therapeia *treatment*) *treatment of disease by religious exercise.*

THEURGY *supernatural intervention in human affairs.*

THES — placing

THESIS [Gr] *a placing;* **THEMA** *the thing laid down*   48

ANATHEMA *anything greatly detested; a ban or curse against an offender,* anathematic, anathematically, anathematization, anathematizer, amathematize.

ANTITHESIS (anti *against* + tithenai *to place*) *extreme contrast; opposition of thought,* antithetical, antithetically.

APOTHESIS *in surgery, the setting of a dislocated bone.*

EPENTHESIS *in grammar, the insertion of a sound or syllable in a word to make its pronunciation easier.*

EPITHEM *in medicine, any external application on the body, other than salve or plaster.*

HYPOTHECATE *to pawn; to pledge in security of some debt,* hypothec, hpothecary, hypothecation, hypothecator.

HYPOTHESIS *a supposition; a theory imagined to account for what is not understood,* hypothesize, hypothetic, hypothetical, hypothetically, hypothetist.

METATHESIS (meta *over* + tithenai *to place*) *transposition of letters or sounds in a word; interchange of elements in chemistry,* metathetic, metathetical.

PARATHESIS *in grammar, apposition,* parathetical, parathetically.

PARENTHESIS *material between curved lines; additional wordage in a complete*

THES
placing

sentence, shown by curved lines or dashes or commas, parenthesize, parenthetic, parenthetical, parenthetically.

PROSTHESIS *in grammar, the addition of a letter or syllable to the beginning of a word; in medicine, substitution of an artificial device.*

SYNTHESIS *a whole made up of elements put together; deductive reasoning,* synthesist, synthesize, synthesizer.

SYNTHETIC *artificial, not genuine,* synthetical, synthetically, syntheticism, synthetist, synthetize.

THEME *a subject on which a person speaks or writes; a musical phrase on which variations develop.*

THESIS *a dissertation for a degree; a proposition defended in argument.*

THETIC *set forth dogmatically,* thetical.

TON
stretch tone

TONOS [Gr] *a stretching, a tone;* TONITRUS *thunder*   54

ASTONISH (ad *to* + tonare *to thunder*) *to fill with wonder,* astonished, astonishing, astonishingly, astonishingness, astonishment, astounding, astoundingly.

DETONATE *to explode violently,* detonating, detonation, detonative, detonator.

HYPOTENUSE *in a right angle triangle, the side opposite the right angle.*

TONE *a pitch of the voice that expresses the feeling of the speaker,* toneless, tonetic, tonetics.

SEMITONE *in music, the half step in a diatonic scale,* semitonic.

INTONE *to chant; prolonged monotones,* intonation.

TONIC *physically and morally invigorating,* tonicity.

ATONIC *an unaccented word or syllable.*

ATONY *lack of bodily tone; lack of stress in phonetics.*

BARITONE (barys *deep* + tonos *tone*) *deep-toned male voice.*

DIATONIC *the eight notes of the standard scale without the chromatic intervals.*

ISOTONIC (isos *equal* + tonos *tone*) *having equal tones; equal tension.*

MONOTONE *repetition of the same tone,* monotonic, monotonically.

MONOTONOUS *talking about the same old thing,* monotonist, monotonously, monotonousness, monotony.

TUNE *a melody; a rhythmic succession of musical tones,* tuneful, tunefully, tunefulness, tuneless, tuner; attune.

UNTUNE untunable, untuned, untuneful.

THUNDER (A-S thunor) *sound caused by lightning,* thundering, thunderingly, thunderless, thunderous, thunderously.

TOR
twist
pain

TORQUEO, TORQUERE *to twist,* **TORTUM; TORMENTUM** *extreme pain*   **45**

CONTORT *twist out of shape,* contorted, contortion, contortionist, contortive.

DISTORT *twist out of natural shape; alter from the true meaning,* distorter, distortion, distortive.

EXTORT (ex *out* + torquere *to twist*) *to wring from by physical force or threats,* extorter, extortion, extortionary, extorionate, extortioner, extortionist.

INTORT *to twist inward,* intortion, intorsion.

RETORT *to answer an argument in kind,* retorter, retorsion, retortion, retortive.

TORMENT *extreme pain or anguish,* tormented, tormenter.

TORTURE *any severe physical or mental pain,* tortuable, torturer, torturingly, torturous; self-torture.

TORSE *in heraldry, a wreath.*

TORSEL *a timber laid in masonry to support a crossbeam.*

TORSO *a trunk of a human body or statue.*

TORT *in law, a wrongful act (aside from Contracts) from which an injured party can bring civil action,* tortious, tortiously.

TORTUOUS *full of twisting curves,* tortuosity, tortuously, tortuousness.

TORQUE *the force that produces a twisting or rotating motion called torsion.*

TORTOISE *a slow moving, shell-covered animal.*

TRACT
draw

TRAHO, TRAHERE *to draw,* **TRACTUM**   **152**

ABSTRACT (abs *from* + trahere *to draw*) *"to draw from"; a summary of the substance of a treatise,* abstractedly, abstractedness, abstracter, abstraction, abstractional, abstractionalism, abstractionalist, abstractive, abstractively, abstractiveness, abstractly, abstractness.

ATTRACT *"to draw to"; to get admiration,* attracter, attractile, attractingly, attraction, attractive, attractively, attractiveness, attractivity, attractor.

BETRAY *to violate a trust,* betrayal, betrayer, betrayment; unbetrayed.

CON'TRACT *(n) an agreement between two or more.*

CONTRACT' (com *together* + trahere *to draw*)(vb) *"to draw together"; to shrink; to bargain,* contractant, contractedly, contractedness, contractability, contractible, contractibleness, contractile, contractility, contraction, contractive, contractor, contractual; precontract *to stipulate beforehand.*

DETRACT *"to draw from"; a taking away,* detracter, detractor, detractress, detractingly, detraction, detractive, detractiveness.

TRACT
draw

DISTRACT *"to draw apart"; to divert to another viewpoint,* distracted, distractedly, distractedness, distracter, distractible, distracting, distraction, distractive; undistracted, undistracting.

DRAG (*A-S* dragan) *to draw along the ground by force,* dragging, dragnet.

DRAW *to pull; to attract,* drawable, drawback, drawer, drawing.

EX′TRACT (*n*) *an excerpt.*

EXTRACT′ (*vb*) *"to draw out" by effort,* extractable, extraction, extractive, extractor.

INTRACTABLE (in *not* + tractare *to handle*) *"hard to handle"; obstinate,* intractability, intractableness, intractably, intractile.

PORTRAIT *a picture of a person,* portraitist, portraiture.

PORTRAY *"to draw forth"; to make a picture of,* portrayal, portrayer.

PROTRACT *"to draw out"; to prolong or delay,* protracted, protractile, protraction, protractive; unprotracted.

PROTRACTOR *a mathematical instrument for drawing or measuring angles.*

RETRACT *"to draw back"; to withdraw a statement or offer,* retractable, retractile, retractility, retraction, retractor; unretracted.

SUBTRACT (sub *under* + trahere *to draw*) *"to draw under" or take away,* subtracter, subtraction, subtractive.

TRACE *to follow the trail or development,* traceable, traceably, tracer; traceless, tracelessly.

TRACK *marks of an animal; a path; a sequence of ideas,* trackage, tracker; trackless, tracklessness.

TRACT *a stretch of land; a leaflet,* tractability, tractable, tractableness, tractably, tractate, tractation, tractator, tractrix.

TRACTILE *ductile; capable of being drawn out,* tractility.

TRACTION *the pulling power of a motor; pulling a dislocated bone or muscle into place,* tractional.

TRACTOR *a powerful vehicle for pulling machinery.*

TRADE *exchanging commodities; an occupation,* trade-in, trade-off, trader, tradeless.

TRAIL *to follow tracks; to hang behind,* trailer, trailing.

TRAIN *to guide mental and physical development; a transportation unit,* trainable, trainer, training, trainless.

TRAIT *a distinguishing characteristic.*

TRAITOR *one who betrays his country,* traitress, traitorous, traitorously, traitorousness.

TRACT
draw

TREASON *"to deliver over"; violation of allegiance to one's country*, treasonable, treasonableness, treasonably, treasonous.
TRAWL *fishing with a long line, hooked and bouyed*, trawler.
TREAT *to behave toward others in a certain manner*, treatable, treatably, treater, treatment; mistreat.
ENTREAT *to ask earnestly; to implore*, entreater, entreatingly.
ENTREATY *earnest petition*.
MALTREAT *treat roughly; abuse*, maltreatment.
TREATISE *a formal essay on some subject*, treatiser.
TREATY *a formal agreement between two or more nations*, treaty-making.

TRIBUT
give

TRIBUO, TRIBUERE *to give, allot,* TRIBUTUM   32
ATTRIBUTE *to consider as belonging to*, attribution, attributive, attributively.
CONTRIBUTE *to give in common with others*, contributable, contribution, contributional, contributive, contributor, contributory.
DISTRIBUTE (dis *apart* + tribuere *to give*) *to give or bestow in portions*, distributable, distributary, distributee, distributer, distribution, distributional, distributive, distributiveness, distributor, distributorship.
REDISTRIBUTE *to distribute again*, redistribution.
RETRIBUTION *deserved punishment for evil done*, retributor, retributory.
TRIBUTE *money paid as acknowledgement of subjugation*, tributer, tributarily, tributariness.
TRIBUTARY *money paid in tribute; a stream that flows into a larger body of water*.

TRUD
thrust

TRUDO, TRUDERE *to thrust,* TRUSUM   35
ABTRUSE *"to thrust away"; difficult to comprehend*, abtrusely, abtruseness, abtrusion, abtrusity.
DETRUDE *"to thrust down,"* detrusion, detrusive, detrusor.
EXTRUDE *"to thrust out,"* extrusion, extrusive.
INTRUDE *to push something on; to force oneself on others without being welcome*, intruder, intrudress.
INTRUSION intrusional, intrusionist, intrusive, intrusively, intrusiveness.
OBTRUDE *"to thrust against"; to urge upon when not desired*, obtruder.
OBTRUSION obtrusionist, obtrusive, obtrusively, obtrusiveness; unobtrusive.
PROTRUDE *"to thrust forward,"* protrudable, protrudent.
PROTRUSION protrusive, protrusively.

TUM
swelling

TUMEO *I swell;* **TUMULUS** *a heap of earth*   **33**

CONTUMACY *insubordination; in law, a willful contempt of a court order,* contumacious, contumaciously.

CONTUMELY *insolence, contempt,* contumelious, contumeliously, contumeliousness.

TUMID *swollen, distended,* tumidity, tumidly, tumidness.

TUMESCENCE *a swelling,* tumescent, tumefacient, tumefaction, tumefy.

INTUMESCE *to enlarge or swell,* intumescence, intumescent.

TUMBLE *to fall suddenly; to do acrobatic feats,* tumbler, tumbling.

TUMOR *a benign or malignant swelling in the body,* tumored, tumorous.

TUMULOSE *full of mounds,* tumulous, tumulosity.

TUMULT *commotion of a multitude,* tulmulter, tulmultuous, tumultuously, tumultuousness.

TURB
turmoil

TURBO, TURBARE *to throw in discord,* **TURBATUM**   **33**

DISTURB (dis *apart* + turbare *throw in confusion*) *to discompose; to make uneasy,* disturbance, disturber; undisturbed.

PERTURB *to throw in disorder,* perturbability, perturbable, perturbate, perturbation, perturbative, perturbedly, perturber.

IMPERTURBABLE *impassive,* imperturbability, imperturbably, imperturbation, imperturbative, imperturbed.

TROUBLE *to annoy and confuse,* troubler, troublesome, troublesomely, troublesomeness, troubly.

TURBID *muddy, cloudy, confused,* turbidity, turbidly, turbidness.

TURBULENT *disorderly, unruly,* turbulence, turbulency, turbulently.

TURMOIL *commotion, confusion, disturbance.*

TUT
secure

TUEOR, TUERI *secure,* **TUTUS**   **23**

INTUITION *instant realization without thought,* intuitional, intuitionalism, intuitionalist, intuitionism, intuitionist, intuitive, intuitively, intuitiveness.

TUITION *money paid for instruction,* tuitional, tuitionary.

TUTELAGE *the functions of a guardian,* tutelar, tutelary.

TUTOR *a private teacher; a teaching assistant,* tutorage, tutoress, tutorial, tutorially, tutorly, tutorship; untutored.

UND
wave

UNDO, UNDARE *to flow,* **UNDATUM**   27

ABOUND *to possess in great quantity*, abounding; superabound.
ABUNDANCE *a great plenty*, abundant, abundantly.
SUPERABUNDANCE *more than needed*, superabundant, superabundantly.
INUNDATE *to overflow, to deluge*, inundant, inundation, inundator, inundatory.
REDOUND (re *again* + undare *to surge*) *to come back; to react on a person's record*, redounding.
REDUNDANT *superfluous*, redundantly, redundance, redundancy.
UNDULATE *to cause to move up and down or to and fro*, undulately, undulating, undulatingly, undulation, undulative, undulatory.

UNI
one

UNUS *one*   44

UNIDIRECTIONAL *moving only in one direction*.
UNIFORM *always the same*, uniformal, uniformly, uniformity, uniformness; disuniform.
UNIFY (unus *one* + facere *to make*) *make into one*.
UNILATERAL *involving only one of several persons; taking in account one side only*, unilaterally, unilaterality.
UNION *a combining for mutual benefit*, unionism, unionist, unionistic, unionize, unionization; disunion; reunion.
UNIQUE *single; different from all others*, uniquely, uniqueness.
UNISON (unus *one* + sonus *sound*) *two or more giving a single sound*, unisonal, unisonance.
UNIT *one*, unitable, unitage.
UNITARIAN *one who denies the Trinity and divinity of Jesus, but holds to God as a single being*, Unitarianism.
UNITE *to join together as one*, unitive, unitize, unity; disunite, disuniter, disunity; reunite.
UNIVERSAL *pervading all or the whole*, universality, universalistic, univeralization, universalize.
UNIVERSITY *where all colleges combine in one school*.

US
use

UTOR, UTI *to use,* **USUS**   53

ABUSE *to maltreat, to treat harshly*, abusable, abuseful, abuser, abusive, abusively, abusiveness; inabuse.
DISABUSE *cessation of the practice*.
MISUSE *treat or use improperly*, misusage, misuser.

US
use

PERUSE *to read with attention,* perusable, perusal, peruser.
USE *the act or state of being used,* usage, usance, usability, useable, useful, usefully, usefulnes, user; useless, uselessly, uselessness.
UNUSED unuseful, unusefully.
USUAL *customary, common, frequent,* usually, usualness.
UNUSUAL *not expected; strange, exceptional,* unusually, unusualness.
USURP *to take possession by force,* usurpation, usurpatory, usurper, usurpingly.
USURY *the act of lending money at an excessively high rate of interest,* usurer, usorious, usoriously, usoriousness.
UTENSIL *any implement or tool used in the kitchen or farm.*
UTILITY *usefulness; public services,* utilizable, utilization, utilize.

VACU
empty

VACO, VACARE *to empty*   15

EVACUATE (e *out* + vacuus *empty*) *to make empty,* evacuation, evacuative, evacuator, evacuatee.
VACATE *to make vacant,* vacancy, vacantly.
VACATION *a time of recreation from work,* vacationer, vacationist.
VACUUM *a space with most of the air removed, a void.*
VACUOUS *lack of intelligence, interest, or thought,* vacuousness, vacuity.

VAD
go

VADO, VADERE *to go,* VASUM   14

EVADE (e *out* + vadere *to go*) *keep out of the way; elude,* evasible, evasion, evasive, evasively, evasiveness.
INVADE *to intrude upon; to enter with hostile intentions,* invader, invasion.
PERVADE *to spread or be diffused throughout,* pervasion, pervasive.
WADE (A-S wadan) *to move forward with difficulty,* wader.

VAG
wandering

VAGO, VAGARI *to wander,* VAGATUS   23

VAGABOND *drifting from place to place,* vagabondage, vagabondish, vagabondism, vagabondize.
VAGARY *an odd or unexpected conduct,* vagarious, vagarish, vagarity.
VAGRANT *in law, an idle or disorderly person whose way of living makes him subject to arrest,* vagrancy, vagrantly, vagrantness.
VAGUE *not clearly or precisely expressed,* vaguely, vagueness.
EXTRAVAGANCE (extra *beyond* + vagari *to wander*) *going beyond reasonable conduct,* extravagancy, extravagant, extravagantly, extravaganza.
NOCTIVAGANT *wanderer in the night (as animals for prey),* noctivagation.

VAL
strong

VALIDUS *strong;* **VALERE** *to be strong, powerful*   **63**

AVAIL (ad *to* + valere *to be strong*) *to take advantage of an opportunity,* availabililty, available, availableness, availably; unavailable, unavailing.

COUNTERVAIL *to use equal force against.*

PREVAIL *to gain the superiority,* prevailing, prevailingly.

CONVALESCENCE *to recover health after an illness,* convalescent, convalescently.

EQUIVALENCE (equi *equal* + valere *to be strong*) *equal in value, etc. to another,* equivalency, equivalent, equivalently.

EVALUATE (e *from* + valere *to be worth*) *to determine the worth of,* evaluation.

PREVALENCE *widespread existence,* prevalency, prevalent, prevalently.

VALETUDINARIAN *sickly or anxiously concerned about one's health,* valetudinarianism, valetudinariness, valetudinary.

VALIANT *brave and courageous,* valiantly, valiantness.

VALID *having legal force; substantiated by evidence,* validate, validation, validity, validly, validness; unvalidated.

INVAL'ID (a) *having no force or effect,* invalidate, invalidation, invalidity, invalidly, invalidness.

IN'VALID (n) *a person who is infirm or disabled,* invalidism.

VALOR *courage, bravery,* valorization, valorize, valorous, valorously; invalorous.

VALUE *the worth of a thing at a particular time,* valuable, valuableness, valuably, valuation, valuator, valueless; overvalue.

UNDERVALUE undervaluing, undervaluation.

VEN
come

VENIO, VENIRE *to come,* **VENTUM**   **90**

ADVENT *the coming of Christ,* Adventism, Adventist, Adventual.

ADVENTITIOUS *accidental, casual,* adventitiously, adventitiousness.

ADVENTURE (ad *to* + venire *to come*) *a bold and hazardous undertaking with the outcome uncertain,* adventurer, adventuress, adventuresome, adventuresomeness, adventurous, adventurously, adventurousness; misadventurous; unadventure.

AVENUE *a thoroughfare bordered by trees.*

CIRCUMVENT (circum *around* + venire *to come*) *to go around something and trick or prevent it,* circumvention, circumventive, circumventor.

CONTRAVENE *to oppose or violate an agreement or ruling,* contravener, contravention.

VEN
come

CONVENE (com *together* + venire *to come*) *to bring together,* convener, convenable; reconvene.

COVENANCE *that which is proper with established custom.*

CONVENIENCE *fitness, comfort; that which makes work less difficult; a handy device,* convenient, conveniently.

INCONVENIENCE inconveniency, inconvenient, inconveniently.

CONVENTION *a periodical assembly of an organization; a general agreement on the customs of social life.*

CONVENTIONAL *customary, based on tradition,* conventionalism, conventionalist, conventionality, conventionalization, conventionalize, conventionally.

CONVENT *the buildings holding a community of nuns (sometimes monks) who live under strict religious vows.*

COVENANT *a binding agreement by two persons or parties to do or not to do something,* covenantee *to whom made,* covenanter *who makes the covenant.*

EVENT (e *out* + venire *to come*) *that which comes, especially an incident of importance,* eventful, eventual, eventuality, eventually, eventuate, eventuation; uneventful.

INTERVENE (inter *between* + venire *to come*) *to come between, as an influencing force, so as to settle an argument or action,* interventionist, intervener, interventor.

INVENT *to devise in the mind; to originate a new device or process,* inventor or inventer, inventress, inventful, inventible, inventibleness, invention, inventional, inventive, inventively, inventiveness.

INVENTORY *an itemized list of goods, stock or property,* inventorial, inventorially.

PREVENT (pre *before* + venire *to come*) *to keep something from happening,* preventability, preventable, preventative, preventer, preventingly, prevention, preventional, preventive, preventively.

REVENUE (re *back* + venire *to come*) *the income return from property or investment.*

SUPERVENE *something unexpected to the normal course of events,* supervenient, supervention.

VENG

VINDICO, VINDICARE *to avenge,* VINDICATUM   **31**

AVENGE *to get revenge by punishing the injuring party,* avengeful, avengement, avenger; unavenged.

VENG
VIND
avenge

REVENGE (re *again* + venger *take vengeance*) *to retaliate for an injury or insult suffered*, revengeable, revengeance, revengeful, revengefully, revengefulness, revenger, revengefully; revengeless; unrevenged.

VENGEANCE *the return of an injury for an injury*, vengeful, vengefully.

VINDICATE *to clear from censure by evidence; to defend against opposition*, vindicability, vindicable, vindication, vindicative, vindicativeness, vindicator, vindicatory, vindicatress.

VINDICTIVE *revengeful in spirit*, vindictively, vindictiveness.

VER
true

VERUS *true;* VERAX, VERACIS *veracious*   17

AVER *to declare to be true.*

VERACITY *truthfulness of statement*, veracious.

VERDICT (vere dictum *"truly said"*) *a judgment; in law, the answer of the jury to the question put to it.*

VERIFY (verus *true* + facere *to make*) *to prove to be true by demonstration or evidence*, verifier, verifiable, verification, verificative.

VERISIMILAR (verus *true* + similis *like*) *probable; having the appearance of truth*, verisimilitude.

VERISM *the theory that art and literature should adhere closely to reality.*

VERITABLE *genuine; having the distinctive qualities of the person or thing*, veritably, verity *truthfulness.*

VERY *in the fullest sense*, verily *certainly.*

VERB
word

VERBUM *a word*   24

VERB (verbum) *that part of speech enabling an assertion or denial to be made.*

VERBAL *by means of words; spoken, literal*, verbalism, verbalist, verbally, verbalize, verbalization.

VERBATIM *following the original word by word.*

VERBICIDE (verbum *word* + caedere *to kill*) *perverting the meaning of a word; punning.*

VERBIAGE *wordiness; superabundance of words.*

VERBOSE *abounding in words; wordy*, verbosely, verboseness, verbosity.

VERVE *enthusiasm; vigor and energy in expression of ideas.*

ADVERB *a word to modify a verb, adjective, or other adverb*, adverbial, adverbally, adverbalize.

VERB PROVERB (pro *before* + verbum *a word*) *a maxim expressing a well known truth learned by experience and observation*, proverbial, proverbialist, proverbally, proverbalize.

VERS
VERT
turn

VERTO, VERTERE *to turn*, VERSUM   **183**

ADVERSE (ad *to* + vertere *to turn*) *opposite; contrary to one's interests*, adversative, adversatively, adversely, adverseness, adversity *misfortune, calamity*.

ADVERSARY *an opponent or antagonist*.

ADVERT *to turn the mind to*, advertence, advertent, advertently.

INDAVERTENCE *negligence, oversight*, inadvertency, inadvertent, inadvertently.

ADVERTISE (advertir *to inform*) *to publish a notice of*, advertisement, advertiser, advertising.

ANIMADVERT (animus *mind* + ad *to* + vertere *to turn*) *to perceive, criticize or censure*, animadversion, animadversive, animadversiveness, animadverter.

ANNIVERSARY (annus *year* + vertere *to turn*) *returning each year at a stated time*.

AVERT (a *from* + vertere *to turn*) *to turn from, to ward off*, averter, avertible.

AVERSE *disliking, unwilling*, aversely, averseness, aversion.

CONTROVERSY (contra *against* + vertere *to turn*) *in a discussion on a question in which opposing opinions clash*, controversial, controversialist, controversially, controvert, controverter, controvertible, controvertibly, controvertist.

CONVERT *to change into another substance or form*, converter, convertibility, convertible, convertibleness, convertibly.

CON'VERSE (*n*) *the opposite; a thing reversed in position*, conversely, converser, conversible, conversion.

CONVERSE' (*vb*) *to have free communication of thoughts*.

CONVERSANT (com *together* + vertere *to turn*) *having a thorough understanding*, conversable, conversableness, conversably, conversance.

CONVERSATION *informal exchange of ideas*, conversational, conversationalist, conversationally.

DIVERT *to deflect(stream); to distract (children)*, diverter, divertible, divertingly, divertingness, divertimento *a light instrumental composition;* divertissement *a short ballet between acts;* undiverted.

DIVERSE *capable of assuming different forms*, diversely, diverseness.

VERS
VERT
turn

DIVERSIFY (di *apart* + vertere *to turn* + facere *to make*) diversifiability, diversifiable, diversification, diversified, diversifier; undiversified.

DIVERSION *distraction of attention*, diversionary.

DIVORCE *a legal dissolution of the bonds of matrimony*, divorceable, divorcement, divorcee.

INTERVERT *to turn to another course or use.*

INTROVERT (intro *from* + vertere *to turn*) *to turn one's interest upon oneself; to introspect*, introvertive, introversion, introversive.

INVERSE *directly opposite; reversed in order,* inversely, inversion, inversive, invert.

OBVERSE *turned toward the viewer, opposite of reverse,* obversely; obvert *to turn toward.*

PERVERSE (per *through* + vertere *to turn*) *deviating from what is right,* perversely, perverseness; perversion *an abnormal form; sexual acts deviating from the norm,* perversity; pervert *to cause to turn from what is considered right and natural,* perverted, perverter.

RETROVERT *a turning or tilting backwards,* retroverted, retroversion.

REVERT (re *back* + vertere *to turn*) *to return to a former practice or opinion,* reverter, revertible, revertive, revertively; unreverted.

REVERSE *a change to the opposite,* reversely, reverser, reversibility, reversible, reversibly, reversion, reversionary; unreversed.

IRREVERSIBLE *incapable of being reversed,* irreversibleness, irreversibly, irreversibility.

REVERSION *a return to a former condition or belief,* (the following are legal) reversional, reversionary, reversioner.

SUBVERT (sub *under* + vertere *to turn*) *to overthrow or destroy; to undermine morals,* subverter, subvertible; subversion, subversionary, subversive.

TRANSVERSE (trans *across* + vertere *to turn*) *crosswise,* transversely, transversion.

TRAVERSE *to pass over or examine thoroughly,* traverser; untraversed, untraversable.

UNIVERSAL (unus *one* + vertere *to turn*) *considered as constituting a whole,* universalistic, universality, universalization, universalize, universally.

UNIVERSITY *a single institution composed of various colleges.*

VEER *to change direction,* veerable, veeringly.

VERSATILE *competent in many things,* versatility, versatileness.

VERSE (versus *a turning*) *metrical writing or speaking.*

VERS
VERT
turn

VERSIFY (versus *a turning* + facere *to make*) versifier, versification.
VERTIGO *a sense of dizziness*, vertiginous.
VERSION *an account showing one point of view; a variation or translation*, versional, versionist.
VERSUS *"turned in the direction of"; one party in sports, law, or debate against another.*
VERTEBRA *a single segment of the spinal column*, vertebrae (pl), vertebral, vertebrally.
VERTICIL *in botany, where the leaves or flowers surrounded the stem in a circle on the same plane*, verticillate.
VERTICAL *perpendicular or in a upright position*, verticality, verticalness.
VERTEX *top, apex, summit.*
VORTEX (vertere) *a whirling mass of water; a powerful eddy of air; an activity that resembles an irresistible power*, vortical, vortically.

VEST
clothe

VESTIS *a garment*   19
DEVEST *in law, to take away a title or estate.*
DIVEST *to strip of rank or rights*, divestible, divestiture, divestment, divesture.
INVEST *to install in office with ceremony; to put money in business etc. for profit*, investitive, investiture; uninvested.
INVESTMENT *the laying out of money to purchase some kind of property*, investor.
REINVEST *to invest anew*, reinvestment.
REVEST *to vest again with office or possession or power.*
VEST *a short sleeveless garment; to put a person in control.*
VESTMENT *an official robe or gown.*
VESTRY *a room in church for putting on vestments; a room where prayer meetings, etc. are held.*
VESTURE *in law, everything except trees that grows on the land.*

VECT
VEH
carry

VEHO, VEHERE *to carry*, VECTUM   28
VEX *to irritate in minor ways*, vexation, vexatious, vexatiously, vexatiousness; unvexed.
CONVEX (com *together* + vehere *to bring*) *having a surface that curves outward*, convexedly, convexedness.
INVEIGH (in *in* + vehere *to bring*) *to make strong denunciations*, inveigher.
INVECTIVE *a violent verbal attack*, invectively.

VECT, VEH — *carry*

VECTION *passage of disease from an infected to a healthy person.*
VECTOR *a line drawn from its point of origin to its final position.*
VEHEMENCE (vehere *to carry* + mentis *mind*) *intense feeling,* vehemency, vehement, vehemently.
VEHICLE *any means of conveying or communicating,* vehicular.
WEIGH (A-S wegan) *to measure by scale, estimate; consider and choose carefully,* weighable, weighing.
WEIGHT *heaviness as a quality,* weightily, weightiness, weightless.

VIA — *way*

VIA *a way;* VOIE [Fr] *a way*   51
WAY (A-S weg) *path, journey, route; method,* wayfare, wayfarer, wayfaring; waylay *to accost by surprise,* waylayer; wayward *willful, erratic.*
DEVIATE *to turn from the common or right course,* deviation, deviant, deviator, deviatory; undeviating, undeviatingly.
DEVIOUS *roundabout; going astray, crooked,* deviously, deviousness.
OBVIATE (ob *against* + via *way*) *prevent obstacles by effective measures,* obviation.
OBVIOUS *easy to see or understand,* obviously, obviousness.
PERVIOUS *penetrable, having a mind open to influence or argument,* perviousness; impervious, imperviously.
PREVIOUS (pre *before* + via *way*) *happening before something else,* previously, previousness.
TRIVIAL (tri *three* + via *way*) *when persons on three roads meet, little is accomplished,* trivia *unimportant matters,* trivialism, triviality, trivially, trivialness.
VIA *by way of passing through,* viaduct *a bridge to carry traffic over a land depression.*
CONVEY *to transport from one place to another,* conveyable, conveyance, conveyancer, conveyer; reconvey, reconveyance.
CONVOY *to escort for protection.*
ENVOY (in *on* + via *way*) *a deputy who transacts business with a foreign government.*
VOYAGE *a long journey,* voyageable, voyager, voyaging.

VID

VIDEO, VIDERE *to see,* VISUM   124
ADVISE *to counsel or offer an opinion worthy to be followed,* advice, advisability,

VID
VIS
see

advisableness, advisably, advisedly, advisedness, advisement, adviser or advisor, advising, advisorily, advisory.

PROVIDE (pro *before* + videre *to see*) *to procure beforehand; to make available*, providable, provider, providing.

PROVIDENCE *preparation; timely care; guidance by God or nature*, provident, providential, providentially, providently, providentness.

PROVISION *preparatory arrangements made in advance for some future needs; a legal clause stipulating some specific thing*, provisional, provisionally, provisionary, provisioner.

PROVISO *a legal clause that restricts an agreement or contract*, provisory, provisorily.

PROVISOR *an appointee by the Pope before the death of the incumbent*, provisorship.

REVISE (re *again* + visere *to see*) revisable, revisal, reviser, revision, revisional, revisionary, revisionism, revisionist; unrevised.

SUPERVISE (super *above* + *visus* see) *to direct the work or project*, supervision, supervisor, supervisorship, supervisory.

EVIDENCE (e *from* + videre *to see*) *that which tends to prove; ground for belief*.

EVIDENT *easy to see or perceive*, evidential, evidentially, evidentiary, evidently, evidentness.

SELF-EVIDENT *certainty of an idea without proof*, self-evident, self-evidently.

ENVY (in *in, upon* + videre *to see*) *ill will because of another's advantage*, enviable, enviableness, enviably, envier, envious, enviously, enviousness.

INVIDIOUS *likely to invoke envy; discriminating unfairly*, invidiously, invidiousness.

PURVEY (providere *to foresee*) *to provide provisions*, purveyance, purveyor.

SURVEY (super *over* + videre *to see*) *to examine carefully as to precise state or value*, surveyable, surveyance, surveying, surveyor, surveyorship; resurvey.

VIEW *range of vision; visual aspect of something*, viewer, viewpoint; viewless, viewlessly.

INTERVIEW (inter *between* + videre *to see*) *a face to face meeting to confer on something*, interviewer, interviewing.

REVIEW (re *again* + videre *to see*) *to view in retrospect*, reviewable, reviewal, reviewer.

VISA *an endorsement stamped on a passport*.

VISAGE *the face, expression, countenance*.

VISIBLE *that can be seen*, visibility, visibleness, visibly.

VID / VIS — *see*

VISION *the sense of sight; the ability to perceive something not actually visible,* visional, visionariness, visionary, visionist, visionless.

VISTA *a view through tress with a view framed.*

VISUAL *that can be seen,* visuality, visualization, visualize, visualizer, visually; supervisual *beyond ordinary visual power.*

VISOR *projection on cap to protect eyes; moveable shade on car windshield.*

VISIT *to come and see or stay with a friend; a professional meeting,* visitable, visitant, visitation, visitorial, visitor or visiter, visitress, visiting; revisit, revisitation; unvisited.

VINC / VICT — *conquer*

VINCO, VINCERE *to conquer,* VICTUM   50

CONVINCE (*originally, to overcome*) *persuade by evidence or argument,* convincer, convincible, convincing, convincingly, convincingness; inconvincible, inconvincibly; unconvinced.

EVINCE (e *from, out* + vincere *to conquer*) *to show in a clear manner,* evincement, evincible, evincibly, evincive.

PROVINCE *a part of the country removed from the capital,* provincial.

PROVINCIALISM *behavior peculiar to a province,* provincialist, provinciality, provincialize, provincially, provinciate.

VINCIBLE *capable of being conquered or subdued,* vincibility, vincibleness.

INVINCIBLE *that cannot be overcome,* invincibility, invincibleness, invincibly.

CON'VICT (n) *a person sentenced for a crime.*

CONVICT' (v) *to prove guilty of a crime,* convictible, convictism, convictive, convictively, convictiveness; self-convicted.

EVICT *to lawfully expel from property occupying,* eviction.

VICTOR *one who wins in a contest,* victress, victorious, victoriously, victoriousness, victory.

VANQUISH *to overcome or defeat in any contest,* vanquishable, vanquisher, vanquishment; unvanquished.

VIV — *life*

VIVO, VIVERE *to live,* VICTUM; VITA *life*   58

CONVIVAL *social, jovial; fond of eating and drinking,* convivialist, conviviality, convivially.

REVIVE (re *again* + vivere *to live*) *to come back to health; to flourish after a decline,* revivable, reviver, revivify, revivification, revivingly, reviviscence, reviviscency, reviviscent.

VIV — life

REVIVAL *a fervid religious meeting; return of a play*, revivalism, revivalist, revivalistic.

SURVIVE (super *above* + vivere *to live*) *to outlive*, survival, surviver or survivor, surviving, survivorship.

VIABLE *able to live*, viability.

VITAL *essential to the existence of something*, vitalic, vitalism, vitalist, vitalistic, vitality, vitalization, vitalize, vitalizer, vitally, vitals.

VIVACITY *sprightliness of behavior*, vivacious, vivaciously, vivaciousness.

VIVID *full of life, brilliant, striking*, vividity, vividly, vividness.

VIVIFY *to animate*, vivificate *chemical reduction to metallic state*, vivification *conversion of food into living matter through assimilation*.

VIVARY (or vivarium) *raising plants and animals under conditions similar to their natural environment.*

VIVIPAROUS *bringing forth living young (as do mammals)*, viviparity, viviparously, viviparousness.

VIAND *an article of food.*

VICTUAL *supply with provisions*, victualage, victualer.

VITAMINS *organic substances found in most foods and essential, in small amounts, for body functioning.*

VOC — call

VOCO, VOCARE *to call,* **VOCATUM**   116

ADVOCATE (ad *to* + vocare *to call*) *one who pleads the cause of another in court; one who defends a cause by argument*, advocacy, advocateship, advocation, advocator, advocatory, advocatus diaboli *the devil's advocate.*

CONVOKE (com *together* + vocare *to call*) *to summon to meet*, convocation, convocational, convocationist, convocator.

EQUIVOCATE (equi *equal* + vocis *voice*) *to express one's opinion ambiguously so as to deceive*, equivocal, equivocacy, equivocally, equivocalness, equivocation, equivocator, equivacatory, equivoke.

UNEQUIVOCAL *plain, clear, straightforward*, unequivocally, unequivocalness.

EVOKE (e *out, from* + vocare *to call*) *to summon, to elicit*, evocable, evocation, evocative, evocator.

INVOKE *to call on a divinity for blessing or inspiration; to implore, entreat*, invocation, invocatory.

PROVOKE (pro *forth* + vocare *to call*) *to arouse, exasperate, irritate*, provocation, provocative, provocativeness, provokable, provoker, provoking, provokingly; unprovoked, unprovoking.

VOC — call

REVOKE (re *back* + vocare *to call*) *to rescind, cancel, annul,* revocability, revocable, revocableness, revocably, revocation, revocatory, revokable, revokement, revoker, revokingly.

IRREVOCABLE *incapable of being recalled; cannot be reversed,* irrevocability, irrevocableness, irrevocably.

VOCAL (vocalis *sounding*) vocable *sound rather than meaning,* vocalic *consisting of vowels,* vocalism *use of the voice,* vocalist, vocality, vocalization, vocalize, vocally, vocalness, vocative.

VOCABULARY *all the words used by a person or class or profession,* vocabulist.

VOCATION *any career, profession or occupation,* vocational, vocationally.

AVOCATION *something one does in addition to his regular work,* avocatory.

VOCIFERATE *a violent outcry,* vociferance, vociferant, vociferation, vociferator, vociferous, vociferously, vociferousness.

VOICE *human sound made through the mouth,* voiceful, voicefulness, voicer; voiceless, voicelessly, voicelessness.

VOWEL *a letter that refers to a single sound; a, e, i, o, u; not consonants,* vowelist, vowelization, vowelize, vowelly; vowelless.

VOUCH *to affirm; to give evidence for,* vouchee, voucher, vouchsafe.

AVOUCH *to declare or assert with positiveness,* avouchable, avoucher, avouchment.

AVOW *to declare openly,* avowable, avowal, avowance, avowant, avowantly, avowedly, avower.

DISAVOW disavowal, disavower, disavowment.

VOL — roll

VOLVO, VOLVERE *to roll,* VOLUTUM   61

CONVOLVE *to roll together,* convolute, convolution.

DEVOLVE (de *down* + volvere *to roll*) *pass on to others duties and responsibilities,* devolution, devolvement.

EVOLVE (e *out* + volvere *to draw*) *to develop gradually,* evolvement, evolvent.

EVOLUTE *in geometry, a special curve.*

EVOLUTION *the theory that all plants and animals developed from earlier forms by hereditary transmission with slight variations in successive generations,* evolutional, evolutionary, evolutionism, evoluntionist.

EVOLUTILITY *the capacity of an organism to change as a result of nutrition.*

INVOLVE *to bring into connection; to occupy the attention of; to entangle in trouble,* involvedness, involvement.

INVOLUTE *intricate; curled in a spiral,* involution, involutional, involutionary.

VOL
roll

INTERVOLVE (inter *between* + volvere *to roll*) *to wind together or be involved*, intervolution.

OBVOLUTE *overlapping; turned into*, obvolution, obvolutive, obvolent.

REVOLT (re *again* + volere *to roll*) *to mutiny; to refuse to accept authority*, revolter, revolting *also disgusting*, revoltingly, revolute.

REVOLUTION *turning a body around a center of axis; overthrow of a government or social system*, revolutionary, revolutioner, revolutionist, revolutionism, revolutionize.

REVOLVE (re *back* + volvere *to roll*) *to move in a circle or orbit around a point*, revolvable, revolvement, revolvency, revolving.

REVOLVER *a pistol with a revolving cylinder for cartridges*.

VOLUME *originally a scroll; a book; quantity, bulk, mass*, voluminal.

VOLUMINOUS *great magnitude, writing to fill volume*, voluminosity, voluminously, voluminousness.

VOLUBLE *speaking fluently; glib and garrulous*, volubility, volubleness, volubly.

VOLUTE *a spiral scroll or whorl*, volution, volutoid.

VOLT *a circular tread; a sidewise horse gait; a fencing move to avoid a thrust; a unit of electromotive force*.

WALLOW *to roll in a mire; to indulge oneself in riches, vice, etc.*, wallerer.

VOL
wish

VOLO, VELLE *to wish*   18

BENEVOLENCE (bene *well* + volens *wish*) *good will, act of kindness*, benevolent, benevolently, benevolous.

MALEVOLENCE (male *badly* + volens *wish*) *ill will, personal hatred*, malevolent, malevolently.

VOLITION *exercise of the will*, volitional, volitionally, volitive.

VOLUNTARY *by one's own free choice*, voluntarily, voluntariness, voluntarism, voluntaristic, voluntarism, volunteer.

VOT
vow

VOVEO, VOVERE *to vow*, **VOTUM**   30

DEVOTE (de *from* + vovere *to vow*) *to apply oneself to some purpose*, devotedly, devotedness, devotee, devoteeism, devotement, devoter.

DEVOTION *deep affection*, devotional, devotionist, devotionally, devotionist.

DEVOUT *expressing piety, sincere*, devoutful, devoutfully, devoutly, devoutness; devoutless, devoutlessly, devoutlessness.

VOW *to promise solemnly*.

VOT
vow

VOTE *a decision expressed on a proposal or election of a person,* votable, voter, voteless.
VOTARY *an ardent supporter of a cause, ideal or religion,* votress.
VOTIVE *a consecrated fulfillment of a vow,* votively, votiveness.

VULG
people
publish

VULGO, VULGARE *to publish,* **VULGATUM**   **20**
DIVULGE (di *apart* + vulgare *to make public*) divulgence, divulger, divulsion, divulgator, divulgation; undivulged.
PROMULGATE (promulgatus) *to publish or make known officially,* promulgation, promulgator.
VULGAR *common to the great mass of people; lack of refinement,* vulgarian, vulgarism *an expression of coarse speech,* vulgarity, vulgarization, vulgarize, vulgarly, vulgarness; unvulgarize.
VULGATE *the Catholic fourth century Latin version of the Bible.*

VULS
tear out

VELLO, VELLERE *to pluck, tear out,* **VULSUM**   **16**
AVULSE *to pluck, to pull off,* avulsion.
CONVULSE (com *together* + vellere *to pluck*) *to cause to shake with laughter, grief or rage,* convulsion, convulsionary, convulsionist, convulsive, convulsively; anticonvulsive *medically effective for convulsions.*
DIVULSION *a tearing apart,* divulsive.
REVULSION *withdrawal; a violent reaction in sentiment,* revulsive.
VELLICATE *to cause to twitch convulsively (i.e. muscles),* vellication, vellicative.

MINOR ROOTS

Minor Roots is an arbitrary division of less important roots. They often have only one core word and few prefixes.

ACE/ACI	*sour, sharp*	acetify, acidity, acrimonious, acerbity.
ACOUS	*hear*	acoustics, acoustical, acoustically.
ACRO	*height*	acrobat, acrophobia, acronym, acropolis.
AGON	*struggle*	agony, antagonize, protagonist, agonize.
AGR	*field*	agriculture, agrarian, agriculturist, agronomy.
ALB	*white*	album, albumen, albino, albatross.
ALI	*another*	alias, alibi, alien, alienate, inalienable.
ALI	*nourish*	alimony, alimentary, alimental, coalition.
ALT	*high*	altitude, altar, alto, exaltation.
ALTER	*other*	alteration, unaltered, altercation, alternative.
AMA	*love*	amicable, amiability, amateur, paramour.
AMBUL	*walk*	amble, perambulate, somnambulist, ambulance.
AMPL	*large*	ample, amplification, amply, amplitude.
ANG	*choke*	anger, angina, anguish, anxious, anxiety.
ANGL	*angle*	angle, angular, triangle, quadrangular.
ANN	*a year*	annals, anniversary, annually, annuity.

ANTHRO	*man*	anthropology, misanthrope, philanthropy.
ANTIQU	*ancient*	antique, antiquary, antiquated, antiquity.
APT	*fit*	apt, aptness, aptitude, adapt, inept.
AQUA	*water*	aquarium, aquatic, aquanaut, aqueduct.
ARB	*judge*	arbiter, arbitrage, arbitrarily, arbitrate.
ARBOR	*tree*	arbor, arborist, arboretum, arborescence.
ARC	*bow, arch*	arc, arch, arcade, archery, archeress.
ARCH	*ruler, chief*	hierarchy, monarch, oligarchy, anarchy.
ARCHA	*ancient*	archaeology, archaic, archaistic, archaeologist.
ARD/ARS	*burn*	ardent, ardor, arson, arsonist.
ARISTO	*best born*	aristocrat, aristocracy, aristocratically.
ARM	*weapon*	armory, armaments, armada, armistice.
ART	*skill*	artful, artifice, artificial, artistically.
ARTIC	*joint*	article, articulate, inarticulate, arthritis.
ASP	*rough*	asperate, asperity, exasperate, exasperation.
ASTR	*star*	astronomy, astronaut, asterisk, disaster.
ASTUT	*crafty*	astute, astutely, astuteness, astuciously.
ATHL	*contest*	athlete, athletically, decathlon, pentathlon.
ATMOS	*vapor*	atmology, atmosphere, atmospherically.
ATROC	*cruel*	atrocity, atrocious, atrociousness.
AUDI	*hear*	audible, audition, audience, auditorium.
AUG	*increase*	auction, augment, August, augmentation.
AUGU	*omen*	augur, inaugural, reinaugurate, uninaugurated.
AURI	*ear*	auricle, auricular, aurist, auriscope.
AUSPIC	*soothsay*	auspice, auspiciously, inauspicious.
AUTO	*self*	autocracy, autonomy, autobiographic, automate.
AVI	*bird*	aviator, aviatrix, aviate, aviary.
AXIOM	*evident*	axiom, axiomatic, axiomatically.
BAC	*a staff*	bacteria, bacterial, bacillus, bacillar.
BALL	*dance*	ballroom, ballad, ballerina, ballet.
BAPT	*dipped*	baptism, baptize, Baptist, Anabaptist.
BARB	*savage*	barbarian, barbarity, barbarism, barbarous.
BARK	*a ship*	embark, debark, disembark, embarkation.
BARO	*weight*	barometer, barograph, baroscope, isobar.
BAS	*base, low*	basic, basis, basement, bassoon, debasement.
BATT	*battle*	embattled, battle fatigue, battlefield, battleship.
BELL	*war*	bellicose, belligerent, rebel, rebellious.

BENE	*well*	benefit, benediction, benevolent, beneficient.
BI	*two*	biennial, bigamist, binocular, biscuit.
BIO	*life*	biology, biographer, biopsy, antibiotic.
BLA	*censure*	blasphemy, blasphemous, blame, blameless.
BON	*good*	bonus, boon, bounty, bona fide.
BOTAN	*plant*	botany, botanical, botanically, botanist.
BRAC	*arm*	brace, bracelet, bracero, embrace.
BREV	*short*	brevity, brief, abbreviate, breve.
BRONCH	*windpipe*	bronchial, bronchitis, bronchitic, bronchoscope.
BRUT	*bestial*	brute, brutal, brutish, brutality.
CAL	*glow, heat*	calorie, caloric, caldron, scald.
CAMERA	*chamber*	camera, chamber, bicameral, unicameral.
CAMP	*plain*	campus, encamp, decamp, campaign.
CAP	*hold*	capable, incapable, capacious, capacity.
CAPR	*leap*	caper, caprice, capriciously, capriciousness.
CARP	*seize*	carp, carper, discerptive, excerpt.
CAUS	*burn*	caustic, cauterize, cautery, holocaust.
CENS	*appraise*	censor, censorious, censure, census.
CERT	*determine*	certain, certify, certificate, ascertain.
CHAOS	*abyss*	chaos, chaotic, chasm, chasmal.
CHARI	*grace*	charity, charitable, uncharitable, uncharitably.
CHAST	*pure*	chaste, chastity, chastise, castigate.
CHOL	*bile*	cholera, choleric, melancholy, melancholic.
CHOR	*sing*	choir, choral, chorister, chorus.
CHROM	*color*	chromatic, chrome, chromosome.
CHRON	*time*	chronic, anachronism, chronology, synchronize.
CINC	*gird*	cincture, precinct, succinct, succinctness.
CIRC	*round*	circle, circular, circus, semicircle.
CLASS	*rank*	class, classical, classify, classification.
CLEM	*mild*	clement, clemency, inclement, inclemency.
CLER	*assigned*	clergy, cleric, clerk, clerkship.
COCT	*cook*	concoct, concoction, precocious, precocity.
COD	*a tablet*	code, codicil, codify, codification.
COLOR	*hue*	color, coloration, discolor, uncolored.
COM	*festivity*	comedy, comic, encomium, tragicomedy.
COMP	*with bread*	company, companion, accompany.
CONCIL	*win over*	conciliate, conciliatory, irreconcilable.

CONTRA	*opposed*	contrary, contrariously, contrast, counteract.
COPULA	*couple*	copulate, copulation, couple, couplet.
CORN	*a horn*	cornet, unicorn, cornea, capricorn, cornucopia.
CORON	*a crown*	corollary, coronation, coroner, crown.
COSM	*universe*	cosmic, cosmetic, microcosm, cosmopolitan.
COUNT	*reckon*	account, discount, recount, uncounted.
COURT	*royally*	courtly, courtesy, cortege, discourteous.
COVER	*hide*	cover, discover, covertly, undiscovered.
CRAT	*rule*	aristocrat, autocracy, theocracy, democratic.
CRE	*burst*	crevice, crevasse, decrepit, discrepancy.
CRIT	*judge*	critic, criticism, criterion, critique, hypocrite.
CRUC	*cross*	crux, crucial, crucifixion, excruciate.
CRYPT	*secret*	apocryphal, crypt, cryptic, cryptogram.
CULP	*blame*	culpable, culprit, exculpate, mea culpa.
CUMU	*heap*	accumulate, cumulus, cumulative, accumulative.
CURT	*short*	curtly, curtail, curtailing, curtailment.
CURV	*bent*	curvation, curvilinear, curvity, recurve.
CUS	*cause*	accuse, accusation, excuse, unexcusable.
CUSTOM	*manner*	accustom, custom, customary, unaccustomed.
CYCL	*circle*	cyclist, motorcycle, cyclone, cyclometer.
CYN	*doglike*	canine, cynicism, cynosure, cynegetics.
DEC	*ten*	decimal, decimate, decade, December.
DECOR	*to befit*	decor, indecorous, decorate, decorum.
DELET	*erase*	delete, indelible, delible, deleterious.
DELIC	*delights*	delicious, delicacy, delicately, indelicate.
DEMN	*penalize*	condemn, condemnation, indemnify, damnable.
DENS	*thick*	condensable, condensation, density, recondense.
DERM	*skin*	dermatitis, dermatology, epidermis.
DEXT	*right hand*	dexterity, dexterously, dextral, ambidextrous.
DI	*day*	diary, diurnal, per diem, dial.
DIGIT	*finger*	digit, digital, digitalis, prestidigitator.
DISCI	*learn*	disciple, discipline, disciplinarian.
DOL	*grieve*	doleful, dolorous, condole, indolent.
DOM	*house*	domestic, domestication, domicile, dome.
DOMIN	*master*	dominate, domineer, dominion, predominant.
DORM	*sleep*	dormant, dormer, dormitory, dormouse.
DOX	*belief*	orthodox, paradox, unorthodox, heterodox.

DUBI	*uncertain*	dubiously, dubitable, indubious, indubitably.
ELEG	*select*	elegance, elegant, elegantly, inelegantly.
EBR	*drunk*	ebriety, ebrious, inebriate, sobriety.
EDI	*build*	edifice, edification, edify.
ELEM	*first principle*	element, elemental, elementary.
EMIA	*blood*	anemia, uremia, hemoglobin, anemic.
EMUL	*imitate*	emulate, emulative, emulator, emulous.
ENNI	*year*	biennial, perennial, decennial, centennial.
ENVIR	*encircle*	environs, environment, environmentalist.
EQUIP	*fit out*	equipt, equipment, unequipped.
EQUUS	*a horse*	equestrian, equine, equerry, equitation.
ERC	*press*	coerce, coercive, exercise, unexercised.
ERG	*work*	erg, energy, energetic, synergistic.
ESOT	*inner*	esoteric, esoterical, esotericism, esoterically.
ESTH	*feeling*	esthetics, estheticism, anesthesia, anesthetic.
ESTI	*value*	esteem, estimable, estimate, inestimable.
ETH	*customs*	ethics, ethical, ethically, unethical.
ETHN	*nation*	ethnic, ethnical, ethnological, ethnocentric.
EU	*good*	eugenics, eulogy, euphony, euthanasia.
EXAM	*test*	examine, examinee, examiner, examination.
EXT	*out*	exterior, external, extreme, extrinsic.
FABUL	*speak*	fable, fabulous, confabulate, ineffable.
FABR	*worker*	fabric, fabricate, fabrication, fabricator.
FACET	*wit*	facetious, facetiously, facetiousness.
FAM	*report*	famous, infamy, defame, defamation.
FAMI	*hunger*	famine, famish, famishment.
FAMIL	*household*	familiar, familiarize, family, unfamiliar.
FAN	*temple*	fanatic, unfanatical, profane, profanity.
FAN/FAT	*speak*	infant, infantry, fate, fatalistic.
FANT	*imagine*	fancy, fantasy, fantastic, fantasticalness.
FARC	*stuffed*	farce, farcical, farceur, farcically.
FASCI	*enchant*	fascinate, fascinator, fascinatingly, fascination.
FASTID	*disdain*	fastidious, fastidiously, fastidiousness.
FATU	*silly*	fatuous, fatuity, infatuate, infatuation.
FAVOR	*befriend*	favorable, unfavorable, favorite, favoritism.
FEAS	*perform*	feasible, feasibility, malfeasanse, nonfeasance.
FED	*league*	federal, federalize, confederation, federate.

FELIC	*happy*	felicity, felicitate, felicitous, infelicity.
FEMIN	*woman*	effeminate, femininity, feminine, female.
FER	*fierce*	ferocious, ferocity, fierce, fierceness.
FEST	*joyful*	feast, festival, festoon, fete.
FEV/FEB	*fever*	fever, feverish, febrile, febrifugal.
FILI	*sibling*	filial, filicide, affiliate, affiliation.
FINAN	*pay*	finance, financial, refinanced, unfinanced.
FISC	*monetary*	fiscal, confiscate, confiscation, confiscatory.
FLAGR	*burn*	flagration, flagrantly, flagrance, conflagration.
FLAT	*blow*	flatulent, flatulence, inflation, reflate.
FOLI	*leaf*	foliage, folio, interfoliate, foil.
FORTU	*chance*	fortuitous, fortunate, misfortune, unfortunate.
FRANK	*free*	frank, frankly, frankness, franchise.
FRAT	*brotherly*	fraternal, fraternity, fraternize, fratricide.
FRAUD	*deceit*	fraud, fraudulent, fraudulency, defrauder.
FREQ	*often*	frequent, frequenter, frequency, infrequent.
FRIC	*rub*	friction, frictionless, frictionally, dentifrice.
FRIG	*cold*	frigid, frigidity, refrigerate, refrigeration.
FRING	*border*	fringe, fringeless, infringe, infringement.
FUM	*smoke*	fume, fumeless, fumigate, perfume.
FUR	*rage*	fury, furious, furiously, infuriate.
FUT	*disprove*	confute, confutation, refute, refutation.
GAG	*pledge*	engage, disengagement, reengage, mortgage.
GAM	*marriage*	bigamy, polygamy, monogamy, misogamy.
GEL	*frost*	congeal, gelative, jelly, congealment.
GERM	*a sprout*	germ, germinate, germane, germicide.
GLOR	*honor*	glorious, glorification, ingloriously.
GLOT	*tongue*	epiglottis, gloss, glossary, polyglot.
GLU	*tenacious*	glue, glutinous, agglutination.
GLUT	*swallow*	glut, glutton, gluttonous, gluttony.
GON	*angle*	diagonal, hexagon, octagon, trigonometry.
GORG	*throat*	gorge, gorgeous, gargle, disgorge.
GOVERN	*command*	government, misgovern, regovern.
GRA	*pleasing*	graceful, disgrace, gratuitous, ingratiate.
GRAND	*great*	aggrandize, grandfather, grandeur.
GRU	*agreeing*	congruent, congruously, discongruity.
GUST	*a tasting*	gustation, gusto, disgust, disgusting.

GYR	*revolve*	gyrate, gyroscope, autogyro, gyrostabilizer.
HAL	*breathe*	inhale, inhalation, halitosis, exhalation.
HARMON	*fitting*	harmony, harmonics, harmonica, harmonize.
HAUST	*draw out*	exhaust, exhaustible, inexhaustible.
HELI	*spiral*	helix, helical, helicograph, helicopter.
HEM	*bloodlike*	hemorrhage, hemorrhoids, hematin.
HERB	*a plant*	herbaceous, herbal, herbalist, herbivorous.
HERO	*protect*	hero, heroine, heroic, unheroic.
HETERO	*different*	heterodox, heteronym, heterogeneous.
HIER	*sacred*	hierarchy, hierology, hieroglyphic.
HOLO	*whole*	catholic, holograph, holohedral, holocaust.
HOMO	*same*	homogeneous, homogenize, homonym.
HON	*respect*	honor, honorless, dishonor, honesty.
HORR	*dreadful*	horrify, horridness, abhor, abhorrence.
HORT	*encourage*	hortatory, hortation, exhort, exhortation.
HOST	*an enemy*	hostile, hostility, unhostile.
HYPN	*sleep*	hypnotism, hypnotic, hypnotist, hypnotize.
IDEA	*conception*	idea, ideal, idealization, ideology.
IDENT	*the same*	identify, identical, identity, identification.
IDIO	*peculiar*	idiocy, idiom, idiosyncratic, idiotic.
IGN	*fire*	ignition, igneous, ignite, ignescent.
IGNO	*not know*	ignore, ignorance, ignorant, ignoramus.
IMI/IMA	*likeness*	imitate, inimitable, image, imagination.
INSUL	*island*	insulate, insulin, island, peninsula.
INTEG	*whole*	integer, integral, integration, integrity.
INTERP	*explain*	interpret, interpretation, misinterpretation.
IRE/IRA	*anger*	ire, irate, irascible, irritation.
ITER	*again*	iterate, iterance, iterative, reiterate.
JOURN	*[Fr] a day*	adjourn, journey, journal, sojourn.
JUBIL	*cry of joy*	jubilant, jubilee, jubilation.
JUG	*yoke*	abjugate, conjugal, subjugate, subjugation.
JUVEN	*youth*	juvenile, juvenal, juvenility, juvenescent.
KIN	*move*	kinescope, kinetic, cinema, cinematography.
LABOR	*work*	labor, collaborate, laboratory, elaborate.
LAM	*wail*	lament, lamentation, lamentable, lamentational.
LANGU	*weak*	languor, languidly, languish, languishment.
LAPSE	*slip*	lapse, collapse, elapse, relapse.

Root	Meaning	Examples
LATERAL	*side*	lateral, collateral, equilateral, multilateral.
LAUD	*praise*	laud, laudable, laudatory.
LAX	*loose*	laxity, laxative, relaxation, laxation.
LEN	*mild*	lenient, leniency, relent, relentless.
LIBR	*book*	library, librarian, libel, libretto.
LIBRA	*balance*	libration, deliberate, deliberately, equilibrium.
LIC	*permitted*	licit, illicit, license, licentious.
LIMIT	*boundary*	illimitable, limit, limitless, unlimited.
LINGU	*tongue*	lingual, linguistics, lingulate, bilingual.
LITIG	*strife*	litigate, litigation, litigious, litigiosity.
LOGUE	*discourse*	monologue, dialogue, prologue, catalogue.
LONG	*lengthen*	along, longevity, oblong, prolong.
LUSTR	*brighten*	lustre, lustrous, illustrate, illustrious.
MACH	*a device*	machinery, machinist, machinate, machinations.
MACUL	*a spot*	maculate, maculation, immaculate, immaculately.
MANI	*madness*	mania, maniacal, manic-depressive.
MAR	*border*	margin, marginal, marque, demarkation.
MAR	*sea*	marine, maritime, marinade, submarine.
MATER	*matter*	material, materialism, immaterial.
MECH	*contrive*	mechanic, mechanism, mechanical, mechanize.
MELIOR	*better*	meliorate, meliorable, ameliorate, amelioration.
MEND	*mistake*	amend, amendment, mend, emendable.
MENDA	*lying*	mendacious, mendaciousness, mendacity.
MERCI	*tenderness*	mercy, merciful, merciless, unmerciful.
MERIT	*deserve*	merit, meritorious, demerit, unmerited.
MICRO	*little*	microcosm, micrometer, microphone.
MIM	*imitate*	mime, mimic, mimicry, pantomime.
MIN	*threats*	minacious, minacity, comminatory, menance.
MINEN	*project*	eminence, pre-eminent, prominence.
MINIS	*serve*	minister, ministerial, administer, administrator.
MIS	*hatred*	misanthrope, misanthropic, misogamy.
MISER	*wretched*	miserly, miserable, misery, commiseration.
MITIG	*soften*	mitigate, mitigation, unmitigated, unmitigable.
MOL	*mass*	mole, molar, molecule, demolish, demolition.
MOLEST	*trouble*	molest, molester, molestation, unmolested.
MOR	*bite*	morsel, mordacious, remorse, remorseless.
MORPH	*shape*	amorphous, anthropomorphic, metamorphic.

MUS	*song*	muse, museum, music, musicality.
MUTIL	*maimed*	mutilate, mutilator, mutilation, unmutilated.
MYST	*conceal*	mystery, mysterious, mystic, mysticism.
MYTH	*a fable*	mythical, mythologist, mythological.
NARR	*tell*	narrate, narration, narrator, unnarrated.
NEC/NEX	*tie*	connect, disconnect, nexus, annex.
NECESS	*needful*	necessary, necessity, necessitous, unnecessary.
NEO	*new*	neon, neophite, neoclassic, neocosmic.
NEUT	*neither*	neuter, neutral, neutralization, neutron.
NIHIL	*nothing*	nihilistic, nihilism, annihilate, annihilator.
NOBL	*well known*	noble, nobility, ignoble, ennoble.
NOCT	*night*	equinoctial, noctuary, nocturnal, nocturne.
NYM	*name*	anonymous, patronym, metonymic, synonym.
OCUL	*eye*	oculist, binocular, inoculate, monocle.
OD	*a way*	episode, method, methodical, period.
ODOR	*smell*	odor, odorous, inodorous, malodorous.
OMIN	*an omen*	abominate, abominable, omen, ominous.
OMNI	*all*	omniformity, omnipotent, omniscient.
ONER	*a burden*	onus, onerous, exonerator, exonerate.
OPIN	*think*	opine, opinion, opinionated, opinionless.
OPT	*see*	autopsy, dioptic, myoptic, optical, optician.
OPT	*choose*	option, adoption, co-opt, readopt.
OPUL	*wealthy*	opulent, opulently, opulence, inopulent.
ORB	*circle*	orb, orbit, orbitary, exorbitance.
ORI	*begin*	orient, aboriginal, origin, origination.
ORN	*furnish*	ornate, adornment, suborn, subornation.
ORTH	*straight*	orthodox, unorthodox, orthography, orthology.
OV	*egg*	ova, oval, ovarian, ovum, ovulate.
PAC	*peace*	pacify, pacification, repacify, appeasement.
PACT	*bind*	pact, compact, impact, recompact.
PALA	*taste*	palate, palatable, palatability, unpalatable.
PALP	*touch*	palpable, palpability, palpitation, impalpable.
PAR	*bring forth*	parent, parentage, parentless, parturition.
PARL	*speak*	parlance, parley, parliamentarian, parlor.
PAST	*pasture*	pastor, pasture, repast, unpastoral.
PAU/POV	*poor*	pauperism, poorly, poverty, impoverished.
PECCA	*sin*	peccable, peccadillo, impeccable, impeccability.

PECT	*breast*	pectoral, parapet, expectorate, expectoration.
PELL	*call*	appellant, appellation, appeal, repeal.
PENE	*pierce*	penetrate, penetration, impenetrable.
PENT	*five*	pentachord, pentagon, pentathlon, pentacostal.
PERI	*try*	experiment, experienced, expertly, inexpert.
PERP	*entire*	perpetual, perpetually, perpetuation, perpetuity.
PEST	*plague*	pest, pestiferous, pestering, pestilence.
PETR	*stone*	petrify, petrification, petrol, petroleum.
PHIL	*love*	philanthropy, philanderer, philosophical.
PHON	*sound*	antiphony, cacophony, euphony, polyphonic.
PHREN	*the mind*	phrenologist, frenetic, frenzy.
PHYS	*nature*	physical, physician, physiological, metaphysics.
PIL	*rob*	pilfer, pillage, compile, compilation.
PIO/PIE	*religious*	pious, impious, piety, impiety.
PLA	*lament*	complain, plaint, plaintiff, plague.
PLOR	*cry out*	deplorable, implore, exploratory, unexplored.
PLU	*more*	plural, plus, pluperfect, surplus.
PLUM	*a feather*	plume, plumeless, deplume, implume.
POE	*compose*	poem, poet, poetically, impoetic.
POL	*a pole*	pole, polar, polarity, polarization.
POLI	*polish*	polish, polishable, polite, impolite.
POLY	*many*	polygamy, polygram, polygraph, polysyllable.
PONT	*bridge*	pontiff, pontificate, pontoon.
POR	*passageway*	pore, porous, porosity, imporosity.
PORC	*pig*	pork, porcine, porcupine, porpoise.
POST	*demand*	postulant, postulatory, expostulate.
POSTER	*after*	posterior, postern, posterity, preposterously.
POT/POS	*drink*	potable, potion, compotation, symposium.
PRAV	*wrong*	depraved, depravation, depravity, undepraved.
PRED	*plunder*	prey, predatory, depredate, depradation.
PREG	*with child*	pregnant, impregnate, reimpregnate.
PROTO	*first*	protocol, protoplasm, protozoa, prototype.
PUD	*modesty*	impudence, impudently, repudiate, repudiation.
PULV	*dust*	pulverable, pulverize, pulverization.
PUNI	*punish*	punitive, impunitive, punish, unpunished.
PUR/PUS	*fester*	purulent, suppuration, pus, pustule.
PUTR	*rotten*	putrid, putrification, unputrified, putrescence.

PYR	*fire*	pyre, pyrite, empyrean, pyrotechnical.
QUAL	*kind, sort*	quality, qualification, disqualify, unqualified.
QUAN	*how much*	quantity, quantification, quantum.
QUOT	*how many*	quote, quota, quotient, quotability.
RANC	*stale*	rancid, rancidity, rancorous, rancorousness.
RANG	*order*	arrangement, deranged, disarranged.
RASE	*rub off*	erase, erasure, raze, abrasion.
RE	*thing*	real, realist, realization, unreal.
REND	*restore*	render, rendition, surrender, surrenderee.
RHY	*measured*	rhyme, rhythm, rhythmical, unrhymed.
RID/RIS	*to mock*	ridicule, deride, risibility, derision.
RIG	*stiff*	rigid, rigorousness, rigor, rigor mortis.
RIT	*of rites*	ritual, ritualistic, ritualize, ritualism.
ROB	*strength*	robust, robustness, corroboration.
ROT	*a wheel*	rote, rotary, rotund, routine.
RUB	*red, ruddy*	rubicund, rubric, ruby, erubescence.
RUD	*rough*	rude, rudiment, erudite, erudition.
RUMIN	*muse on*	ruminant, ruminate, ruminator, unruminated.
RUR/RUS	*country*	rural, ruralistic, rustic, rustication.
SAGA	*perceive*	sagacity, sagacious, sagaciousness, presage.
SAL	*salt*	salt, salary, salad, sauce, salami.
SAN	*sound*	sane, sanctuary, sanitarium, insanity.
SANG	*blood red*	sanguine, sanguinary, consanguinity, sang-froid.
SARC	*the flesh*	sarcoma, sarcophagus, sarcasm, sarcastic.
SATIR	*censure*	satirist, satire, satirical, satirize.
SCAND	*disgrace*	scandal, scandalize, scandalous, scandalizing.
SCHOL	*school*	scholar, scholastic, school, unscholastic.
SCIND	*to cut*	abscind, prescind, rescind, scissors.
SCINT	*spark*	scintilla, scintillate, scintillation.
SCRUP	*doubt*	scruple, scrupulous, unscrupulously.
SCRUT	*search*	scrutable, scrutiny, inscrutable, inscrutability.
SCURR	*scoffer*	scurrility, scurrilous, scurrilously.
SECR	*hidden*	secret, secrecy, secretary, undersecretary.
SEMI	*half*	semiannual, semicircle, semilunar, semitone.
SEMIN	*seed*	seminal, seminary, disseminate, insemination.
SEN	*old*	senate, senescence, senility, seniority.
SEX	*six*	sextant, sextuplets, sexagenarian, sexennial.

SICC	*make dry*	desiccate, desiccative, siccative.
SIDER	*star*	consider, desideratum, sidereal, inconsiderate.
SIMUL	*same time*	simultaneous, simultaneity, simultaneousness.
SINIST	*left hand*	sinister, sinisterly, sinistrous.
SINU	*winding*	sinuate, sinuosity, insinuate, insinuation.
SKEPT	*doubt*	skeptic, skeptical, skepticism, skepticalness.
SOL	*comfort*	console, consolation, disconsolate, solace.
SOLIC	*anxious*	solicit, solicitation, solicitude, unsolicited.
SOLID	*firm*	solidly, solidarity, consolidate, soldier.
SOMN	*sleep*	insomnia, somnolent, somnabulist.
SOPH	*wisdom*	philosophy, sophistry, sophistication.
SORB	*drink in*	absorb, absorption, sorbent, unabsorbable.
SORT	*a kind*	sort, assortment, consortable, resorting.
SPER	*hope*	despair, desperate, desperado, prosper.
SPERS	*scatter*	asperse, aspersion, disperse, intersperse.
SPHER	*a ball*	spheroid, spherically, atmosphere, hemisphere.
SPLEN	*to shine*	splendid, splendor, resplendid, resplendence.
SPOIL	*take from*	spoil, aspoliate, despoiled, unspoiled.
STA	*a standing*	apostacy, ecstasy, hypostasis, static.
STELL	*star*	stellar, constellation, subconstellate.
STILL	*drop*	still, distill, distillery, instill.
STIMU	*a goad*	stimulus, stimulation, unstimulated.
STIN	*fix*	destine, predestine, predestination, obstinacy.
STRAT	*spread out*	stratum, unstratified, stratagem, prostration.
STUP	*senseless*	stupid, stupefy, stupor, stupendous.
SUBLIM	*exalted*	sublime, sublimity, sublimate, sublimation.
SUC	*draw in*	suck, suckle, suction, succulent.
SUMM	*chief part*	summary, summit, consummate, inconsummate.
SUPER	*above*	superb, superable, superior, supreme.
TAC/TIC	*silent*	tacit, taciturn, reticent, reticence.
TAIL	*cut*	tailor, detail, entail, retail.
TAL	*that kind*	tally, tallying, retaliate, retaliation.
TARD	*dilatory*	tardy, tardiness, retard, retardation.
TAST	*to feel*	taste, tasteless, distaste, untasted.
TAX	*arrangement*	syntax, taxidermy, taxonomy, tactics.
TECH	*art, skill*	technical, technology, polytechnic, technique.
TELE	*distant*	telescope, telegraph, telephone, television.

TEMP	*regulate*	temperature, temperate, intemperance.
TEMPT	*try*	tempt, temptation, attempt, reattempt.
TENU	*thin*	tenuous, attenuate, extenuate, extenuation.
TER	*clean*	terse, terseness, deterge, detergent.
TERR	*fright*	terror, terrible, deterred, unterrified, deter.
THEO	*observe*	theorem, theory, theoretician, theoretical.
THERM	*heat*	thermal, thermometer, thermos, thermostat.
THRON	*king seat*	throne, dethrone, enthrone, unthrone.
TIM	*fear*	timid, timorous, intimidate, intimidation.
TIN	*tinge*	tinct, tincture, tinge, taint.
TITL	*title*	title, titular, entitled, untitled.
TOLER	*bear*	tolerable, tolerant, intolerant, intolerable.
TORP	*benumb*	torpidity, torpor, torpescent, torpedo.
TOTAL	*entire*	total, totality, teetotaler, totalization.
TOX	*poison*	toxic, antitoxin, intoxicate, intoxication.
TRAD	*hand down*	tradition, traditionally, traitor, traitorous.
TREM	*quake*	tremble, tremulous, tremor, tremulousness.
TREPID	*trembling*	trepid, trepidation, intrepid, intrepidity.
TRI	*three*	triangular, triennial, trisect, trivial, triad.
TRIC	*entangle*	trickery, intricate, intrigue, extricate.
TRIT	*rubbed*	trite, attrition, contritely, detrimental.
TRUNC	*cut off*	trunk, truncheon, truncate, detruncate.
TUBER	*swelling*	tuberous, tubercular, protuberant.
TURG	*swell*	turgid, turgidity, turgescence.
TUS	*bruise*	contusion, obtuse, pertusion.
TUT	*protect*	tutor, tutoress, tutelage, untutored.
TYRA	*despotism*	tyrant, tyranny, tyrannical, tyrannize.
UBER	*abundant*	ubertous, uberty, exuberance, exuberantly.
ULC	*a sore*	ulcer, ulceration, ulcerousness.
ULTI	*beyond*	ultimate, ultimatum, ulterior, penultimate.
UMBR	*shadow*	umbrage, umbrella, inumbrate, somber.
UNC	*anoint*	anoint, inunction, unctiousness, unguent.
URB	*city*	urbane, urbanity, suburb, suburban.
URG	*press on*	urge, urging, urgently, unurged.
UST	*burn*	ustulate, combustion, incombustion.
VALV	*revolving*	valvelet, valvular, bivalve, univalve.
VAN	*empty*	vain, vanity, vauntingly, evanescent.

VAN	*before*	van, vanguard, advance, disadvantage.
VAPOR	*breathe*	vapor, vaporize, evaporate, vaporousness.
VARI	*diverse*	variously, variety, invariable, unvaried.
VARIC	*straddle*	prevaricate, prevaricator, prevarication.
VAST	*large*	vast, vastness, devastate, devastation.
VEN	*sell*	vend, vendor, venal, venality.
VENER	*reverence*	venerate, venerable, unvenerable.
VENT	*the wind*	vent, ventilation, ventilator.
VENTR	*the belly*	ventral, ventricle, ventriloquist.
VERBER	*send back*	reverberate, reverberation, reverberating.
VERD	*green*	verdant, verdure, verdurous, unverdant.
VERE	*feel awe*	revere, reverence, reverend, irreverence.
VERG	*tend*	verge, converge, diverge, divervingly.
VERM	*a worm*	vermin, vermicule, vermifuge, worm.
VESTIG	*footprint*	vestige, vestigial, investigate, uninvestigated.
VIC	*instead*	vicar, vicariously, vice-president, vicissitude.
VIGOR	*strength*	vigor, vigorously, invigorate, reinvigorate.
VIL	*mean*	vile, vilify, revile, reviling.
VIOL	*injure*	violate, violence, inviolable, unviolated.
VIR	*manliness*	virtue, virtuoso, virtually, virility.
VIRU	*poisonous*	virus, virulent, virulently, virulence.
VIT	*avoid*	evitable, inevitable, inevitability.
VITR	*glassy*	vitreous, vitrify, vitrescence, vitriolic.
VOR	*gluttonous*	devour, voracious, carnivorous, omnivorous.
ZO	*animal*	zoo, zoological, zoologist, zodiac, protozoa.